For my wife Sandra,
who knows the story off by heart
but listens anyway ...

And in Memory of
My aunt, Tilda Templeton, Ballycarry, (1937–1986),
and our Scottish cousin Andrew Keatings,
Bellshill, Lanarkshire, (1927–2008)

The title of this book refers to the passage in the Bible which was the inspiration for the naming of the emigrant ship the *Eagle Wing*. The ship was built in Groomsport, County Down, in 1636, with the aim of taking two Presbyterian congregations to America. Unfortunately, it did not reach its destination and was forced to turn back in mid-Atlantic due to storms. In the next century at least 300,000 Ulster Presbyterians successfully charted the waters to a new life in America.

"Ye have seen what I did unto the Egyptians, and how I
bare you on eagle's wings, and brought you unto myself.
Now, therefore, if ye will obey my voice indeed, and
keep my covenant, then ye shall be a peculiar treasure
unto me above all people: for the earth is mine."
Exodus 19: 4–6

The journey of the Ulster Scots and Scotch-Irish

Dr David Hume MBE

Published 2011 by
Colourpoint Books
Colourpoint House, Jubilee Business Park
Jubilee Road, Newtownards, BT23 4YH
Tel: 028 9182 6339
Fax: 028 9182 1900
E-mail: info@colourpoint.co.uk
Web: www.colourpoint.co.uk

First Edition
First Impression

A catalogue record for this book is available from the British Library.

Designed by April Sky Design, Newtownards
Tel: 028 9182 7195
Web: www.aprilsky.co.uk

Printed by GPS Colour Graphics Ltd, Belfast

ISBN 978-1-906578-96-1

EAGLE'S WINGS

The journey of the Ulster Scots and Scotch-Irish

Dr David Hume MBE

Photo: Rowland White

The Author

Dr David Hume is a native of Ballycarry, County Antrim, and can trace his Ulster Scots ancestral roots in County Antrim back to the seventeenth century. He is a graduate of the University of Ulster and a past pupil of Ballycarry Primary School and Larne High School. A former newspaper journalist, he was also employed at the start of his career as a research assistant to a Northern Ireland Member of the Westminster Parliament.

Active in many aspects of local community life, he was founding chairman of Ballycarry Community Association, and co-founder in 1993 of the Broadisland Gathering, the longest-established Ulster Scots family festival in Northern Ireland. He was one of those principally involved in the twinning of Larne with Clover and York County in South Carolina. His efforts in this latter regard resulted in him having the title of Honorary Citizen of Clover conferred by the American city council in 1996.

Married with three sons, he is author of several historical studies, including *For Ulster and Her Freedom: the story of the April 1914 gunrunning*, *The Spirit of 1798 and Presbyterian Radicalism in Ulster*, *The Ulster Unionist Party 1972–1992*, *Far From the Green Fields of Erin: Ulster emigrants and their stories* and *People of the Lough Shore*, a local history study. He is a regular contributor to *The Ulster-Scot* newspaper, the official organ of the Ulster-Scots Agency.

Dr Hume was awarded the MBE by Her Majesty the Queen for services to the community in Ballycarry and Larne in 2007. He is Director of Services of the Grand Orange Lodge of Ireland, a post he has held since 2003. In 2011 he was appointed as a member of the Ministerial Advisory Group on the Ulster-Scots Academy.

CONTENTS

INTRODUCTION

In the summer of 1865 the *Larne Weekly Reporter* informed readers that atmospheric conditions on the previous Sunday evening had been such as to render the Scottish coast particularly distinct and that the cottages scattered along the hillsides there were clearly visible:

> "Every feature on the Highland mountains was so marked and prominent that the scene was beautiful in the extreme; and the Craig of Ailsa, as it stood bold and gigantic in the unruffled waters and seemingly only a few miles distant from our shores, presented an appearance both grand and beautiful. We have not in our recollection witnessed such a delightful view of the channel and Scotch shore as we did on the evening in question …"[1]

It was a reminder, if any were needed, of the close proximity between the land masses on both sides of the North Channel.

The North Channel, linking Scotland and Ulster, is not a geographical barrier. In fact, through history it has served more often as a channel of communication. Viewing the Scottish and Ulster coasts from the air, it becomes clear how little distance really separates the two. In ancient times it was safer and more convenient to use the waves as a means of travel as opposed to journeying overland through forests and difficult landscape. For example, in the Scotland of the Stone Age, around 10,000 years ago, there is archaeological evidence that ancient man, who was engaged in making flint axe heads, traded with and imported articles from settlements across the channel in Antrim.[2] A site at Ballygally on the Antrim coast was excavated in 1995 after evidence of a flint factory was unearthed. Several tons of worked flints were eventually removed from the site, which also produced evidence of stone which was indigenous to the island of Arran in Scotland. It is clear that, from the earliest times, there were common linkages across the North Channel. The most ancient recorded people of the islands, the Picts, may have crossed from Ireland to Scotland, although it is now in the latter that they are more commonly recalled by historians. They were found in areas north of the Forth, and hill forts have been found in the Pentland Hills and in the area around the Pentland Forth; indeed the name Pentland is said to derive from an early form of the word Pict.[3]

Ballygally Head, County Antrim, site of an ancient settlement which traded with Scotland.

Place names are often important pointers

to the past. In County Antrim, for example, there is a Cairnalbanagh (Cairn of the Scots) in the Glens of Antrim and a Ballyalbanagh (the place of the Scots) near Ballyclare, and in Scotland the name Argyll derives from the word *Earraghaidheal* (coastland of the Gaels).[4] In the nineteenth century, observers could reflect on the clearly Scottish background to many areas in Ulster. For example, the 1837 Ordnance Survey Memoir for the Parish of Donaghadee in County Down states that "The dialect of the people is almost completely Scotch and they have altogether a great resemblance to their Scotch neighbours."[5] One local Ulster newspaper in an 1870s article, entitled 'Scotch Nomenculture', reflected that "When we examine the names of many of the families in the North of Ireland, and especially in our immediate neighbourhood, we find, singular to say, that they represent a whole host of towns in Scotland, thus testifying the Scottish origin of the people referred to ..."[6] The article went on to speculate that those with surnames in the area such as Ayr, Balfour, Barr, Blackburn, Fenwick, Girvan, Hamilton, Irvine, Johnston, Kelso, Kilpatrick, Moffat, Nairn, Stirling and others were probably derived from a town of origin. In the case of the Girvan family of Larne, for example, the first of the line is said to have been a David Girvan, who came from the town of Girvan in Ayrshire in 1606 and settled at Ballyriland townland, Raloo.

A house plaque erected by John Girvan at Larne, County Antrim, in 1776.

The family would play a part in early Ulster Scots history through David Girvan's son, also David, who helped to build the *Eagle Wing*, a ship which set sail for America in September 1636. The ship never reached its destination due to storms and returned its Presbyterian emigrant passengers to Belfast Lough. The Girvan family, however, continued to prosper. John Girvan, the grandson of the original settler, was a bailiff of the parish and a friend of the Downshire family, which owned Raloo at that time. Lord Downshire made Girvan's youngest brother, David, manager of a mill at Tullylish on the River Bann and he became prosperous. The carving of the Girvan family name on their homestead above Larne was a sure sign of such prosperity. The family also had connections with the Houstons of Ballyboley, ancestors of General Sam Houston, who won fame by his victory over a Mexican army at San Jacinto in 1836, and the securing of Texan independence.

The port of Girvan in Scotland, the ancestral home of Girvan families in Ulster and elsewhere.

The ancient links continued through the centuries. In medieval times there were feudal connections with Scotland, such as Robert the Bruce, through intermarriage with the family of the Earl of Ulster, holding title to lands in County Antrim. One of his Royal Mandates was issued from Olderfleet Castle at Larne[7] and it is supposedly on the island of Rathlin, close to his own shores, that Robert the Bruce spent time in hiding, where he watched and was inspired by a spider, which kept weaving its web despite adversity. However, it is fair to say that there are other caves on the Scottish coast laying claim to the honour of being home to Bruce's spider.

Mercenary soldiers from Scotland, known as Gallowglasses, were engaged from time to time by Irish chieftains in Ulster, adding another element to the population mix. In the fifteenth century came the strongest medieval link of all when the MacDonnells intermarried with the Bisset family (who were originally Scots as well) and became heirs of the title to the Glynnes or Glens of Antrim. All of this was before the Plantation of Ulster, which brought thousands of Scots to the Ulster counties from 1609 onwards. However, from 1606 the private efforts of Sir James Hamilton and Sir Hugh Montgomery, two Lowland Scots, would see much of County Down and the eastern part of Antrim becoming home to a sizable Scots population, certainly of much greater scale and proportion than any earlier Scots settlement. This legacy from the Plantation period is probably the most relevant in the context of modern history, for it has been of immense importance socially, culturally and politically.

A statue of Robert the Bruce in Stirling.

In his impressive work, *The Ulster Scot*, James B Woodburn (1872–1957) highlighted denominational population statistics which showed that the Scottish population was particularly strong in Antrim, Down, Londonderry City and County and Belfast.[8] However, this does not detail the complete story, since denominational break-down in the twentieth century is only one means of identifying the strong Scottish connection and the links which existed and remain. The late Professor Robert Gregg, in his research in the 1960s, highlighted strong Ulster Scots linguistic regions in North Down, East and Mid Antrim, parts of Londonderry and East Donegal, based on the criteria of language, surname and denomination.[9] Political studies have helped identify that support for the Ulster Liberals in the nineteenth century was strongest among Presbyterian communities, particularly in the areas of Down, Antrim, Londonderry and East Donegal.[10] The contention could be made that this cultural and political legacy extended back to the roots of the Scots presence in Ulster, but most particularly from the eighteenth century onwards.[11]

The legacy of the Ulster Scots extends over centuries and across continents. This book aims to provide a layman's guide to the history of the Ulster Scots and the landscape which they altered by their presence and which still bears testimony to their legacy. The story of the Ulster Scots is an amazing historical journey, which is still being undertaken and whose chapters have not yet been fully written.

Archaeologists work on a seventeenth century Plantation house at Linford, County Antrim, in 1990. Evidence of pottery from Devon was unearthed at the homestead, which was only a short distance from an earlier Neolithic settlement site. Courtesy of the *Larne Times*

ENDNOTES

1 *Larne Weekly Reporter*, 15 July 1865
2 Glover, Janet, R, *The Story of Scotland*, London: Faber & Faber, 1977, p13
3 Glover, *op cit*, p17
4 Thomson, *Companion to Gaelic Scotland*, Oxford: 1983, p54
5 OS Memoir for Parish of Donaghadee, 1837, Belfast: Institute of Irish Studies, 1991, p50
6 *Larne Weekly Reporter*, 18 March 1871
7 Barrow, GWS, *Robert the Bruce and the Community of the Realm of Scotland*, Edinburgh: Edinburgh University Press, 1988, p163
8 See Woodburn, James, B, *The Ulster Scot*, London: 1915
9 Smyth, et al, *The Academic Study of Ulster-Scots: Essays for and by Robert Gregg*, Cultra, 2008, pays tribute to the efforts of the late Professor Gregg, who laid the foundations for academic study of Ulster Scots.
10 Walker, Brian, *Ulster Politics, The Formative Years 1868–86*, Belfast: 1989
11 Hume, David, *To Right Some Things That We Thought Wrong*, Belfast: 1998

Chapter One

ANCIENT TIMES AND ANCIENT LINKS

Archaeologists refer to what they call the 'Irish Sea Province' in ancient times, highlighting the close links that existed between the shores of the British Isles basin. Wales and southern Ireland were closely connected, as were Scotland's western coast, England's Lancashire and Cumbrian coastlines and the north of Ireland.[1] These links, it would appear, were about more than geography in many cases. In his study of Celtic migrations, WA Hanna suggests that population movement of the Celts is readily identifiable from modern place names. He details that Wales gets its name from the old continental Celtic tribe, the Volcae, a name which as Wolch and later Walsch meant 'stranger' or 'foreigner' to their German neighbours, whose Anglo-Saxon descendants applied the derivative Waelas to the Britons in general. Similarly, those in Strathclyde were once called Straecled Waelas, while it is suggested that the Cornovii tribe, highlighted by Ptolemy's maps in the second century, had migrated from the Welsh borders to south-west Britain, where they were known as the Corn Wealas.[2]

Hanna also suggests that the tribe noted in Ptolemy's early maps as the Voluntii was one of several small septs of the British branch of the Brigantes and inhabited the coastal region of Lancashire. They migrated from there to the north of Ireland, where as the Uluti and later the Ulaid their tribal descendants gave their name to Ulster.[3]

In the Scotland of the Stone Age, ancient man was engaged in making flint axe heads and imported some of these from Antrim.[4] In recent years a site at Ballygally on the Antrim coast was excavated after evidence of a flint factory was unearthed. It was discovered by a local man out walking, who noticed worked flints on the surface of a development site. Subsequently an archaeological dig was carried out and several tons of worked flints were removed from the site. Evidence of stone which was indigenous to the island of Arran in Scotland was also discovered. It is clear that, from the earliest times, there were common linkages across the North Channel. The earliest connection is believed to be that of the Picts, the most ancient recorded people of the British Isles. Found in both ancient Ireland and Scotland, historians differ over whether they originally came to Ireland from Scotland, or vice versa. Either way, whenever settlers from Ulster sailed east in the fifth and sixth centuries, the Picts were the people they came into most immediate contact with, and it is generally argued that this had a negative impact on the Pictish people.

Archaeologists at work at Ballygally on the Antrim coast, where a large quantity of worked flints and also stone indigenous to the island of Arran in Scotland were unearthed, providing trade links in Neolithic times between Scotland and Ulster.

Historians believe that the Dal Riata, who were to found a joint kingdom between Ulster and Scotland, had initially won lands in Munster. There is some suggestion that a famine in Munster led them to move north into Ulster, from whence some crossed the channel into Pictland. It is likely that 150 or 200 years before Fergus Mor was crowned King at Dunadd there was a Dalriadian settlement in Scotland. Cairpre Riata is described in early accounts as being the founder of Dal Riata in both Ireland and Scotland.[5]

Ballygally Head on the Antrim coast, as seen from the Sallagh Braes. This area was the site of an ancient promontory fort and settlement overlooking the North Channel to Scotland.

Legend tells of how in AD500, King Fergus Mor of Antrim set sail for Dunadd on the Scottish coast, where he was to be crowned ruler of the joint kingdom of Dalriada. Fergus was said to have taken with him the *Lia Fail* or Stone of Destiny. According to legend, this stone played not only an important part in Fergus' coronation but also in the coronation ceremonies of all subsequent Scots and British monarchs. This legend is an extremely strong one. Debate exists as to whether the Stone of Destiny which resided in Westminster Abbey was that same stone, whether it was the Biblical Jacob's Pillow, and who exactly these people who brought it were. Such stories are the stuff of legend and have excited much discussion.[6]

We know from the tenth century *Senschus fer nAlban* (Tradition of the Men of Scotland), which is believed to have been drawn from earlier sources, that Fergus Mor was crowned King at Dunadd and can assume that since there was no conflict or invasion that a settlement already existed, having been established in Argyll at an earlier date. Irish legend adds further to this, suggesting that Ulstermen and women had settled ten generations before Fergus, equating to a date in the third century or earlier. The Venerable Bede, a seventh century author and religious scholar, who is regarded as the father of English history, also suggested a similar situation in Argyll. Some others have suggested that it is likely that the movement of people involved a single dynasty and was not a large-scale folk invasion, although this may more closely relate to the actual arrival of Fergus among his people in the sixth century, the earlier population movement having taken greater numbers over a period of time.[7]

The Stone of Destiny under the Coronation Chair in Westminster Abbey. The ancient artefact was brought north to Scotland in 1996 and is now located in Edinburgh Castle.

The joint kingdom lasted until AD637 when internal disputes led to the separation of the territory. However, a legacy had been handed down and it was one which extended far beyond the fact that one of Fergus' grandsons, Comgall, gave his name to the Scottish district of Cowal. The people who crossed from Antrim to settle on the west coast of Caledonia were known as *Scotti* to the Romans, signifying that they were raiders, or Scots to modern historians. It is believed that the root word *Riata*, as used in Dal Riata, signifies 'travelling' and this is appropriate when we consider the movement of the Scots throughout history. In time the settlers would bequeath their greatest gift to their new land, which is today known as Scotland. The cultural ties between the lands on both sides of the North Channel were strong in ancient times, as one author has highlighted by referring to a single cultural province: "Gaelic-speaking Scotland and Ireland constituted a single culture-province down into the seventeenth century …"[8]

Coisir Og Dhail Riata, the young choir of Dalriada, highlighted ancient linguistic and cultural links between Argyll and Antrim when they performed in Scots Gaelic at the 2010 Broadisland Gathering Ulster Scots Festival in Ballycarry, County Antrim. Members are seen here singing with local children in the village primary school.

The Scots of Ulster found themselves in competition with other peoples in the new land to which they had migrated; the Picts were their most immediate neighbours and history records that the Dalriadian King Aedan was in conflict with the Picts for 13 years despite, or perhaps because, he was married into the Pictish Royal Family. In later years King Brude of the Picts is believed to have given the island of Iona to Colm Cille (St Columba), who was instrumental in converting Brude Mac Malcolm to Christianity. Brude died in AD584 and Columba in AD595. The Picts were to be lost to history as an identifiable people through Kenneth McAlpin, who became King of Dalriada in AD841 and reigned for 16 years. One ancient chronicle informs us that Danish pirates had wrought devastation on the west coast and many Picts had been wiped out defending their homes. Kenneth then moved into the territory "… and after slaying many, drove the rest to flight. And so he was the first of the

Scots to obtain the monarchy of the whole of Albania, which is now called Scotia …"[9] The Scots line continued when in AD1005 Malcolm II became King of the Picts and the Scots, and was succeeded by his grandson Duncan, made famous in Shakespeare's *Macbeth*.[10]

The word *Pict* is a Roman one, used from the late third century AD onwards and refers to a group of people of whom we know little, and who have left us little to understand them by. This has, of course, added to the mystery and the legend about them. However, in more recent years, more research has led to a greater level of understanding about the Picts and our basis of knowledge is extending beyond pure archaeology.

The term Pict may have been applied by the Romans as a term of abuse for the peoples they encountered in the north of Britain. It literally means 'the painted people', most likely alluding to the designs with which they were said to tattoo or prick their bodies. As Lloyd and Jenny Laing point out in *The Picts and the Scots*, the term was probably not used for one exclusive group of people, but for all those who inhabited the lands beyond the Antonine Wall and who were a threat to Roman Britain:

> "Research suggests that there were many tribal groups in northern Scotland who, during the early centuries AD, grouped and re-grouped, partly in response to Rome, partly in response to their own internal economic and social development, and we cannot really at this early period, or later, speak of a 'kingdom of the Picts'. The Pictish lands comprised many lands with changing boundaries, and first one kingdom, then another held supremacy over its neighbours."[11]

However, they go on to remark that both the peoples of northern Scotland and their neighbours saw them as having some kind of underlying unity.

It has been noted that in terms of metalwork and stones with Pictish symbols, these most generally represent articles of high-status. Mundane articles are uniform across Scotland north of the Forth-Clyde line, but the Picts may have been a ruling class. Some have suggested that the term Pict should perhaps be regarded as denoting a ruling class of certain Celtic tribes as opposed to a total society.[12] Similarly, the ancient society of Ulster was dominated at the top level by the Ulidians, while the majority of the society were known as the Cruithni.

Most of the documentary evidence for the Picts has been left for us by others, whose accounts have been added to by archaeology. Some of these accounts were probably added to by the imagination of the writer or the generation. For example, a twelfth century Icelandic chronicler in the *Historia Norvegie* describes the Picts as pygmies who "did wonders in the mornings and the evenings but at mid-day lost their strength and hid in holes in the ground". Although fanciful, this may have underlined the fact that the Picts were seen as a people about whom myths could be made, and also that their use of souterrains, or underground chambers, was common.

There was greater interest in the Picts in the sixteenth century, spurred on by discoveries relating to native peoples in the Americas. John White, who is famous for his drawings of American Indians on the Roanoke voyages of Sir Walter Raleigh, in the period after 1584, attempted to draw what he believed the Picts would have looked like. While he saw them as 'noble savages', William Camden regarded them as less noble than savage and recounted how their activities had contributed to the break-up of Roman Britain. Camden went against the tide of opinion which regarded the Picts as having come from Scythia, suggesting that they were natives of Britain who had migrated north at the time of the Roman conquest. In 1695 he wrote:

> "But for this name of the Picts, the authority of Flavius Vegetius will clear all doubts concerning it. He in some measure demonstrates that the Britains us'd the word Pictae to express a thing coloured, in the very same sense that the Romans did. For he says that the Britains call'd your Scout-pinnaces Pictae, the sails and cables thereof being dy'd blue, and the mariners and soldiers clad in habits of the same colour. Certainly if the Britains would call ships from their sails of blue-dye Pictae, there is no reason in the world, why they should not give the name Picti to a people that painted their bodies with several colours, and especially with blue (for that is the dye that woad gives)."[13]

The first actual written reference to the Picts which has survived comes in AD297 when Eumenius, in a piece of Classical Literature, refers to them in such a way that suggests their name was well enough known to an educated Mediterranean readership so as not to require explanation. Classical sources seem to indicate that there were two main tribal groups among the Picts, at least between the early third century AD and the fourth. These were the Caledonians, who were active against the late first-century Roman general Agricola when he came north, and the Maeatae, mentioned in AD197–200, when they also attacked the Romans.

Writers may have speculated but the 'problem with the Picts', as historians termed it, was that little physical – or identifiable physical – trace had been left behind. Prominent remains include Pictish sculptured stones but even these have left few clues to the entire society that they represent. There are elaborate carvings and language guides on these stones but the Pictish language was lost in time, replaced by Scots Gaelic and later Latin sources written by monks. Authors Lloyd and Jenny Laing point out that "When people no longer spoke Pictish, they were not inclined to transcribe in an obsolete language." It is a logical fate which has affected other languages in more recent times. The decline of the Ulster Scots or Ullans language in the twentieth century came about as it was the language of the rural and often uneducated classes, and was seen as merely crude English, which had to be corrected. While the Ulster Scots language enjoyed a revival in the late twentieth and twenty-first century, the fate of Pictish was more depressing.

The Ballylumford Dolmen at Islandmagee in County Antrim is one of many such structures of ancient culture which survive in Ireland, north and south, and probably dates back around 4,000 years to the Middle Bronze Age. This one appears to have been part of a ceremonial and burial site.

The Scots, who emerged on the scene, fostered no interest in the history of their Pictish neighbours, whom they had subsumed.[14] This added to the problem of the survival of the language, while other historical factors, including removal of Scottish records to London in the thirteenth century (where they were not cared for and lost as a result) and destruction of archives in Scots monasteries in the Reformation of the sixteenth century also played a part in the process which almost wrote the Picts out of history. However, two copies of one important document did survive, a Pictish King list, giving the names of the rulers in Pictish form and also providing a chronology of those who ruled the Picts.

The contemporaries of the Picts were the Cruithni people of Ulster, who had their capital at Emain Macha, now Navan, County Armagh. There were two main groups of people in Ulster in this pre-Christian and early Christian period. The Cruithni comprised the majority but the Ulaid were the Celtic overlords. Both had their individual tribal kings, and either Ulidian or Cruthinic kings could be overking, or *Ard Ri.* Both groups faced a common threat with the consolidation of Gaelic tribes in the south and west. One of the greatest pieces of ancient Irish literature, *The Cattle Raid of Cooley (Táin Bó Cúalnge)*, tells of the invasion of Ulster by the combined armies under Queen Maeve of Connaught. In this saga the greatest warrior was Cuchulainn, who was trained by a woman warrior on the Scottish island of Skye, highlighting a Scottish connection. When the Scots moved across the channel, Skye remained a Pictish area, while Islay, Iona and Argyll were Scot strongholds, thus the Ulster link with Skye at the time of Cuchulainn is significant.

As the encroachment by Gaels continued the Cruithin were driven out of

Donegal and the area now comprising Londonderry. In AD627 one of the greatest Cruithin kings, Congal, became High King of Ulster and the following year slew the O'Neill High King. However, in 637 at Magh Rath (Moira, County Down) he was killed in battle and his army defeated, in what the antiquarian and poet Sir Samuel Ferguson described as the greatest battle fought within the bounds of Ireland. The Scot Dalriadians had sent soldiers to the assistance of Congal at Moira, and defeat also effectively spelt the end of their involvement in the affairs of what was their homeland.[15] The independent Ulster kingdom remained until 1084, when the Ulidians were defeated in a battle at the Boyne by the O'Neills.

The O'Neills in turn added something to the legends of the ancient period. Their symbol of the Red Hand of Ulster has quite a story behind it, supposedly relating to a member of the dynasty who had fallen behind in a race to reach the shore and touch the land, thus claiming ownership of it. The legend is that he cut off his hand and threw it to the shore in order to win. However, it has been suggested that the red hand stems from a much earlier period, when the warrior knights of Ulster were known as the Knights of the Bloody Hand or the Red Branch Knights. Thus the red hand is seen as a very ancient symbol indeed. By laying claim to it, the O'Neills, in a fairly rational process, sought to legitimise their replacement of the old rulers and the beginning of their dominance of the landscape, which lasted until the seventeenth century.

Even more ancient legends are to be found in the *Irish Book of Invasions*, which records the waves of invaders to these shores. Among them were the Tuatha de Danaan, who were said to have come from the east and were associated with the Druids and magic. According to legend, the *Lia Fail* (Stone of Destiny), which roared beneath a righteous king, rightly belonged to them. Mythology also claimed that when they were defeated in battle by new invaders they retreated to a spirit or underworld. Echoes of this story remain in the belief in fairies and little folk, who were otherworldly but occasionally appeared in our own.

There are many legends as to the origins of the Scots. Our understanding comes from ancient and medieval texts, and the 1320 Declaration of Arbroath in particular seeks to set out a genealogy of the Scots. It was drawn up by Scottish nobles in an attempt to assert Scottish independence and sent to the Pope of the day, who was then a temporal as well as spiritual leader. The Declaration claimed that the ancestors of the Scots came from Greater Scythia (southern Russia) by way of the Mediterranean and Spain:

> "the nation of the Scots, has been distinguished by many honours; which, passing from the greater Scythia through the Mediterranean Sea and the Pillars of Hercules, and sojourning in Spain among the most savage tribes through a long course of time, could nowhere be subjugated by any people however barbarous; and coming thence one thousand two hundred years after the outgoing of the people of Israel, they, by many victories and infinite toil, acquired for themselves the possessions in the West which they now hold ..."

The writer Nennius, five centuries earlier, suggested that the origins of the Scots lay in ancient Egypt and with a Scythian who was expelled by the Egyptians after the disastrous attempt to cross the Red Sea. They were fearful he, being of noble birth, would lay claim to their territory in the wake of the loss of so many of their leaders.

The legends may be problematical in terms of timescale, and, it should be said, probably also fanciful in a general sense, but they all seem to point to the Mediterranean as the source of the Scots. In support of this we find references to a migration by Egyptians under Scotia and her husband Gaythelos, the Scythian, to north-west Spain, where a town was established called Brigantia. This was noted in Roman times and more recent authors have made much of its presence and the archaeological remains, which seem to point to Egyptian links. According to ancient texts:

> "one of the sons of Gaythelos, Hyber by name, young in years but strong of purpose, was roused to war and took up arms … He killed some of the few inhabitants whom he found and enslaved the rest, but he claimed the whole land as a possession for himself and his brothers, calling it Scotia after his mother's name."[16]

History records that the ancient name for Ireland was Scotia, and that the original Scots moved across to Alba. The movement of peoples into Ireland was considerable and is retold in the *Irish Book of Invasions*, which lists various peoples, many endowed with supernatural powers, that settled and made a new home on the westernmost edge of Europe. Among those listed are the Milesians, descendants of one Miledh or Miletus, a name that is believed to trace the individual to the town of Miletus, principal port of the Greek province of Caria in Asia Minor. Legends also separately tell us that Gaythelos was the son of Neolus, from the same location.

It has been suggested that this migration of people, who are arguably the ancestors of the Scots and the Welsh, took place around the seventh century BC.

Is this the story of the origins of the Scots? It could be. The Scots had to come from somewhere, ultimately, and often legends, while not factual, have elements of truth within them. We should remember, however, that the Declaration of Arbroath was a document aimed at encouraging the Pope to recognise the right of Scotland to be a nation, and therefore it was in the interests of the nobles of the time to encourage a strong pedigree and sense of identity.

We may not know much about the origins of the peoples in this period or the truth behind their legends but we do know quite a lot about their everyday lives.

The Picts and Scots are usually both defined as Celts, although the former may have pre-dated the Celts. The term Celt is primarily a linguistic one, denoting a group of Indo-European languages and the people who spoke them. They were emerging as a recognisable people in an area comprising Bavaria, Switzerland, Austria, Hungary and Bohemia around 500 BC. In the sixth century BC they had spread over much of France and part of Northern Italy, and could be found in Rome, Greece and Asia Minor by the third century. They gave their name to Gaul (Roman: *Galli*) and left place names including *bri* (hill), *mag* (a plain), and *dun* (a fort).

Archaeologists appear increasingly unsure about the validity of linking what appears to be a common linguistic base across Europe to a wider sense of community, and this is a debate which seems likely to continue.[17] However, it is clear that 'Celtic culture', as defined by occurrence of artifact types and styles of art, would appear to have reached a high water mark around 200 BC, stretching across Europe, including Spain, Ireland and Scotland, and beyond. It is believed that Celtic peoples may have moved into Ireland in at least two time phases, generally accepted to have been through Northern Spain and France and also from Britain, outnumbering and assimilating Picts and other Pre-Celtic people perhaps as early as 500 BC. However, a genetic research project based at Trinity College Dublin suggested in 2004 that Irish people had commonality with people from Portugal, Spain, North Africa, and Scandinavia,[18] perhaps giving some credence to the traditional legend of a migration from Iberia to Ireland, the Scandinavian connection being accounted for through Viking settlements.

Our current understanding is that the Ireland of the Celts was largely a rural society with no cities or towns. The ordinary homestead was the Rath, often erected on a hilltop and surrounded by a circular rampart and fence. This is reflected in many local place names such as Rathfriland, and there are remains of many raths dotted across the landscape. The Ordnance Survey Memoir of the 1830s and 1840s includes many references to raths, often termed 'forts', while making us aware that many of them had disappeared by that time. In the landscape of the County Antrim village of Ballycarry, for example, one of the townlands is named Forthill, but the rath after which it was named has long since disappeared from the landscape.

Milk, cheese and meat formed a main part of the diet for the rath dwellers, with corn being used to make a variety of porridges. Cattle were kept for milk rather than meat, while pork was very popular and the main meat eaten at feasts. Fish was also eaten and they gathered fruit such as raspberries, blackberries and strawberries, but apple was the only fruit that was cultivated in any way. These Pre-Christian people had many gods and goddesses and believed in a supernatural world called *Tír na nOg* (The Land of Youth). Their priests were the Druids, who were widely believed to be skilled in magic and had to study for 20 years to earn their title. Part of their training was that they wrote nothing down and instead memorised everything.

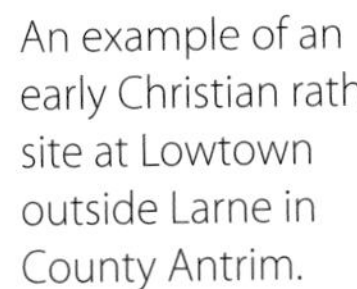

An example of an early Christian rath site at Lowtown outside Larne in County Antrim.

The Celtic year was divided into four seasons, the passage from one to the other marked by a festival. *Samain*, 1 November, marked the end of one year and the beginning of the next, while *Imbolc*, beginning on 1 February, appears to have been connected with the tending of sheep. *Bealtaise*, which began on 1 May saw the beginning of the warm season, and was when cattle were put out to grazing. Great fires were lit across the country in celebration of this season and the changes which it brought. The last of the seasons was *Lughnasa*, which started on 1 August. At that time sacrifices were made to the fertility god Lug to ensure the ripening of the crops and a good harvest. These seasons correspond very closely today with our own present seasons, which isn't surprising since they relate to an agricultural people.

Both Picts and Scots were essentially farmers; archaeological evidence from one site at Dundurn in Scotland, provides an example of the evidence, showing that 61% of the bones found were from cattle, 31% from pigs and 8% from sheep or goat. Virtually all the bones were from domesticated animals. At the Pictish site at Buckquoy in Orkney about 7,000 bones were recovered; cattle accounting for 50%, sheep 30% and pig 20%.[19]

We know that in addition to farming, however, these people also had excellent craftsmen, including blacksmiths. Ironworking evidence has been uncovered at Dunadd, former capital of the Scots, and a blacksmith's tongs, hammer and avil have appeared as Pitctish carved symbols. Iron items found by archaeologists include barrel padlocks, arrow tips, knives, nails and handles. Bronze was also used to provide ornamental work, with clay moulds used for bronze casting found at a number of sites. Archaeologists believe that the moulds were made and ornamentation added while the clay was soft. They were probably set on edge in sand while the hot metal was poured in and the finished castings then trimmed. Items of boneware, such as combs, also survive today. A bone spoon and a knife handle were found at Buckquoy in Orkney, and a quite elaborately decorated leather shoe was found at the Dundurn site in Perthshire.

Other artifacts survive only as representation on sculptures, such as clothing, and leatherwork. Pictish representation in sculpture gives considerable clues as to what people wore. Women seem to have worn long skirts and some form of cloak, with a brooch attaching them, while men wore hooded cloaks and tunics. A stone in Birsay, Orkney, depicts three warriors with ankle-length robes. They appear to have long hair, which reached down their backs and was tied back with headbands.

Distinctive buildings associated with the Picts are the brochs, known in Scotland as Picts' houses. There are around 500 in Scotland, the best example being the Broch of Mousa which stands at 13 metres and was probably originally 15 metres high. It is believed they may have evolved from round, stone-built houses from around 700 BC. From c.200 BC these brochs became the centres of villages or settlements, which clustered around them. Historians speculate that the brochs fell into disuse in Atlantic Scotland by the second century AD when a more settled situation in terms of underlying continuity of population and settlement among the Picts made them unnecessary. The brochs may have been similar in this regard to souterrains, which were thought to be initially created for defensive and protective purposes, but later served in more mundane ways. There are no brochs in Ulster, but souterrains are shared between both Scotland and northern Ireland, suggesting a commonality in both people and historical background.

Inside a souterrain (or underground chamber) at Cairncastle, County Antrim. Souterrains were probably originally built for shelter and defence, and bear resemblance in both Northern Ireland and Scotland.

Courtesy of the *Larne Times*.

Some souterrains date back to at least 500 BC, as is the case in one instance at Douglasmuir, Angus, in Scotland. The typical design of a souterrain is highlighted by that located at Knockdhu, near Cairncastle outside Larne. The entrance is concealed and after crawling along a narrow passageway one enters a chamber, stone-lined, which has a second narrow passageway leading to another chamber. There are, in fact, three such chambers. Another souterrain, discovered while a farmer was ploughing at Liminary outside Ballymena in 1904, also had three chambers descending from the entrance, the largest of which was around 16 feet in length and about five and a half feet high.[20] It appears that the souterrains were constructed by land being excavated, stone structures built and then the soil reinstated on top of them. A different design of a souterrain from those in Ireland has come from Newmill in Perthshire, dating to the first century AD. It was stone walled and stone floored, but probably had a wooden pitched roof which projected, along with part of the wall, above ground level. It was reached from the adjacent hut by means of a ramp which led down to an underground door.[21]

Much has been learned about the pastimes of the Picts and Scots. Sculptures indicate that horse riding was common, horses being ridden both bareback and with saddles. Harnesses are also shown. There is also evidence of board games, with pieces to move around a board, which had peg holes, created from bone knobs with metal shanks. Music appears to have been important and is represented by depictions of instruments on both Pictish and Scottish sculptures. These instruments included various harps; large ones which stood on the ground and are similar to those used today, and smaller, less heavy ones. Harps depicted on the Pictish stone at Nigg and the Scottish stone at Ardchattan are the earliest examples of true harps known in Europe. Blast horns and drums are also depicted on some stones and on a slab at Nigg a figure appears to have cymbals. Drinking was another favourite pastime, and legend has it that the Picts discovered heather ale. At Invergowrie a Pict is portrayed using a drinking-horn with a bird head terminal.

Whatever the truth behind the legends of the Picts and Scots, we at least know the archaeological facts, which point to two remarkable peoples whose societies were elaborate and civilised and whose legacy still remains.

These two peoples became amalgamated in time and their descendants help today to form modern Scotland. That essential unity was brought about by the Celtic Church and another legendary figure, who was associated as the figurehead of that church – Columba of Iona. As was the case with the Scots of Antrim Dalriada, St Columba journeyed across the North Channel to play a role in the future destiny of his adopted home.

St Columba, who was born at Garten in Donegal in AD521, was a major figure in the early history of Scotland. This is probably most significantly because he combined not only a strong ecclesiastical calling, but also was a member of the northern Ui Neill family and a prince in his own right within the family. He thus had a shrewd political sense, which came into play greatly in his adopted home. The circumstances of his departure for Iona, which was to be the powerhouse of his ministry, are said to have related to the fact that significant blood had been shed on his behalf in battle in Ireland and he was atoning for his sense of conscience over this in leaving Ireland forever. Whatever the exact details, Columba's ministry to Caledonia was to ring through the centuries, for he laid the foundations for the modern Scotland.

Both Ireland and Scotland had witnessed a pagan revival at the time of Columba's ministry, and one author outlined that Dalriada, settled by Antrim families, "was the only Christian beach-head available" for an attempt to spread the Gospel in Scotland.[22] There were other holy men in the areas around, but Columba was probably unique in combining a strong sense of political mission as well. While he is probably generally remembered as a saint and leading light in the early Celtic Church, Columba's role was possibly much more significant in encouraging political unity, as noted by one author:

> "... Columba was unique in that his actions displayed an acute political awareness and expertise ... a tradition which remembers him merely as a saintly hermit exiled on a remote Hebridean island does him less than justice."[23]

When the Dalriadian kingship was in a crisis of succession in AD574, for example, Columba's sponsorship of Aedan, one of the two sons of Gabrahn, who would not appeared to have been the most likely successor, was significant. Aedan was descended not only from Gabrahn, a grandson of Fergus Mor of Antrim Dalriada, but his mother was daughter of an earlier Christian King of Strathclyde, and his wife appears to have been a grand-daughter of Brude, King of the Picts. Columba undoubtedly saw the strategic political significance of promoting Aedan, since he had connections to the Dalriadians, Picts and Britons, and it proved an important choice.

In terms of ministry, meanwhile, the links between Ulster and Scotland were clearly displayed in the presence of another of the great figures of the Early Celtic Church, St Comgall of Magheramorne and Bangor, with Columba on a mission to convert the King of the Picts.

The growth of Celtic Christianity in Scotland clearly owes much to the missionaries from Ulster who, in addition to promoting the Christian message, also laid the basis for a political and cultural unity which has remained through the centuries. Even in terms of the movement from Ulster eastward, some authors have suggested that disparate elements of this were involved. The contention would chiefly be that the migration of Cruthni people to Scotland was largely forgotten about, owing to the more significant and influential movement of the Dal Riata or Scots from Ulster, and has not attracted as much historical interest. Remnants of this eighth century, historical linkage remain, however, in the area where the strongest settlement occurred, Galloway, including the fact that churches in Galloway were often dedicated to saints popular in Ulster.[24] The derivative of the name Galloway is said to evolve from *Galwethia*, the origin of which is 'foreigner Irish', according to one writer.[25] The same author points out that at the Battle of the Standard in Scotland in 1138, the Gallowegians in the van of the Scottish army were taunted by the English with cries of "Irish, Irish". The Galloway Irish were thus an important part of the history of the Ulster Scots community.

Below: Slemish mountain outside Broughshane, said to be where St Patrick tended sheep as a slave. Patrick was captured by raiders from Antrim and brought to Ulster as a slave, later returning to spread Christianity across the province.

Bottom: St Patrick's grave, Downpatrick, County Down.

There is also, of course, the debate over the origins of St Patrick, the patron saint of Ireland. A considerable claim has to rest with Dumbartonshire in Scotland, but in any case Patrick was, when he was captured as a slave, on the edge of Roman civilisation in Britain at that time. Given that he was captured by raiders from Ulster (the Scotti) and supposedly ended up on Slemish mountain in Ballymena, his origins being from what became Scotland would make sense. There are many churches associated with him in Northern Ireland, among them *Teampall Phadraig* (Templepatrick) in the parish of Donaghadee, where local history has it that Patrick landed after a journey from Scotland. Aspects of the legend may be fanciful – he is supposed to have left an imprint of his hand and foot on a stone near the shore, for example[26] – but the link to Scotland has some credence at least.

In 575 at Druim Cett near Limavady, the equivalent of an international convention took place to discuss, from a political point of view, the quite unique circumstance of the link to Scotland. The aim of the event was to regularise the situation regarding the Dalriadians, most singularly in respect of how they related to the Ui Neills in Ulster. St Columba (Colum Cille) was once again back on his home territory and was a significant figure and probably also an instrumental voice. The decision of this convention was as follows:

> "their expedition and their hosting belong to the men of Ireland always, for the hostings belongs to the territories always, their tax and their tributes belong to the men of Scotland or their fleet alone belongs to the men of Scotland; all else however belongs to the men of Ireland."

The great convention of Druim Cett took place at what is now known as the Mullagh or Daisy Hill near Limavady. The eminent historian of Dalriada, John Bannerman, says "nothing like it ever happened again in Ireland or Scotland".[27] This event, attended by senior kings and clergy, had the aspect of an international convention and an international agreement. There is a certain irony in the fact that the presence of Ulster Scots in Ireland in the sixth century led to a major agreement as to their position. While Druim Cett may have resolved matters in the sixth century, generations down the line and centuries into the future that same presence presented political conundrums and still, it could be argued, continues to do so.

Beneaghmore stone circle in County Tyrone. Similar structures exist in Scotland from ancient times, providing indications of a common culture on these islands.

HISTORICAL TRAILS
SITES TO VISIT

The following locations may be of interest as historical sites relating to the ancient period:

Dunseverick Castle on the North Antrim coast. It was from here, according to legend, that King Fergus set sail to be crowned King of Antrim and Scottish Dalriada at Dunadd on the west coast of Scotland.

Dunseverick Castle, County Antrim

Dunseverick, on the rugged North Antrim coast, lies near the Giant's Causeway and a few miles west of the village of Ballintoy. It is not a terribly impressive site in modern times, as only part of the keep remains of the once large castle, which dominated the area. The original castle was, according to legend, erected by one Sobhaire, after whom Dun Sohhaire (Dunseveric, or the fort of Severic) is named. Local history details that Severic was killed by sea raiders from Scandinavia, who attacked the coastline having settled in the Orkneys and Hebrides.

Legend has it that King Fergus Mor of the Kingdom of Dalriada left from Dunseverick, with his sons and the famous *Lia Fail* (Stone of Destiny), in order to be crowned King of the joint Dalriadian kingdom, at Dunadd in Scotland. The castle which Fergus would have known can no longer be seen, but the present ruins were probably erected close to the earthen fort (or dun) and are Norman in origin. It is believed that the founder of the Anglo-Norman castle was Alanus De Galweia, Earl of Athol, who had been granted Dalriada by King John in 1210.[28]

Later, the castle was owned by the O'Cahan family, but their involvement in the 1641 Rising and the Civil War brought disaster to the family. Two of them, Gillduff and Turlough Oge O'Cahan, were executed at Carrickfergus in 1653 and the castle was confiscated by the government. The last of the family to live there was Gillduff O'Cahan, whose father was executed, leaving the castle to become a ruin a few years afterwards.

Bangor Abbey, County Down

Bangor Abbey, Bangor, County Down

The modern Bangor Abbey is built on the site of one of the greatest Celtic monasteries in ancient Ireland, founded around AD555, by St Comgall of County Antrim. There were, at one time, 3,000 students attached to the monastery and its sister foundations, and it built up a considerable reputation for scholarship between the sixth and ninth centuries. Bangor Abbey had close association with the Isle of Man and the Abbot of Bangor was chaplain to the King of Man. One of the kings of the island was buried at Bangor in the eleventh century.[29] Comgall was born at Magheramorne in County Antrim and his father was said to be a warrior named Setna. Interestingly this is a Christian name which appears in the Dalriadian settlement in Scotland, as does Comgall. St Comgall was instrumental in undertaking a mission with St Columba to convert Bruce, King of the Picts, to Christianity, a development which opened the way for a closer relationship between the Picts and the Scots.

Ballygally, County Antrim

The prominent coastal landmark of Ballygally Head was the site of an ancient flint working in Neolithic times. Archaeology in a nearby field found evidence of settlement, and several tons of worked flint, suggesting extensive production of flints for tools and weapons. Stones indigenous to the Island of Arran in Scotland were also found there, either having been traded directly or from a route at another site, possibly Tieve Bullagh in North Antrim. The location at Ballygally is surrounded by a number of ancient landmarks, including a promontory fort at nearby Knockdhu. In ancient times the coastal areas were highly settled and trade links developed around what archaeologists refer to as 'the Irish Sea province'.

Dunadd, Scotland

Dunadd in Argyll is the site where the ancient monarchs of Scotland were crowned. It lies south of Kilmartin in the midst of the Great Moss (Moine Mhor), which is a raised peat bog nature reserve. Dunadd towers 176 feet high above the ancient landscape and is believed to have been a Pictish fort prior to the arrival of the Scots. Stone carvings on the rocks at Dunadd show ogham script (ancient alphabet of Pictish origin) as well as the outline of a boar, a hollowed out footprint and a small basin. Historians believe that the footprint and basin are related to the coronation ceremonies of the Dalriadic Scots.

Dunadd fort and farm, Mid Argyll.
Courtesy of Margaret Lister.

In or around AD500, King Fergus Mor of Antrim Dalriada was crowned King of the joint kingdom of Dalriada, which extended across the North Channel to his native Antrim.

Legend has it that the Stone of Destiny was brought to Dunadd and subsequently transferred to Scone Palace. Dispute still surrounds whether this stone (the *Lia Fail*) was the stone taken by Edward the Hammer to London after he subjugated the Scots, and which remained in Westminster Abbey until the 1990s.

Moira, County Down

This is the site of the battle of Magh Rath, described by the antiquarian and poet Sir Samuel Ferguson as the greatest battle fought within the bounds of Ireland. Here, in AD637, King Congal of Ulster was defeated by the Gaels and the kingdom began to wane. However, as late as 1018 the Ulster Cruthin and the Brefni would allay in an attempt to defeat the O'Neills. The links with Dalriada in Scotland were clear at the time of the battle and a contingent of Scots Dalriadians participated in Congal's forces. Congal's defeat led to a decline in the influence of Scottish Dalriada in Ulster affairs, as a consequence of being on the losing side. Today there is little evidence in Moira of the significant battle fought there.

Navan, County Armagh

Navan is the site of the ancient capital of Ulster and an extensive complex of buildings. The enclosure of the site extends to cover an area of around 18 acres of land and archaeology has resulted in an estimate that there was Bronze Age settlement under the mound at Navan in around 700 BC. History records that Concohobar mac Nessa, the greatest King of Emain Macha (Navan Fort), died in AD33. His death coincides with the period in which the influence of Navan was waning. Pressure from the Ui Neill and Airgialla tribes resulted in the ancient kingdom of Ulster being pushed further and further eastward, and eventually Emain Macha was captured and burnt. However, the symbolic importance remained and in 1387 the Ulster King Niall O'Neill built his house at Navan in order to link the O'Neills with the ancient legacy of Emain Macha and its people. St Patrick is believed to have arrived to preach at Armagh while Navan was still relevant and the saint clearly understood the symbolic importance of the site in the context of Ulster history and society.[30]

HISTORICAL QUOTES

"We know, Most Holy Father and Lord, and from the chronicles and books of the ancients gather, that among other illustrious nations, ours, to wit, the nation of the Scots, has been distinguished by many honours; which, passing from the greater Scythia through the Mediterranean Sea and the Pillars of Hercules, and sojourning in Spain among the most savage tribes through a long course of time, could nowhere be subjugated by any people however barbarous; and coming thence one thousand two hundred years after the outgoing of the people of Israel, they, by many victories and infinite toil, acquired for themselves the possessions in the West which they now hold, after expelling the Britons and completely destroying the Picts, and, although very often assailed by the Norwegians, the Danes and the English, always kept themselves free from all servitude, as the histories testify. In their kingdom one hundred and thirteen kings of their own royal stock, no stranger intervening, have reigned."

Scottish Declaration of Arbroath, 1320

A plaque commemorating St Columbanus at Bangor Abbey.

"How much more does it behove us, who believe in the hope of our fruits to be laid up, not on earth but in heaven, to cleanse from vicious passions the field of our heart, and not suppose that we have done enough when we subdue the ground of our bodies by the labour of fasting and of watching, unless we primarily study to correct our vices and reform our morals."

St Comgall of Magheramorne, related through one of his greatest disciples, Columbanus.

HISTORICAL FIGURES

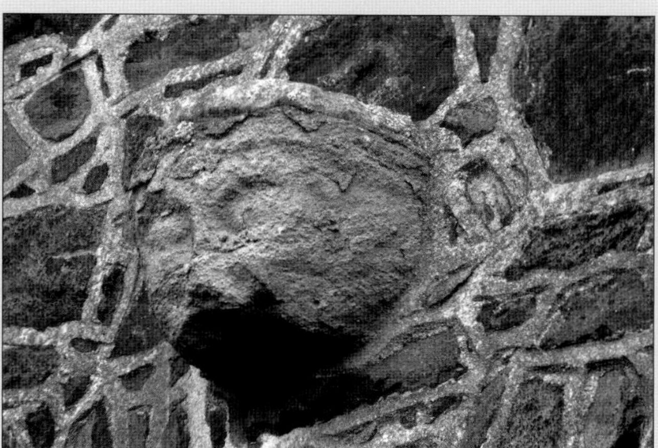

An early Christian sculpture at St Cedma's Church in Larne.

St Comgall of Magheramorne

Comgall of Magheramorne was born around 517, and is said to have been of the Cruithinic race. His father was Setna, described as a warrior, and his mother was named Briga. Magheramorne, located near Larne, is a Celtic place name meaning 'plain of the Mourna'. It is named after a coastal tribe who also gave their name to the Kingdom of Mourne in County Down.

As a young man Comgall is said to have displayed a great sense of vocation in the Christian ministry and was sent to monastic schools at Clonenagh, Clonard and Glasnevin to be educated. As a missionary he showed great zeal and founded a number of monasteries before settling at Bangor in County Down. It is believed that his monastic foundation at Bangor Mor (Bangor the Great as it became known in later years) was established around AD555.[31]

Comgall's monastery would have been similar to other such settlements in the sixth century. The foundation would have been surrounded by a ditch, an essential part of what was known as 'an enclosure'. Inside the enclosure would have been the church, a school, hospice and other buildings. Some sites had craft workshops. Bangor became famous for the type of choral psalmody which was practiced there, and both this and the mission itself spread across Europe as missionaries moved eastward. The most logical expansion was to nearby Galloway, where emigration had resulted in settlements from the east coast of Ulster.

Among the monastic legacies of Bangor Mor were communities founded by Columbanus at Annegray, Luxeuill and Fontaine, all geographically close, in Burgundy. Despite a dispute with St Columba over a Bangor foundation at Ros-Torathair, which resulted in a battle between the Ui Neill and the Cruithin at Coleraine around 579, both Comgall and Columba would share a mission to the Picts in Caledonia. Meanwhile, seven years after he founded Bangor Abbey, Comgall had also founded a monastery on the Scottish island of Tiree.

It is known that monastic life under Comgall's regime at Bangor was quite severe. There was only one meal a day, taken in the evening, while Confession was held in public, before the whole community and acts of penance were taken extremely seriously. Silence was upheld at meal times, conversation restricted at other times and Comgall is said to have arisen in the middle of the night to immense himself in a stream and say his prayers and recite psalms. Despite the strictures, monks were not difficult to attract to the foundation and there were 3,000 students at Bangor and sister churches. One author has made the claim that "The piety and learning of the Bangor monks were unrivalled in Christendom and it was mainly due to them that Ireland became known as the island of saints and scholars."[32]

Comgall died in 603 at the age of 91 years. His bones were to suffer from Viking raids at Bangor in later years and were removed around 823 to Antrim. Among his words which survived are, "Break up your fallow ground and sow not among thorns."

St Columba of Iona

St Columba, also known in history as Colum-cille, was a member of the ruling northern Ui Neill family and said to be a prince in his own right. He was born at Garten in County Donegal in AD521. He is one of the most prominent religious figures in Scottish history. Despite his prominence, Columba remains something of a mystery figure in many ways. Little is known about his earlier life in Ireland, other than that he is said to have been of Royal blood though both his paternal and maternal lines.

He founded monasteries at Derry, Durrow and Kells but later entered into dispute with King Diarmit, who had killed a member of his family. He defeated Diarmit in battle in AD561. It is said that Columba, in order to pay penance for the men who had died in the battle, went into exile as a missionary in Caledonia. Legend has it that Columba went into exile away from Ireland but was careful to select a location from which he could still view his old homeland. Thus, the coast of Argyll was where he began his missionary work, establishing a monastery on Iona off the island of Mull.

St Comgall of Magheramorne undertook a mission with Columba, who converted King Brude of the Picts to Christianity. The conversion of the Picts to the faith of the Scotti of Dalriada was to have long-term implications for the development of history, and the merger of the Picts and Scots under King Kenneth MacAlpin shaped the future development of the country.

Columba died on Iona on 9 June AD597, but the legacy of his foundation lived on. Iona was seen as ecclesiastical centre of Scotland, which is borne out of the fact that there are 48 Scottish kings buried there. Iona remains synonymous with Celtic Christianity today and is a centre of pilgrimage for thousands of people each year.

King Fergus of Dalriada

Born around AD434, history has recorded few details of Fergus Mor, King of Dalriada. This is ironic, given that he was the originator of a political destiny and a kingdom which would project his people, the Scots, into a key role in future development of the land in which they had settled.

He was the son of King Erc of Dalriada, and succeeded him when he died in AD474. His kingdom covered most of coastal County Antrim. Around AD500, Fergus and his sons are said to have crossed the north channel to Kintyre, and it was at Dunadd that he was crowned King of the joint kingdom of Antrim and Scottish Dalriada. Legend records that he took with him the *Lia Fail*, or Stone of Destiny, over which to be crowned. The expedition was regularising a settlement pattern which had already been established, and possibly re-establishing an earlier settlement on the west coast of Scotland.

Fergus died in AD501, a short time after the establishment of the joint kingdom straddling the channel. He was succeeded to the kingship of Dalriada by his son Domangart, who died in AD507. Domangart was succeeded by his son Comgall, who reigned for 32 years. Gabran, another son of Domangart, then ascended to the throne, reigning for 22 years and developing links with Southern Pictland. The Tripartite Life of St Patrick prophesied that the descendants of King Fergus Mor Mac Erc would rule the Dal Riata and the Fortreann (Picts) forever.

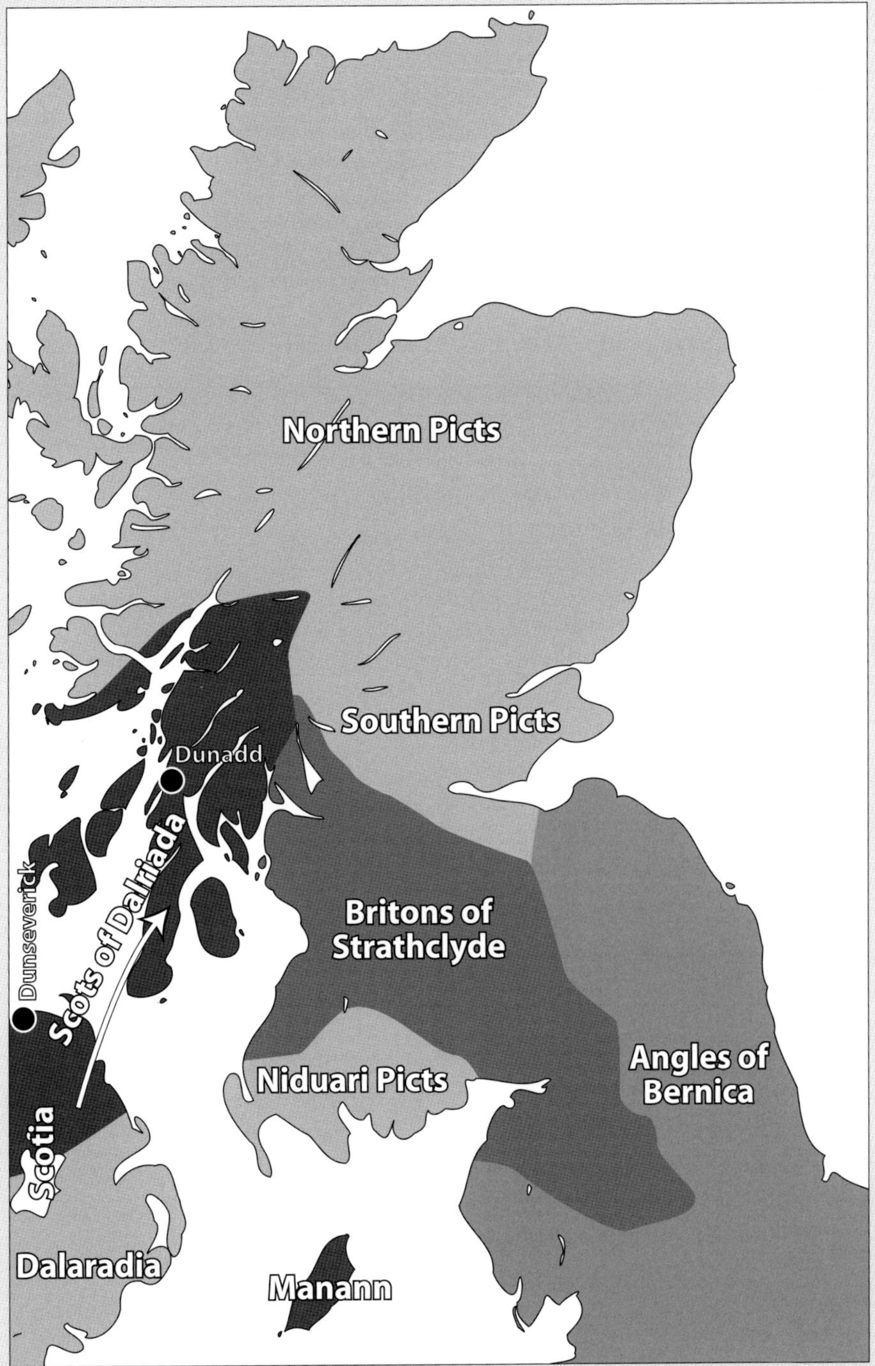
Northern Picts
Southern Picts
Dunadd
Dunseverick
Scots of Dalriada
Britons of Strathclyde
Angles of Bernica
Niduari Picts
Scotia
Dalaradia
Manann

ENDNOTES

1 See, for example, Moore, ed, *The Irish Sea Province in Archaeology and History*, Cardiff: 1970

2 Hanna, WA, *Celtic Migrations*, Belfast: Pretani Press, 1985, p33

3 Hanna, *op cit*, p24

4 Glover, Janet, R, *The Story of Scotland*, London: Faber & Faber, 1977, p13

5 Bannerman, John, *Studies in the History of Dalriada*, Edinburgh: Scottish Academic Press Ltd, 1974

6 An excellent overview of the history of the Stone of Destiny is provided by Nick Aitchison in *Scotland's Stone of Destiny*, Gloucestershire: The History Press Ltd, 2003

7 See, for example, Moore, ed, *The Irish Sea Province in Archaeology and History*, Cardiff: Cambrian Archaeological Association, 1970, p56

8 Bannerman, John, 'The Scots of Dalriada', in Menzies, Gordon, ed, *Who are the Scots?*, BBC, 1971, p72

9 'The Chronicle of Henry of Huntingdon', quoted in Glover, Janet, R, *The Story of Scotland*, London: Faber & Faber, 1977, p39

10 Glover, *op cit*, p39

11 Laing, Lloyd and Jenny, *The Picts and the Scots*, Gloucestershire: The History Press Ltd, 1996, pviii

12 Laing and Laing, *op cit*,, pviii

13 Laing and Laing, *op cit*, p2

14 John Bannerman points out in his *Studies in the History of Dalriada*, *op cit*, p106, that the ruling family of Dal Riata seemed to have been well aware of the advantage of intermarriage with neighbouring royal houses; at least two princes appear to have married into the royal families of Pictland.

15 For a detailed account of the Dalriadian connection, see Bannerman, John, *Studies in the History of Dalriada*, Edinburgh: Scottish Academic Press, 1974

16 This translation is from Laidler, Keith, *The Head of God. The Lost treasure of the Templars*, London: W&N, 1998, p53

17 See, for example, Armit, Ian, *Celtic Scotland*, London: 2005, p12–13

18 Study conducted by Dr Dan Bradley and PhD student Brian McEvoy, and featured in McEvoy, Richards, Forster and Bradley, 'The Longue Durée of Genetic Ancestry: Multiple Genetic Marker Systems and Celtic Origins on the Atlantic Facade of Europe', *The American Journal of Human Genetics*, 1 October 2004, 75(4) pp 693–702

19 Laing and Laing, *op cit*, p66

20 Skillen, Joseph, *Ulster Journal of Archaeology*, vol X, 1904

21 Laing and Laing, *op cit*, p76

22 Williams, Ronald, *The Lords of the Isles: The Clan Donald and the Early Kingdom of the Scots*, London: 1984, p39

23 Williams, *op cit*, p39

24 Hanna, *op cit*, p35

25 Hanna, *op cit*, p37

26 Hughes, AJ, and Hanna, RJ, *Place Names of Northern Ireland*, vol II, The Ards, Northern Ireland Place Name Project, 1992, p195

27 Bannerman, *Studies in the History of Dalriada*, *op cit*, p157

28 McCahan, Robert, 'Dunseveric Castle', in *McCahan's Local Histories*, reprinted by the Glens of Antrim Historical Society, 1988, compiled by Dr Cathal Dallat

29 Carey, JA, *Historical Notes on the Abbey and Parish of Bangor*, Belfast: John Aiken

30 See, for example, Mallory, JP, *Navan Fort: The Ancient Capital of Ulster*, undated, published on behalf of the Friends of Navan by the Ulster Archaeological Society.

31 Adamson, Ian, *Bangor, Light of the World*, Bangor: Fairview Press, 1979

32 Adamson, *op cit*

Chapter Two

KINGS AND INVASION: the Bruce family and the medieval period in Ulster

An artist's impression of the invasion of Edward Bruce at Larne in 1315. Published in a programme for Larne Grand Fete and Fancy Fair, June 1899.

In May 1315 Edward Bruce, the brother of Robert the Bruce, King of Scotland, in an effort to make himself overlord of Ireland, sailed an invasion fleet into Larne Lough, disembarking with 6,000 men at the Corran. These were battle-hardened troops, who had, not long before, taken part in the decisive Battle of Bannockburn, which secured Scottish independence. The portion of land at which they disembarked is not far from the modern harbour area, where modern tourists just arriving from the Scottish coast also come ashore. The Corran juts into the mouth of Larne Lough and was once the site of two castles, the Curran Castle and the Olderfleet Castle. A ruin at the Corran today is known as Olderfleet Castle but is believed to be the ruins of the older Curran Castle. This castle was once host to Robert the Bruce, who was married into the family of the Earl of Ulster and was feudal lord of lands in County Antrim, extending north from Larne along the coast. During the Scottish Wars of Independence, Robert was literally on the run from the English forces and sought refuge on a secluded coastline. There is a famous story of how, while hiding out in a cave, he watched a spider weave its web, patiently rebuilding the construction each time it was damaged by the wind. There are several places that lay claim to having hosted Robert the Bruce at that time, one of which is Rathlin Island off the North Antrim coast. The island's claim is a sound one, as it is convenient to the shores of Scotland and also in territory that was familiar to Robert. With this historic claim in mind, one of the caves in Rathlin Island's impressive cliffs is named 'Bruce's Cave'.

The Corran at Larne, where Edward Bruce invaded Ireland in May 1315.

It was thus hardly a surprise that Edward Bruce would choose the County Antrim coastline as the embarkation point for an attempt to claim the kingship of Ireland. However, his arrival at the Corran was not met with universal approval. While some Irish chieftains and noble families welcomed him, he also found opposition from the Anglo-Normans, who had been settling the area from the period of Edward de Courcy's invasion and seizure of the Earldom of Ulster in 1177.

Archdeacon John Barbour recounted the life and times of Robert the Bruce in his epic historical poem *The Bruce*, written about 1375 and running to 20 books, each containing 500–600 lines of poetry. Included in this poem are references to Robert Bruce's time spent at Rathlin Island, and Edward Bruce's three-year campaign in Ireland. It is interesting that the equivalent of two books of *The Bruce* relate to east Ulster.[1]

Church Bay on Rathlin Island. The Island was said to be a refuge for Robert the Bruce.

After Edward's arrival at Larne, the first battle he fought on Irish soil was at the rural location of Mounthill, a few miles outside the town. The Scots were victorious, along with their O'Neill, McQuillan and McCartan allies, while another battle was believed to be fought at Pathfoot near Glenarm in the Glens of Antrim. After the Battle of Mounthill, Edward moved his army into the countryside and then moved to besiege Carrickfergus. His armies also sacked Downpatrick and did much to wipe out the Norman settlement in the area. He was eventually crowned King of Ireland, but was killed a short time after in battle at Dundalk.

Carrickfergus, the centre of English authority in Ulster in the sixteenth century.

Drawn by WH Bartlett and engraved by JC Armytage. Taken from Willis, NP and Stirling Coyne, J, *The Scenery and Antiquities of Ireland*, London: Virtue Press, 1841

There was a cairn at Mounthill said to commemorate the battle, and to have been erected over the bodies of slain Scots. The Ordnance Survey Memoir for that area states:

> "Within memory three large standing stones stood near it [the scene of the battle], within a distance of each other. They were known as Bruce's Stones. The mound from which the place derived its name was termed Bruce's Cairn. It stood in an adjoining field until the year 1835, when it was finally demolished. It is said to have been raised to one of Bruce's generals who fell in the action. About 80 years since a grave constructed out of large flat slabs, and containing a quantity of black ashes was discovered near the base of the cairn, which was formed of stones."[2]

Another reference notes that earthern cinerary urns, rudely ornamented and containing dust and small particles of bones, had been found in Bruce's cairn and in the vicinity of the 'druidical altars' (an elaborate series of structures including stone circles) in the townland of Ballydown. This suggests that the archaeological site actually predated the 1315 battle and may have been of more ancient origins.

The Ordnance Survey Memoir also records that quantities of coins found in the parish have included those of the reign of Robert Bruce. Another claim for the area was that "There was a fort of stones on Mount Hill Fair green, in digging up of which an urn was found many years ago, when Robert McWilliams destroyed this fort. Tradition states that all his cattle died after he destroyed this fort." If this is not referring to the 'Bruce' cairn, it is indicating that there were other ruins in the area.

Another of the landscape links in the area is the place name of Bruslee, near Ballyclare. Bruslee is said to refer to the camp, or field, of Bruce. It is believed that Bruce and his army moved towards Ballynure to capture a Logan castle there following the battle at Mounthill. Unlike the place name, which has survived over so many centuries, the Logan castle no longer forms part of the landscape.

Among those whom we know sided with Bruce in the struggle from 1315 was Sir Michael of Kilkenan in Islandmagee. In 1320 the Prior of St John of Jerusalem in Ireland complained to the King of the great losses which he had sustained to the Scots and the rebels who supported Bruce, especially through the instrumentality of Michael of Kilkenan and John Fitz Nicholas of Slaine (in the Ards). The King responded by seizing Michael's lands at Portmuck and Kilkenan (now Kilcoan in Islandmagee) and giving them to the Order. The church at nearby Ballykeel was also under the control of the Order of St John of Jerusalem, the rival of the Knights Templar, who had given their support to Robert Bruce, being instrumental, some claim, in the victory at Bannockburn in 1314.

The Macdonnells of the Isles

In the medieval period the MacDonnells of the Isles had established a presence in County Antrim, with John Mor MacDonnell marrying Margery Bisset, heiress of the Bisset family. The Bissets had been expelled from Scotland further along their ancestral tree for the murder of Patrick de Galloway, whose family had held lands in Antrim under King John. John Bisset and his uncle Walter were granted lands in Antrim by Walter de Burgo, Earl of Ulster. The Bissets founded a friary at Glenarm on the Antrim Coast, the remains of which can still be viewed today inside the boundaries of an old cemetery attached to the local Parish Church. Remnants of impressive stone carvings once wrought by stonemasons from Kintyre in Scotland for the old abbey can be viewed inside the modern St Patrick's Church, while a stained glass window erected by one of the Earls of Antrim highlights the family claim to descend from Milesius, King of Spain, and the daughter of one of the Egyptian pharaohs.[3] The Bissets, whose descent continued through Bisset, McEoin and McKeown lines, would continue to feature strongly in North Antrim although they would eventually be superseded by their MacDonnell allies in the 1520s.[4]

A medieval stone carving by Kintyre stonemasons of a horseman from the old Bissett friary at Glenarm. It highlights the connection with Scotland across the North Channel in medieval times. The stone is now housed in St Patrick's Parish Church in Glenarm.

The MacDonnell family with it's claimed ancestry stretching back to ancient times, would stake a strong claim across the short sea channel from their heartland, which can hardly have been a surprise given the geographical proximity of the locations.

The history of the fifteenth and sixteenth century was a turbulent one, and the MacDonnells were often involved in political intrigue and conflict. In the 1400s John Mor MacDonnell, for example, was persuaded by his allies that he was rightful owner of lands south of Ardnamurchan, and went to war with his brother Donald of Islay, then Lord of the Isles. The latter drew to his force MacLeods of Lewis, Mackintoshes, Mackenzies, Camerons, McNeils of Barra and others, all strong fighting men, and drove John Mor MacDonnell and his force out of Kintyre. John fled to Galloway and was forced to take refuge with his wife's family in the Glens of Antrim as the pursuit continued. It was an unhappy affair, brought to a conclusion when John Mor realised that the cause was lost (and his life might be too), and went to Islay to prostrate himself before his brother and plea for those who had joined with him. Donald pardoned his brother, but the chief of the MacFinnon clan, who was blamed for being instrumental in prompting the rebellion, was hanged.[5]

An artist's impression of Dunluce Castle.

Drawn by WH Bartlett and engraved by J Cousen. Taken from Willis, NP and Stirling Coyne, J, *The Scenery and Antiquities of Ireland*, London: Virtue Press, 1841

The Highland Scots' presence is perhaps most graphically underlined by the magnificent ruins of one of the most distinctive sites in Northern Ireland; Dunluce Castle on the North Antrim coast. Dunluce was once the home to the MacDonnells. The famous novelist Sir Walter Scott, upon visiting it in 1814, wrote that the ruins resembled Dunnottar Castle[6] in Scotland, although on a smaller scale: "The ruins occupy perhaps more than an acre of ground, being the level top of a high rock advanced into the sea, by which it is surrounded on three sides, and divided from the mainland by a deep chasm …"[7]

Sir Randall MacDonnell, the first Earl of Antrim, was the first of his family to use the castle as a family residence, and he died there in 1636. His son Randal, succeeded him, and it was during the time when Randal's wife, Catherine Manners, lived there that part of the kitchens fell into the sea, taking nine servants with them. The Duchess, perhaps not surprisingly, left the castle and never returned.

The family seat changed to Glenarm, where it remains, and there are many other sites associated with them or their retainers. At Bonamargey friary outside Ballycastle, where the MacDonnells lived before moving to Dunluce, there is a memorial to John Macnaghten, "first secretaire to the first Earle of Antrim who departed this Life in the yeare of our Lord God 1630". The descendants of the families the MacDonnells brought with them from Kintyre and the Islands remain in the Glens today.

Glenarm Castle, which became the home of the MacDonnell family and remains the seat of the Earls of Antrim.

There is an interesting cultural mix relating to the Plantation period. Under their land re-grant the MacDonnells had to bring a certain number of Scots settlers over to Ulster. Where previously those they had brought from Kintyre had been Roman Catholic, a Lowland plantation had occurred in Kintyre in the interim and the new settlers were Presbyterian. The evidence of this mix can be seen in names and religious denomination in the area today.

Until the building of the Antrim Coast Road in the nineteenth century it is probably quite true to say that there was more connection between the Glens of Antrim and the land on the other side of the Straits of Moyle than there was with many other parts of the north of Ireland. Geographical isolation helped continue the ties of centuries. Indeed, whenever the MacDonnells felt under pressure from those around them in Antrim, they would light bonfires on the cliff tops and support would come from Kintyre and elsewhere on the opposite coast across the straits of Moyle.

Help was often required, for the MacDonnell presence in County Antrim often led to conflict, sometimes with the McQuillans of the Route, the O'Neills or the English authorities. Early in 1565, when Shane O'Neill marched on the Glens from Newry, warning fires were lit along the Antrim Coast in order to hasten reinforcements from the west coast of Scotland for the MacDonnells. The incursion into the Glens resulted in a battle near Bonamargie Friary in Ballycastle, in which the Scots were defeated and James MacDonnell was taken prisoner and left to die in a dungeon. Shane O'Neill was later killed by the MacDonnells in revenge.

In 1575 the MacDonnells found themselves in conflict with the English authorities, a force under the command of John Norris being sent into their territory. Sorley Boy MacDonnell, being aware of the English advance, sent MacDonnell women and children to Rathlin Island for safety, but the English force landed on the island and besieged the unfortunate Highlanders inside Bruce's Castle. Although surrender terms were agreed, around 600 were massacred, the vast majority of them civilians and only 50 being the Scots garrison. Sorley Boy was forced to watch helplessly from the headlands near Ballycastle. Later, Elizabeth I wrote to the Earl of Essex, under whose command Norris had operated, to thank him for his action against "all such Scots as do infest that realme of Ireland ..."[8]

Less than ten years later there was another conflict between English and Scots in the Glens, this time 500 foot and 100 horsemen, along with Irish troops, moving from Carrickfergus and Coleraine into MacDonnell territory, under the command of Henry Bagnall. They met fierce resistance and were forced in that instance to retreat, but there were further attacks on the MacDonnells. The following year a compromise was reached which officially acknowledged the Highland Scots' presence in the Glynnes or Glens of Antrim. Sorley MacDonnell went to Dublin to pledge allegiance to the Queen, and in turn had his lands formally indentured to him.

This might have ended the period of aggression and conflict, but as the sixteenth century drew to an end another situation arose which upset the MacDonnells. Sir James MacDonnell, who had succeeded Sorley Boy, is said to have been greatly provoked by the harshness of a tax-collecting expedition against the MacDonnells in 1597. He raised a considerable force of men and moved south to threaten Carrickfergus, the seat of English authority. The English garrison appears to have responded rashly to the provocation, giving chase to the Scots, who retreated across country.

The English governor, Sir John Chichester, had marshalled his troops and marched out to meet the Scots. Accounts suggest that this retreat continued for at least four miles, from hilltop to hilltop, until the Scots finally stopped in the townland of Aldfreck outside modern Ballycarry. Chichester sought advice from his officers on what should be done, and the response was that, with troops tired from a recent expedition and low on ammunition, caution should be employed. However, a critical change in opinion occurred when one officer, a Captain Merriman, told the Governor bluntly that "it was a shame we should suffer a sort of beggars to brave us in that sort." The Governor appeared interested in talking despite this remark, however, but two horsemen came up and made similar comments to that of Merriman. The die appears to have been cast at this point.

In front of Chichester's smaller force were an estimated 700 Scots on a hilltop, but two miles behind them were Scots bowmen and Irish with swords and pikes numbering another 800. The ground had been chosen well. The English garrison formed into battle formation and advanced on the Scots, who retreated from the hill on which they had placed themselves. Chichester ordered a horse charge, but only a few horsemen seem to have carried this through. Captain Charles Eggerton's account of the battle tells us that "the Governor commanded the lieutenant of horse to charge, which he did, but not above six of his company followed him …"[9] This may have been because the ground chosen for the charge was revealed to be marshy and that horses and horsemen realised this during the charge. Another account details that soldiers were able to conceal themselves in high grass and "some in the ouse up to their shoulders …" which would tend to support the theory that the Scots had chosen their ground well.

The Old Mill Glen, Ballycarry, said to be the location of the Battle of Aldfreck in 1597. However, it is not exactly clear where the battle took place.

In response to the lack of an effective cavalry attack, the Scots wheeled around and attacked the wings of their opponents to devastating effect. Sir Ralph Lanes, one of those present on the day, tells us that the English "were drawn to the shrubby ground where the ambushment lay. And in the skirmish the garrison bands, having spent all their powder, and a troop of the Scots horse having fallen behind the Governor, between the town and the English, offered to charge them upon the rear when suddenly, out of the shrubs, was discharged upon the rest a whole volley of shot." It was a fatal fusillade in what was to be a decisive battle.

The English force had itself given encouragement to the Scots and Irish through panicked shouts of low ammunition and the need for reinforcements; such calls only added vigour to the MacDonnell attack. Scots horsemen came within two pike lengths of the beleaguered English force and inflicted serious casualties. Chichester, at one point in the battle, used his sword on his own men to try and prevent their flight. He was shot a number of times while on his horse and was killed. His body was later beheaded by the victorious MacDonnells. The loss of the Governor only served to add to the panic. Several officers managed to reach Larne Lough a short distance away and swim across to Islandmagee. History tells us that Captains Merriman, Eggerton and Lieutenant Barry were among them. Sir Moses Hill,[10] who had ridden to Carrickfergus for reinforcement, returned too late.

The bleak post-battle landscape undoubtedly had bodies of wounded and dying strewn around, and weapons discarded. Captain Eggerton tells us in his estimation that 160–180 soldiers were killed in the battle with up to 40 injured. Lane suggests 220 footmen slain beside the officers, who included Chichester, Captain Mansell, Lieutenant Price and Lieutenant Walsh and at least seven sergeants. Around 60 of the enemy were killed. It was an unmitigated disaster for the English force. One prisoner, Captain Constable, later noted that MacDonnell, who would be pardoned in time for the episode, had said the relentless pursuit of his men by the garrison made it seem to him that a battle was inevitable. The choice of the ground for the battle, however, suggested rather more premeditation.

Not long after, Sir Arthur Chichester, a brother of Sir John, became Governor and laid the land waste for 20 miles around Carrickfergus. Just over a decade later, new Lowland Scots settlers had begun to arrive in the area with no knowledge of the events of 1597. This was so much the case, in fact, that the location of the battle was lost to history and has remained the subject of local debate.

The battle illustrates for us that the Scots' pre-plantation presence in Antrim was one which was often turbulent. The battle occurred at the end of a century which had seen much bloody conflict between the MacDonnells and the English authorities based in Carrickfergus. In 1555, for example, the Earl of Essex had to march from Dublin to relieve Carrick, which had been besieged by the Scots, and he did so with great slaughter. One of the most famous attacks on the MacDonnells and their allies occurred, as has been noted, when the Earl of Essex massacred women and children on Rathlin Island, where they had been sent for safety. The murderous assault was witnessed from Ballycastle by the MacDonnells, who had been wrong-footed. Aldfreck had something of a retaliatory nature in that sense.

The Battle of Aldfreck also illustrates the point that before the so-called Plantation settlers arrived, there was a strong Scots presence on Ulster's east coast. The MacDonnells simply extended themselves across a channel which was not a barrier but an important means of transport.

HISTORICAL TRAILS
SITES TO VISIT

The following locations may be of interest as historical sites relating to the medieval Scots period:

The ruins of Olderfleet Castle near Larne Harbour.

Olderfleet Castle, Larne, County Antrim

In 1242 the Bisset family, who had moved across the North Channel from Scotland, built a castle at Olderfleet, near Larne Harbour. The ruins of a seventeenth century building can be found in the area today, although there is some confusion over whether this was Olderfleet or Curran Castle, there having been two in the same area. Historians debate the location of the original Olderfleet, but essentially the landscape would have been similar wherever the castle was located. Access to the sea was common to both, and it was from the sea that Edward Bruce arrived in 1315 with a large army.

His arrival at the Corran point in Larne saw some 6,000 men stream ashore. The Bissets were later recorded as having assembled with other Norman knights to attempt to halt the invasion, but there is some doubt as to whether they might also secretly have welcomed the Bruce invasion. Sir Hugh de Bissett had his lands in the manor of Glenarm and at Olderfleet forfeited after the incident, although he was later pardoned and had them returned.

The old names for the area included Wolderfleet and Wolringis Fyrth, as Archdeacon John Barbour referred to it in the fourteenth century. Through time this became anglicised to Olderfleet. An original castle was built in the area by the Vikings and the castle known today as Olderfleet was once under the charge of Sir Moses Hill, ancestor of the family who founded Hillsborough in County Down.

Today little remains of Olderfleet Castle, although an imposing tower has survived the centuries. The site is located in the heavily industrialised port area, which once included the first power station in Ireland, located several hundred yards away on the Curran Point, and two shipyards that were used for the construction of small coasting vessels and for repairs.

Dunluce Castle on the North Antrim coast was the stronghold of the MacDonnell family in the sixteenth century.

Dunluce Castle, North Antrim

Dunluce rests on the edge of North Antrim, a lasting reminder (despite its obvious air of abandonment) of a past that closely links Ulster to Scotland. For Dunluce was once the home to the MacDonnells, Lords of the Isles and Earls of Antrim. Sir Walter Scott, visiting it in 1814, wrote that the ruins resembled Dunnottar castle in Scotland, although on a smaller scale. It is an impressive structure.

Sir Randall MacDonnell, the first Earl of Antrim, was the first of his family to use the castle as a family residence, and he died there in 1636. His son Randal succeeded him. It was during this time, when Randal's wife Catherine Manners also lived there, that part of the kitchens fell into the sea, taking nine servants with them into eternity. The Duchess, perhaps not surprisingly, left the castle and never returned.

Evidence of the MacDonnells abounds in the Glens of Antrim. The family seat changed to Glenarm, where it remains, and there are many other sites associated with the family or their retainers. At Bonamargey friary outside Ballycastle there is a memorial to John Macnaghten, "first secretaire to the first Earle of Antrim who departed this Life in the yeare of our Lord God 1630." The descendants of the families that the MacDonnells brought with them from Kintyre and the islands remain in the Glens today.

Dunluce Castle, which is one of the most distinctive landmarks in Northern Ireland, was probably built around 1300. It was most likely an ancient fortification site, which was also utilised by the Normans, with Richard de Burgh, Earl of Ulster, creating a castle with five circular towers for bowmen connected by a curtain wall. It was occupied by the de Mandevilles and the McQuillans until around 1560 when the MacDonnells arrived in the Glens of Antrim and staked their claim to the site.

The rugged beauty of the Glens of Antrim, an area settled by the Highland MacDonnells and families associated with them.

Downpatrick, County Down

Downpatrick is located south of Belfast and is the County town of Down in Northern Ireland. It was once the capital of the Earldom of Ulster, and the name comes from *Dun Phadraig* (the fort of Patrick), a reference to St Patrick, who is said to have been buried there.

Another name for the settlement there was Rathkelter, referring to the fort of Kelter, one of the Red Branch Knights of Ulster in ancient times. In the period of the Norman invasion of Ulster, John De Courcy and Knights who advanced from Dublin captured the Earldom of Ulster, and made the town the capital. De Courcy built a castle close to the ancient rath site, and the remains of his motte and bailey can still be seen, but nothing remains of the stone built Castle Derras.

When Edward Bruce invaded Ulster in 1315, he pushed south from Larne with his force of battle-hardened troops and laid siege to Downpatrick the following year, later sacking the town and burning down the cathedral which he found there.

Remnants of the Norman presence in the area include nearby Inch Abbey, a fine and imposing ruin on a lakeside within sight of the town. It is believed that the abbey was located on the site of a Celtic monastery which was plundered by Norse invaders in AD1002. In 1187 de Courcy established a Cistercian Abbey there. The Down Cathedral, which is an excellent example of an Anglo-Norman Church, includes the supposed grave of St Patrick in its cemetery and a number of interesting and historical memorials and stained glass windows. Museums include the Down County museum, located at the site of the former County Gaol.

The magnificent statue of Robert the Bruce at Bannockburn.

Bannockburn, Scotland

Immediately south of the city of Stirling in Scotland is the small settlement of Bannockburn, named after the small stream which runs through the area. In 1314 the area was pivotal in the future development of Scottish history after the Scots won a major victory in the Wars of Independence against England.

The Scots had laid siege to the English garrison at Stirling and negotiated a treaty which would permit the garrison to be saved if it held out until a certain date. As the date approached, an English army moved to relieve the city and Robert the Bruce, commanding four schiltrons, or divisions, set up his camp in an area where the soldiers were screened by trees.

On 23 June 1314 the Battle of Bannockburn began. The first action involved an English knight named Henry de Bohun, who, seeing Robert the Bruce riding around to ascertain the strength of the enemy, charged him with his lance extended. The Bruce carefully maneuvered his horse at the last minute, catching de Bohun off guard. As the Englishmen's lance went swiftly past, Bruce raised himself in the saddle and brought his battle axe down hard on the opposing Knight, killing him instantly. It was the start of a military disaster for the English army. The battle continued the next day, but the English were routed and attempts to subjugate Scotland were now in serious doubt.

It is estimated that over 30,000 English soldiers were killed in the fighting at Bannockburn, including many members of the nobility. Scottish losses were very small. English prisoners were ransomed for Scots prisoners including Bruce's wife, daughter and friend the Bishop of Glasgow. Edward II lost an entire supply train of wagons valued at £200,000, an enormous sum for the period, and was hotly pursued across the border by James Douglas, while the castle at Stirling surrendered the next day, to be followed by many of the English garrison castles in Scotland.

The battle is commemorated by a visitor's centre and an imposing statue of Robert the Bruce on horseback, while a Saltire is raised high on a giant flagpole nearby. The memorial plaque at Bannockburn is headed by the slogan "For God and St Andrew", alluding to an epic speech which Bruce made to his men just before the battle. Over the centuries much of the battlefield site has probably been lost in the development of roads, farms and housing, and there is still some debate over the exact location of the battle.

HISTORICAL QUOTES

Extract from the Scottish Declaration of Arbroath, which was drawn up by Bernard de Linton, Chancellor of Scotland, and signed by the nobles of Scotland on 6 April 1320, prior to being sent to Pope John XXII in an effort to win his approval for the Scots in their conflict against England. The Pope at that time was not only a temporal but also a secular leader.

"To the most Holy Father and Lord in Christ, the Lord John, by divine providence Supreme Pontiff of the Holy Roman and Universal Church, his humble and devout sons Duncan, Earl of Fife, Thomas Randolph, Earl of Moray, Lord of Man and of Annandale, Patrick Dunbar, Earl of March, Malise, Earl of Strathearn, Malcolm, Earl of Lennox, William, Earl of Ross, Magnus, Earl of Caithness and Orkney, and William, Earl of Sutherland; Walter, Steward of Scotland, William Soules, Butler of Scotland, James, Lord of Douglas, Roger Mowbray, David, Lord of Brechin, David Graham, Ingram Umfraville, John Menteith, guardian of the earldom of Menteith, Alexander Fraser, Gilbert Hay, Constable of Scotland, Robert Keith, Marischal of Scotland, Henry St Clair, John Graham, David Lindsay, William Oliphant, Patrick Graham, John Fenton, William Abernethy, David Wemyss, William Mushet, Fergus of Ardrossan, Eustace Maxwell, William Ramsay, William Mowat, Alan Murray, Donald Campbell, John Cameron, Reginald Cheyne, Alexander Seton, Andrew Leslie, and Alexander Straiton, and the other barons and freeholders and the whole community of the realm of Scotland send all manner of filial reverence, with devout kisses of his blessed feet.

Most Holy Father and Lord, we know and from the chronicles and books of the ancients we find that among other famous nations our own, the Scots, has been graced with widespread renown. They journeyed from Greater Scythia by way of the Tyrrhenian Sea and the Pillars of Hercules, and dwelt for a long course of time in Spain among the most savage tribes, but nowhere could they be subdued by any race, however barbarous. Thence they came, twelve hundred years after the people of Israel crossed the Red Sea, to their home in the west where they still live today. The Britons they first drove out, the Picts they utterly destroyed, and, even though very often assailed by the Norwegians, the Danes and the English, they took possession of that home with many victories and untold efforts; and, as the historians of old time bear witness, they have held it free of all bondage ever since. In their kingdom there have reigned one hundred and thirteen kings of their own royal stock, the line unbroken by a single foreigner.

The high qualities and deserts of these people, were they not otherwise manifest, gain glory enough from this: that the King of kings and Lord of lords, our Lord Jesus Christ, after His Passion and Resurrection, called them, even though settled in the uttermost parts of the earth, almost the first to His most holy faith. Nor would He have them confirmed in that faith by merely anyone but by the first of His Apostles -- by calling, though second or third in rank -- the most gentle Saint Andrew, the Blessed Peter's brother, and desired him to keep them under his protection as their patron forever.

The Most Holy Fathers your predecessors gave careful heed to these things and bestowed many favours and numerous privileges on this same kingdom and people, as being the special charge of the Blessed Peter's brother. Thus our nation under their protection did indeed live in freedom and peace up to the time when that mighty prince the King of the English, Edward, the father of the one who reigns today, when our kingdom had no head and our people harboured no malice or treachery and were then unused to wars or invasions, came in the guise of a friend and ally to harass them as an enemy. The deeds of cruelty, massacre, violence, pillage, arson, imprisoning prelates, burning down monasteries, robbing and killing monks and nuns, and yet other outrages without number which he committed against our people, sparing neither age nor sex, religion nor rank, no one could describe nor fully imagine unless he had seen them with his own eyes.

But from these countless evils we have been set free, by the help of Him Who though He afflicts yet heals and restores, by our most tireless Prince, King and Lord, the Lord Robert. He, that his people and his heritage might be delivered out of the hands of our enemies, met toil and fatigue, hunger and peril, like another Macabaeus or Joshua and bore them cheerfully. Him, too, divine providence, his right of succession according to or laws and customs which we shall maintain to the death, and the due consent and assent of us all have made our Prince and King. To him, as to the man by whom salvation has been wrought unto our people, we are bound both by law and by his merits that our freedom may be still maintained, and by him, come what may, we mean to stand.

Yet if he should give up what he has begun, and agree to make us or our kingdom subject to the King of England or the English, we should exert ourselves at once to drive him out as our enemy and a subverter of his own rights and ours, and make some other man who was well able to defend us our King; for, as long as but a hundred of us remain alive, never will we on any conditions be brought under English rule. It is in truth not for glory, nor riches, nor honours that we are fighting, but for freedom -- for that alone, which no honest man gives up but with life itself."

Archdeacon John Barbour was Archdeadon of Aberdeen and wrote an epic and voluminous poem in 1375 detailing the dramatic years of Robert the Bruce's struggle for the Scottish throne. *The Bruce* is one of the most outstanding historical sources for the period and was divided into twenty books. This section deals with the invasion of Ulster by Edward Bruce in May 1315. It details the decision of Edward the Bruce to launch a campaign to win the throne of Ireland, and how he assembled a force, with his brother's approval, at Ayr on the Scottish coast and sailed for Wolringis firth (Olderfleet, now Larne Lough). Barbour lists many of the knights who sailed with Edward, and also some of the Norman Knights of Ulster who were arrayed against him.[11]

Original	Modern translation
The erle off Carrik Schyr Edward,	The Earl of Carrick, Sir Edward,
That stoutar wes than a libard	Was stronger than a leopard
And had na will to be in pes,	And had no desire to live in peace
Thocht that Scotland to litill wes	For he felt Scotland was too small
Till his brother and him alsua,	For him and his brother both
Tharfor to purpos gan he ta	Therefore he resolved
That he off Irland wald be king.	That he would be king of Ireland
Tharfor he send and had tretyng	He sent and negotiated
With the Irschery off lrland,	With the Irish in Ireland
That in thar leawte tuk on hand	Who undertook to make him
Off all lrland to mak him king	King of Ireland
With-thi that he with hard fechting	Provided that he with hard fighting
Mycht ourcum the Inglismen	Could overthrow the English
That in the land war wonnand then,	Who were then in that land,
And thai suld help with all thar mycht.	Which they would help with all their might.
And he that hard thaim mak sic hycht	He, hearing them make this promise
Intill his hart had gret liking	Was glad in his heart
And with the consent of the king	And with the consent of the King
Gadryt him men off gret bounte	He assembled men of great courage
And at Ayr syne schippyt he	And took ship at Ayr
Intill the neyst moneth of Mai,	The following month of May
Till lrland held he straucht his wai.	To make his way straight to Ireland.
He had thar in his cumpany	He had in his company
The Erle Thomas that wes worthi	Earl Thomas, a worthy man,
And gud Schyr Philip the Mowbray	And good Sir Philip Mowbray
That sekyr wes in hard assay,	Who was strong under pressure
Schyr Jhone the Soullis ane gud knycht	Sir John Soules, a good knight,
And Schyr Jhone Stewart that wes wycht	And Sir John Stewart, who was brave

Original

The Ramsay als of Ouchterhous
That wes wycht and chevalrous
And Schyr Fergus off Ardrossane
And other knychtis mony ane.
In Wolringis Fyrth aryvyt thai
Sauffiy but bargan or assay
And send thar schippis hame ilkan.
A gret thing have thai undretane
That with sa quhoyne as thai war thar
That war sex thousand men but mar
Schup to werray all Irland,
Quhar thai sall se molly thousand
Cum armyt on thaim for to fycht,
But thocht thai quhone war thai war wicht,
And forout drede or effray
In twa bataillis tuk thar way
Towart Cragfergus it to se.

Bot the lordis of that countre
Mandveill, Besat and Logane
Thar men assemblyt everilkane,
The Savagis wes alsua thar,
And quhen thai assemblit war
That war wele ner twenty thousand.

Modern translation

Also Ramsey of Oughterhouse
Who was brave and chivalrous
And Sir Fergus of Ardrossan
And many other knights.
They arrived at Larne Lough
Safely and without opposition
And then sent their ships home again.
They have undertaken a major thing
That with such a small number as they were
No more than six thousand men
They should attempt to conquer Ireland,
Where there were so many thousands
Come armed to fight against them,
But although few in number, they were brave
And without any dread or fear
They made their way in two divisions
Towards Carrickfergus, to see it.

But the lords of that country,
Mandeville, Bisset and Logan
Assembled all of their men
The Savages were also there
And when they were assembled
There were nearly twenty thousand.[12]

HISTORICAL FIGURES

Robert the Bruce, King of Scots

Robert the Bruce, future King of Scotland, is believed to have been born 12 July 1274 into an aristocratic Scottish family. He was a descendant of Robert de Brus, a Norman Lord who was granted lands in Annandale in south Scotland by David I. Robert the Bruce was second Earl of Carrick and also feudal lord of lands in County Antrim as a result of intermarriage. In 1298, following a time of upheaval in Scottish history, Bruce became a guardian of Scotland along with John Comyn. It was the stabbing of Comyn in the church at Dumfries that led to Bruce being excommunicated by the Pope of the day. Bruce was undeterred by this, and proclaimed his right to the throne. On 27 March he had himself crowned King at Scone. The following year, Bruce was deposed by Edward's army and forced to flee. His wife and daughters were imprisoned and three of his brothers executed. Robert is said to have spent a period on the island of Rathlin off the coast of Antrim during this time, when he was evading the English authorities. He returned to the Scottish mainland to wage a successful guerilla war, which culminated, but did not end, with the Battle of Bannockburn.

Eventually Robert received papal recognition as King of an independent Scotland and in 1327 Edward II made peace with Scotland, removing all claims to sovereignty over the Scots. Robert, who is believed to have suffered from a form of leprosy, died on 7 June 1329 and was buried at Dunfermline. He had wished to take part in a Crusade, and requested that his heart be taken to the Holy Land. The receptacle only got as far as Spain, when Sir James Douglas famously threw it into the middle of a group of Moors as he charged to his death. Bruce's heart was returned to Scotland and buried in Melrose Abbey.

Edward Bruce, Earl of Carrick

Edward Bruce was one of five sons of Robert de Brus, Earl of Carrick, and Majorie, Countess of Carrick. He was the younger brother of Robert the Bruce and took part in the guerilla warfare which culminated in the Battle of Bannockburn. He was a commander at Bannockburn. In addition to being created Earl of Carrick, Edward would also be crowned King of Ireland after his invasion of 1315. It has been suggested that he may have been fostered as a child, as was a common practice among the Scots aristocracy at the time, and that this may have been across the North Channel, helping explain his interest in being King of Ireland.

Bruce had at least one son to Isabella, daughter of John of Strathbogie, ninth Earl of Atholl, and Alexander Bruce succeeded to his father's Earldom.

The invasion of Ireland was costly to Edward Bruce, for, although initially successful, he lost his life in the Battle of Faughart outside Dundalk in 1318. It is believed that his remains were buried in the Cooley peninsula, although a strong tradition in the locality of Larne was that his body was buried under a cairn at Mounthill, site of his first victory on Irish soil. The period was a brutal one, famine gripped Ireland as the result of Bruce's campaign and the 'slash and burn' tactics of his opponents to prevent him having sustenance. It was a costly period for the Bruce family on both sides of the Irish Sea; Edward died in Ireland, and his three brothers, Niall, Thomas and Alexander were all captured and executed by the English during the conflict in Scotland.

Sir James MacDonnell

The intermarriage of the MacDonnell family into the Bissets in County Antrim produced a major medieval dynasty in the Glens of Antrim, but it was not without turmoil and conflict, as was common in the period.

Conflict between the Scots Highlanders, Irish clans and the English authority was still occurring at the end of the sixteenth century. Sir James MacDonnell won the Battle of Aldfreck, outside Carrickfergus, and captured Olderfleet Castle at Larne for a time. MacDonnell eventually received a pardon for his activities in 1597 and, according to legend, is said to have visited St Nicholas Church and been amazed to see a memorial effigy of Sir John Chichester, with his head intact, declaring how he was surprised since he had separated him from his body. Like all good stories, it may simply be that, since there is no record of MacDonnell visiting the Norman Church in Carrickfergus.

The MacDonnells, who dominated the history of the Western Isles, also figure largely in the history of East Ulster. Today the seat of the family remains at Glenarm, where one of the Earls of Antrim erected a window in St Patrick's Parish Church to highlight the family claim to be descended from Milesius, King of Spain, who took part in migration to Ireland. Remnants of stone architecture inside the church are examples of pieces found in the adjacent lands, which once housed a friary established by Robert Bisset and Alexander MacDonnell, Lord of the Isles.

John de Bisset

The Bisset family was Anglo-Norman and probably first arrived in Scotland in the twelfth century, settling in two main areas, Moray and Berwickshire. Those who settled in Ulster were from the latter region, and in 1242 Walter de Bisset and his nephew John Bisset were accused of the murder of Patrick de Galloway, Earl of

Athol, who had earlier killed a Bisset at a tournament. The house in which the murder took place had been set alight to try to conceal the matter, but the Bissets soon had to seek the protection of the King, Alexander II. They eventually fled to Antrim, however, and his lands and those of his family were seized. Walter Bisset is said to have gone to England, while John obtained lands at Glenarm in County Antrim, and the family became established in the Glens of Antrim.

In 1272 it is recorded that Bissets had lands on the coast at Droagh, Cairncastle and Glenarm and that they had three mills, an orchard and a fishery as well as other property.[13]

In AD1400 the heiress of the Bisset family, Margery Bisset, who was daughter of Sir John Bisset, was married to John Mor MacDonald of Isla, thus establishing a strong MacDonald presence in County Antrim. The families appear to have had strong connections for at least a century prior to the marriage.

The Bissets built a castle at Larne harbour, named Olderfleet, and also established a friary at Glenarm, the ruins of which still remain in the churchyard at St Patrick's Church of Ireland in the village. They lived at Glenarm but appear not to have built the castle there, as they were listed as tenants. Descendants of the original John Bisset became known as MacEoin Bisset, from which is said to be derived the modern name McKeown.[14]

ENDNOTES

1 Barbour, John, *The Bruce*, with translation and notes by Duncan, AMM, Edinburgh: 1999

2 OS Memoir for the Parishes of County Antrim (Ballynure and District), Belfast: 1995, p115

3 See, for example, 'Kintyre Masons carved a heritage in stone on Antrim Coast', in *Larne Times*, 29 May 2003

4 For a detailed account of the Bissets and MacDonnells in the Glens of Antrim and the Isles, see MacDonnell, Hector, 'Glenarm Friary and the Bissets', in *The Glynnes*, annual journal of the Glens of Antrim Historical Society, Volume 15, 1987

5 Williams, Ronald, *The Lords of the Isles, The Clan Donald and the Early Kingdom of the Scots*, London: Chatto & Windus, 1984, p181–2

6 Dunnotter Castle near Stonehaven in Aberdeenshire sits on a clifftop, 160 feet above sea level and is linked to the mainland by a narrow stretch of rock. Like Dunluce, it has a considerable history, including being besieged by Cromwell in 1652 and being used to imprison Covenanters in 1684.

7 Quoted in McCahan, Robert, 'The Giant's Causeway and Dunluce Castle', in *McCahan's Local Histories*, a series of pamphlets on North Antrim and the Glens (1923), compiled by Dallat, Cathal and reprinted by the Glens of Antrim Historical Society, 1988.

8 See Wallace Clark, *Rathlin, It's island story*, Coleraine: 1993

9 See, for example, Hume, David, 'The Unanswered questions of a Ballycarry battle four hundred years ago', *Broadisland Journal*, Ballycarry: 1997

10 Hill was the ancestor of the Downshire family, after whom Hillsborough, County Down, is named.

11 For a reprinting of *The Bruce*, complete with a modern translation, see Barbour, *op cit*

12 Based on AAM Duncan's translation in *The Bruce*, Edinburgh: Canongate Books, 1997

13 McKillop, Felix, *Glenarm, A Local History, Belfast*, Belfast: Ulster Journals, 1987, p11

14 McKillop, *op cit*, p11

Chapter Three

THE STEEL BONNETS AND THEIR PLACE IN HISTORY

A memorial statue to the Reivers, the riding clans of the Scots Borders, in the town of Galashiels.

The Scots Borderers have often been compared with the Highlanders, and there are many similarities in terms of the clan system. However, what distinguishes the Borderers from the Highlanders is that the former "were all horsemen".[1] Nothing underlines this more in the modern world than the annual festivals, known as 'Riding the Marches', that take place in Scottish towns such as Kelso, Jedburgh and Selkirk. These colourful events involve horsemen and women riding through the towns and surrounding countryside, complete with much pageantry. These festivals may be a celebration of heritage in the modern world, but they also point to more dangerous times, when securing the marches or boundaries of an area could be a deadly affair. In her study *The Mother Town. Civic Ritual, Symbol and Experience in the Borders of Scotland*, Gwen Kennedy Neville outlines the potency of the Selkirk Common Riding, and the past from which it draws:

"The common riding has been held faithfully in Selkirk for generations on the first Friday after the second Monday in June. In the drama that unfolds early on the common riding morning, the most spectacular aspect is the appearance of four or five hundred horses and riders following the royal burgh standard bearer down High Street, across the river, and around the boundaries of the old town's common lands. The horses are led outward by the town's silver band playing a medley of local songs in the same order and at the same places every year. After the band comes the stream of walkers in a pattern of segments, each behind the flag of a ceremonial organisation – merchants, weavers, hammermen, fleshers, ex-soldiers, and colonials. These are then followed by the town citizenry overflowing into the streets in a flood of revelry and singing. Riders have arrived early from other towns, and Selkirk folk visiting from overseas have come to visit home, adding to the merriment and celebration ... The day begins at 5:00 AM with the first drum and then the singing of 'Hail Smilin' Morn'. By 9:00 the riders have ridden the marches and returned, coming up the hill at a gallop past the old toll, and ending their ride in the market square. There the burgh flag is handed back to the town's provost, and the young standard bearer ceremonially reports to the assembly that he is returning it 'unsullied and untarnished.'"[2]

A Common Riding at the Broadisland Gathering in Ballycarry was an annual event for several years but ceased due to insurance costs.

Courtesy of Peter Rippon and the *Larne Times.*

These Ridings of the Marches are an important and colourful reminder of a past which was often bleak and uncompromisingly tough. Similarly, Hadrian's Wall, built to keep the Picts and the Scots from northern Britain, stands as physical reminder of an area where peace was not permanent and danger often lurked. The Scottish Borders were long an area of conflict and devastation. As a frontier between England and Scotland they were often the first point of contact for an invading army, which spread devastation and mayhem in its wake. The result was that many of those living in the borders had a precarious lifestyle, which led to lawlessness not only as a means of survival but also regulated lawlessness as a way of life. The Borders, as others have noted, gave us negative words such as 'blackmail' and 'bereaved',[3] which say something about the type of area and the nature of some of the people who lived there.

A borders landscape.

Yet this was also an area which bred people who were survivors. Many families who settled in Ulster in the seventeenth century were Borderers, and they brought with them a unique heritage and culture, and a steely resolve which would be tested again in and beyond Ulster. The Borders also gave much to the United States of America. Prominent border historian, George MacDonald Fraser, makes an interesting point from modern history:

> "At a moment when President Richard Nixon was taking part in his inauguration ceremony, he appeared flanked by Lyndon Johnson and Billy Graham. To anyone familiar with Border history it was one of those historical coincidences which send a little shudder through the mind: in that moment, thousands of miles and centuries in time away from the Debatable Land, the threads came together again ... Lyndon Johnson's is a face and figure that everyone in Dumfriesshire knows; the lined, leathery Northern head and rangy, rather loose-jointed frame belong to one of the commonest Border types … Billy Graham has frequently addressed his Scottishness, perhaps a little thoughtlessly, since there are more Grahams on the southern side of the line than on the northern, but again, the face is familiar. Richard Nixon, however, is the perfect example. The blunt, heavy features, the dark complexion, the burly body, and the whole air of dour hardness are as typical of the Anglo-Scottish frontier as the Roman Wall. It is difficult to think of any face that would fit better under a steel bonnet ..."[4]

The area generally accepted as constituting the Borders stretches from Berwick-on-Tweed to the Solway Firth, following closely the line of the Cheviot Hills and crossing some of Britain's most wild and most beautiful landscapes. The Border region not only includes the valleys of the Tweed and the Teviot but also the Solway plain and Galloway. In the fourteenth century the region on the Scottish side was divided administratively into a number of sectors which were to continue to be of importance in the seventeenth century. These were known as the West, Middle and East Marches.

The area was essentially a rural and agricultural one and this was highlighted even during times when there was conflict. It is notable that many of the raids, for example, would take place outside the summer season (when men had work to perform on the farms). Lord Wharton, Lord Deputy General of the English Marches, ordered watch to be kept throughout the extent of the Border from the beginning of October until mid-March, by day on the heights and by night on the fords. Sir Robert Carey wrote in 1597 of the English Borderers that "the last moneths in the yeare are theyr cheiffe time of steallinge, for then are the nightes longest, theyr horse hard at meat and will ride best, cattell strong and will drive furthest ..."[5] Invasion on the other hand was usually in the summer because grass was available then. The battle of Otterburn in 1388, as was recalled in one famous folk song:

> "fell upon the Lammastide
> When the muir-men win their hay"[6]

The borders had always been a troubled region, the first point where invasion from England was felt. In 1296, for example, Edward I, known as the Hammer of the Scots, launched a series of devastating incursions across the Scots border. The aim was to totally demoralise the Scots and the method was to burn castles, villages, farmsteads, devastate crops, put whole communities to the sword and steal sheep and cattle. The Scots inevitably retaliated in similar fashion, and as the war continued both governments encouraged their people to constantly harass their Borders neighbours through incessant raiding. The Borderland was a wasteland in medieval times, where no one was safe and no property was sacred. The tradition

Melrose Abbey on the Scots Borderers is a good example of the scale of the great Border abbeys.

of Riding of the Marches relates to the protection of the boundaries of an area (the term 'March', an English medieval one, has also made its way to Northern Ireland where we talk of 'marches' between neighbours, 'march ditches' and so on).

Borderers quickly realised that no government could assist them against the incessant raiding that occurred. They saw their own strength as being in their families or clan, and that was all that counted. Surviving on the harsh frontier lands became the most important aim in life, and raiding or 'reiving' across the border became, literally, a way of life. Sometimes the reivers 'crossed the line' in other ways too, and their excursions took place nearer home as well as across the border. As events developed, clan rather than a concept of any wider identity became the most important factor.

This process occurred on both sides of the frontier; the Bishop of Carlisle, writing of the English Middle March in 1518, noted that there was more extortion and theft from English than by all the thieves in Scotland.[7] In Hexham every market day he said there were four score to a hundred thieves openly loitering, hardly something which was encouraging to those of a more honest bent. On many occasions English and Scots alliances were formed. The ability to slip across the Border when necessary was not lost on malcontents on both sides. Thomas Musgrave, one harassed Border official, noted that, "They are people that will be Scottishe when they will and English at their pleasure".[8]

Whenever a raid occurred, those who suffered could give immediate chase (within six days) in an ancient custom known as a 'Hot Trod'. Honoured under Border Law, it allowed those who had been 'spoyled' to mount a pursuit, crossing the border if necessary, and follow with hound and horn, hue and cry, those who had stolen their property. It was the duty of all neighbours between the ages of 16 and 60, whether receiving payment from the injured party or not, to join the Trod. The legality of the Hot Trod was symbolised by a piece of burning turf held aloft on a spear point, and the posse had the right to recruit help from the first town which it came to. Failure to comply in supporting the Hot Trod meant that waverers were judged "partakers to the enemies and used as Traitors".

It was the role of the Wardens of the Marches to try and maintain law and order, although this was often difficult and not assisted by family and clan ties. Nevertheless the wardens were the only symbol of authority on the Borders and held a thin line on behalf of the monarch.

Reivers, meanwhile, were most vulnerable when returning home with their fray, which is when many who were caught were tracked down. In 1596 Sir Robert Carey gave an account of an encounter with some reivers. He was on a patrol with 20 men from his garrison looking for activity from the Burnes, well-known Reivers of Teviotdale, when they appeared, driving 'goods' before them which they had stolen. Two of them were killed outright, a third seriously wounded and the fourth escaped into the night.[9]

Many other reivers ended their days on the gallows at Carlisle or Newcastle, where sometimes 20 or 30 were hanged at the time. One of them, Geordie Burn, left a confession prior to being hanged in 1596 that he had spent a life of "whoring, drinking, stealing and taking deep revenge for slight offences."[10]

Those who did escape could have a complaint filed against them with the March Warden and be answerable at the next Truce Day, another unique event. The Wardens of the Marches were a thin law of lawful authority, and were the constables of the region on both sides of the Border. The English wardens were often appointed from the southern part of England, as it was believed that this would make them more balanced and less likely to he overly influenced. The Scottish wardens were often the 'heids' of Clans within the Borders, the view being that they were the only people likely to exert enough authority to give the role validity. Appointed by their respective governments, they were backed up by Deputies, Keepers, Captains, Land Sergeants and Troopers, and were expected to meet with their opposite numbers on regular Truce Days, the aim being to administer the Border Laws and 'keep the wild people of the three Marches in order'; something which occurred with varying degrees of success.

Truce Days were supposed to be held each month although they often stretched for longer periods, and would involve both English and Scottish wardens, and those whom complaints had been issued against. Traditionally they were most often held on Scottish soil, and formality was also a necessity. Each side in turn would send riders to seek assurances of safety and safe passage. The wardens would then select 12 men – 6 from England and 6 from Scotland – to act as a jury for the cases which could not be resolved. Interestingly, justice of some sort must have been seen to be done at these gatherings, otherwise they would not have survived as long as they did. If someone summoned to answer a charge failed to appear, this lead to them being judged guilty – an interesting legal point.

In some cases the accused simply admitted his guilt and paid up. This was the case, for example, with Thomas Musgrave, Captain of Bewcastle, who admitted theft of over 1,200 cattle and was fined £2,000. The process was supposed to occur as follows: the reiver paid the fine or compensation to his warden, who then paid it to the warden of the complainant, who then in turn was paid. However, as George MacDonald Fraser notes, "Knowing the time and the people, it seems unlikely that the payment would invariably arrive intact."[11]

Not surprisingly, perhaps, some felt justice could be best administered by themselves. MacDonald Fraser comments, "For those dissatisfied, of course, there was only one obvious remedy, which was to swallow disappointment, wait for the next full moon, and take compensation the hard way. It was doubtless quicker than legal action, and much more satisfying ..."[12]

Despite the efforts to maintain a semblance of lawful authority, the Borders remained essentially lawless. Even the wardens often involved themselves in such activity or, at best, turned a blind eye. MacDonald Fraser suggests it was the best they could or would do, and it was better than nothing.[13]

It was the ascension of James I, who was also James VI of Scotland, to the throne of England which made it possible to subdue the worst excesses of the Borders. James was embarrassed that the region transcending both his kingdoms was in such a lawless state and embarked on a policy of pacification, some of which progressed quite brutally. The end result was that the English and Scottish borders ceased to be hostile frontiers, having a common monarch, although not yet united as one political unit. This allowed for a more robust response to the general lawlessness of the Borders, and whenever the Armstrongs raided into northern England, the Captain of Berwick led an Anglo-Scots force in their Liddlesdale heartland, blowing up towers, damaging crops and driving off livestock. Although difficulties with the Reivers continued until 1609 and 1610, the problem had largely been resolved. The Armstrongs were largely tamed, and another particular target of the authorities were the numerous Grahams, regarded as the worst offenders of all the Border Clans. Many were exiled, there was a scheme to plant them in Tipperary in Ireland, some were hanged and others sought a new life within the armies of Europe. The new plantation in Ulster became home to many Armstrongs, Grahams and others. The Grahams in some cases sought to maintain a low profile from the authorities by changing their names, for example, to Meharg, which is Graham backwards, in parts of County Antrim.[14]

Matt Meharg, a well-known East Antrim folklorist. The surname Meharg is Graham reversed and was a device to avoid the unwelcome attention of the authorities in the seventeenth century.

Courtesy of Sam Cross, Larne.

In addition, Parliament prohibited the possession of arms and armour and of ownership of a horse valued at more than 20s value (other than for noblemen and gentry of good repute).[15] This was enforced by a Commission under George Home, Earl of Dunbar, who hanged "above 140 of the noblest and most powerful thieves in all the borders ... and fully reduced the other inhabitants ther to obedience." Home's method of hanging first and trying afterwards was infamously known as 'Jeddart justice'. Many men were rounded up for service in the army overseas at this time, while others left voluntarily, among them 200 Buccleuchs who went to fight in Holland. The outcome of all of these measures was that by July 1609 it was deemed that the Borders had been pacified, and proprietors found that the agricultural development of their estates was at last worthwhile. However, as one author noted, "Not until the eighteenth century ... did these southern shires fully recover from their experiences in the three hundred years, during which they had held against England the frontier of the Scottish realm."[16]

The reiving tradition did not end in 1609, although it was considerably curtailed. In the 1640s a rump of reivers, with fewer places to hide and less strength in numbers, continued to operate in well-organised gangs, terrorising the countryside by day and carrying out "outrages, felonies and nefarious crymes" in the evenings. While the authorities raised what amounted to local vigilante forces against them, they continued to hide out in solitary areas, including what had been the Debatable Land until well into the seventeenth century. They were probably akin to the dispossessed Irish that were known as the 'kern' or 'woodkern' in Ulster during the Plantation years. Following the Flight of the Earls in 1607, the Crown had seized their land on the basis that they had committed treason. Their flight was taken as clear evidence that they had been uncovered plotting against the Crown and had left before they could be brought to book.

It was during the Pacification that the reivers were encouraged to look elsewhere for settlement, either directly by the authorities or indirectly by the pressure that was brought to bear on them. The example of the Grahams of the Borders is an interesting and informative one. Attempts to imprison members of the Graham clan proved dangerous, with some escaping from prison and Rob's Fergie Graham, a fugitive from the law, ambushing key government officials near Dumfries in 1606. The Government decided that something had to be done about the Grahams, since neither licensed murder nor banishment to the Low Countries had worked. It was therefore decided to transport them to Ireland, with a Roscommon landowner, Sir Ralph Sidley, agreeing to settle them on his estates for short leases unless the King decided they should be extended permanently. The Border Commission made efforts to raise subscriptions for this project and pressure was brought to bear on those who were dilatory in raising subscriptions. A note from the Privy Council to the Commissioners in 1606 details that the King wished to know the names of those who refused to contribute; a broad enough hint that action was required.[17]

As it turned out there were not, by this time, so many Grahams to be transported. MacDonald Fraser explains that death, banishment and outlawry had reduced one of the biggest border clans to a pitiful remnant. In the event 50 families and 124 individuals appear to have made the journey in September 1606. The land which they were transported to was not, however, as fertile as at home. Indeed it was more of a wasteland, without wood and water, which were fairly basic constituents to success and survival. The rents were dear and labourers, who were few, demanded high wages and did not speak in the same language. Neither did the Grahams have any money, for the funds raised to transport and settle them appeared to have been pocketed by a corrupt government official. Not surprisingly, the enterprise was anything but successful.

Within two years there were reckoned to be only half a dozen families by the name of Graham in Roscommon, the remainder having scattered elsewhere, some even returning to Scotland. When the scattered Grahams in Ireland were still seen as a problem to some, it was suggested they should be moved to Ulster. The Lord Deputy of Ireland, however, expressed the view that, "They are now dispersed, and when they shall be placed upon any land together, the next country will find them ill neighbours, for they are a fractious and naughty people".[18]

The authorities may have succeeded in quelling the Grahams for a time, but the presence of the unusual name Meharg, mentioned earlier, is only one instance of how they remained. For example, after the Second World War, Graham was the most common name in the Carlisle telephone directory.[19]

In terms of the Ulster Plantation, if we look at the situation in County Fermanagh as an example, we find that those bearing the surname Graham are, as Peadar Livingstone puts it, "all over the county".[20] Another strong borders family, the Elliotts, were also commonly found in the county, at places such as Castlecoole, Magheraboy and Tirkennedy. Two main strands of Johnstons, one from south and one from north Scotland, also settled in great numbers and were more numerous than any other Planter family. In 1641 up to 260 of their menfolk enlisted in the forces of Sir William Cole against the Irish Rising. As early as 1619, finally, Armstrong tenants were common, and this carried down to the 1960s when it was the county's third most common British name.[21]

Enniskillen, County Fermanagh. Many of the Scots Plantation families such as Humes, Elliotts, Armstrongs and Grahams made their way to the area during the Plantation.

The Borders created a tough people, who often raided across the frontier for food and property, and had little respect for the authorities on either the Scottish or the English side. The clan system provided security in such a climate. Even the very title accorded to these clans – the steel bonnets – underlines a very different situation than elsewhere in Scotland. Unlike other clans, the Borderers did not wear soft bonnets, but helmets made of steel, which were designed to protect against swords and other weapons. The image of the 'riding clans' with their helmets says much about their lifestyle and it was no coincidence that the Reivers gave the word 'bereaved' as one of their lasting legacies to the English language. The presence of the Riding Clans in Ulster at the time of the Plantation led one author to draw the conclusion that these people were a frontier's breed, wherever they were to be found; "God's Frontiersmen" as they labelled them in the context of Scotland, Ulster and America.[22]

Can an understanding of outlook be usefully gained by examining the Borders story? Is it possible for a Borderers Culture to have survived from their Border homeland to Ulster and the United States?

Jedburgh, one of the great Border abbeys, was built in 1138 by David I of Scotland. It suffered at the hands of the invading English armies on several occasions in the fifteenth and sixteenth centuries.

This is an interesting point. Under Keesing's definition, a culture is "a system of more or less shared ideational designs for a living characteristic of a particular people".[23] This would suggest that Borders culture could not, ultimately, survive beyond the Borders and, say, their pre-1630s situation. Yet it could be argued that some cultural elements seem to continue into the Ulster Plantation and the American experience. This may be because, either consciously or through fate, Borderers ended up in new frontier situations, which meant that the situation producing the culture essentially remained the same. What Keesing would refer to as the 'sociocultural system' in its environment was not much different than it had been in the Borders. Thus we could say that there are certainly elements of ability and willingness to conflict with others to preserve one's position and well-being, and also disinclination to respect any authority present in the new Borders, where Riding Clan families made their homes.

It is worth reflecting, however, that the Borderers, while fierce in their own interests, could also display extremely positive traits. An English spy once wrote of two Border thieves, whom he employed as guides, "that they would not bewray any man that trusts in them, for all the gold in Scotland and France".[24] Contrasting this with the comment of one Richard Fenwick, in 1597, that "If Jesus Christ were emongst them, they would deceave him, if he woulde heere, trust and followe theire wicked councells ..." it becomes clear that we have essentially a complicated people. One noted Border historian makes the point that it is reasonable to assume that the people of the Borders have not essentially changed a great deal over the centuries. George MacDonald Fraser comments that they were not, to put it at its most tactful, the most immediately lovable folk in the United Kingdom. Newcomers may have found them difficult to get to know, and they had a tendency to be suspicious and taciturn. Such characteristics could also be argued in the personalities of the Ulster Scots and the Scotch-Irish of America, but sometimes nations need frontiersmen and women. MacDonald Fraser continues that perhaps the greatest virtue of the Borderers is their ability to endure. Not only did they do so in the land between Scotland and England, but they also followed this pattern in Ireland and in America. Somehow the old anti-Home Rule slogan of Ulster Unionists – pledging to ensure that "Not an Inch" of their lands would be ruled by a Dublin parliament in the earlier twentieth century – seems to spring from the psyche of men and women of the sixteenth and seventeenth centuries back home on the Marches.

The Flodden Memorial in the Borders town of Hawick commemorates those who fell in one of the many battles with an English army throughout Scottish history.

HISTORICAL TRAILS
SITES TO VISIT

An old image of Hume Castle near Coldstream on the East Marches.

Hume Castle

Hume Castle was built in the thirteenth century by the Earl of Dunbar and is located on a hillside in the heart of Berwickshire, with magnificent views to the border at Coldstream. The castle was the main stronghold of the Humes and featured in many of the dramatic events of the Borders. The Scots later captured the castle and James II of Scotland was killed in front of it when a siege cannon exploded in 1460. The castle was captured and recaptured on a number of occasions in the sixteenth century. In 1547, Lady Home surrendered it to the Earl of Somerset, who was returning south to England after the Battle of Pinkie, in which her husband was killed. Somerset brought her captured son to the front of the castle and threatened to hang him unless the castle was handed over to him. The threat had the desired effect. The Scots recaptured it the following year and killed the English garrison.

During the Cromwellian era, the castle was captured by the forces of the Lord Protector and effectively ceased to be a fortress from that time. In February 1804, when there were concerns over a Napoleonic invasion, beacons were assembled at various points as a means of warning of a French landing. The man in charge of the beacon at Hume Castle mistook an accidental fire in Northumberland for an invasion warning and lit his beacon, which led to others following suit. As men were assembled to combat the invasion, the keeper of the beacon at St Abb's decided that it was unlikely that news of a French landing would come from inland, and thus mitigated the panic.

The large walled enclosure of Hume Castle today was built in the nineteenth century by Sir Hugh Purves Hume Campbell of Marchmont to enclose the ruins of the much earlier structure. The small hamlet of Hume rests below the castle.[25]

Tully Castle in Fermanagh was built by Sir John Hume in 1613. Following a massacre there in 1641 against the Scots settlers by the native Irish, it fell into disuse. Today the castle is in state care.

Tully Castle

In 1610 Sir John Hume of Polwarth, Berwickshire, was granted 2,000 acres of land under the Ulster Plantation scheme at Tully (then known as Carrynroe) in Fermanagh. He built a castle there in 1613, the ruins of which still remain as an imposing example of the presence of the Border in Ulster. Sir John Hume died in 1639 and was succeeded to his estate by his son, Sir George Hume.

The Irish Rebellion broke out in October 1641 and on Christmas Eve of that year, Rory Maguire and a large force arrived outside Tully Castle, determined to capture it on behalf of the Irish chiefs, led by the O'Neills. Most of the men folk were not there and Lady Mary Hume surrendered the castle, on condition of a safe conduct for all who were there. On Christmas Day 1641, however, the Maguires slaughtered 60 women and children, and 15 men, only the Humes being spared. The castle was burnt by the rebels and was never rebuilt.

There was also a village of 24 families close to the castle, something which was typical of Plantation development.

Tully was itself typical of Scottish lowlands architecture, with characteristic projecting turrets and a perimeter wall that had four towers at the corners, which protected this bawn structure. However, there were some architectural differences. The roof of the three-storey castle was thatched, which was uncommon in castle roofing in Scotland, but borrowed from the Irish tradition of thatching properties.

The ruins of Tully, located just off the main Enniskillen to Belleek road, give an excellent impression of what the castle would have looked like in its brief heyday. A Plantation garden has been laid out to provide an idea of the landscape of the Plantation, with herb and flower beds. There is evidence to suggest that there was quite a formal layout for seventeenth century Plantation gardens, with carefully laid out squares and rectangle beds for flowers, vegetables, fruit or herbs. In addition to being recreational, the gardens at places such as Tully were also highly functional.

Carlisle Castle, one of several fortified settlements on the Borders.

Carlisle

Carlisle, the largest settlement in Cumbria, is the location of the excellent Tullie House Museum, which includes the story of the Border Reivers, as well as the general story of the Borders and many artifacts from the Roman settlement. The 900 year old Carlisle Castle was once the main English border stronghold against the Scots. The castle has an excellent military museum with many artifacts, medals, and memorabilia belonging to soldiers of the Border Regiment.

The Romans erected a fort in the last quarter of the first century AD at this site and a town which developed around it was known as Luguvallium. Throughout its long and eventful history, Carlisle has dominated the English side of the Borders.

The history of the Civil War, the Restoration, the Jacobite rebellions of the eighteenth century and other periods have all provided a chapter for the history of the town, which was captured by Bonnie Prince Charlie in 1745 on his route into England. One of the more famous prisoners at Carlisle Castle was Mary, Queen of Scots, who spent enforced time there in 1567.

The centre of the modern city of Carlisle is compact and includes not only the Castle and Tullie House Museum, but also Carlisle Cathedral and an excellent shopping district known as The Lanes. There are many buildings of architectural merit.

Carlisle Cathedral possesses the largest east window of any cathedral in Europe, and its history includes part of the building that was demolished by Oliver Cromwell during the English Civil War to reinforce the nearby castle.

The mother of Ulster Scot, US President Woodrow Wilson, Janet Woodrow, was born in Carlisle and the President visited the city on a number of occasions. There is a plaque on the wall at Carlisle City Church, Lowther Street, commemorating his 1918 visit.

Kelso

Kelso lies at the confluence of the rivers Tweed and Teviot. It is one of the Scottish border towns where you can view a Common Riding, or Riding of the Marches. This ceremony dates back to the days when locals maintained guard on the town boundaries. It is a market town, with cobbled streets, a cobbled market square and a bridge designed in 1803 by John Rennie, who later built Waterloo Bridge in London.

Pronounced 'Kelsae' locally, the town owes its origins to the erection of Kelso Abbey in 1128. The ruins of the abbey, along with the Floors Castle, still attract many tourists to the town today. It is believed that the earliest settlement was located on a rocky outcrop and the town was known as Calkou at that time. The town has a long connection with the Ker family, one of the prominent Borders families, who virtually owned the entire town in the 1600s.

On the opposite bank of the river Tweed was the royal burgh of Roxburgh, which has now completely vanished. It is supposed to have been the first town in the borders and was a favoured location of King David I of Scotland. The town was an interface between English and Scots armies, and was burned on a number of occasions during an eventful history. The ruins of Roxburgh Castle lie close to Kelso, although only a few broken walls remain, located on an eminence around 50 feet above the junction of the rivers Tweed and Teviot.

HISTORICAL FIGURES

A representation of James VI of Scotland and I of England. His influence was significant in terms of the Borders.

James I

Born in 1566, James VI of Scotland and I of England was a prime motivator in the Plantation of Ulster, encouraging Scottish nobles to participate in the scheme. He succeeded Elizabeth I, the last Tudor monarch, and ruled England, Scotland and Ireland for 22 years. He often used the title King of Great Britain, although this was not a legal designation.

He was the only child of Mary, Queen of Scots, and her second husband, Henry Stuart, Duke of Albany (Lord Darnley). His father was murdered in February 1567 and his mother was unpopular, not least among Protestant nobles in Scotland, who viewed her with suspicion. Her marriage to the fourth Earl of Bothwell, who was suspected of murdering her husband, added to this disquiet, and she was arrested, imprisoned and forced to abdicate. Her son became King at the age of one year, and his kingdom was ruled by James Stewart, Earl of Moray, as regent on his behalf.

At the coronation ceremony of James, the sermon was preached by John Knox, the Scottish Reformer, while the young boy was educated by the historian and poet George Buchanan. He was married to Anne of Denmark and the couple had three children, one of them Charles, the future Charles I of England.

In 1603, on the death of Elizabeth I, James was proclaimed King of England and made his way south to govern his joint kingdom from London. On 5 November 1605, an attempt was made to kill James and blow up parliament by Guy Fawkes, adding further to mistrust of Roman Catholics at that time. James did encourage leniency on those who took an Oath of Allegiance, which included a denial of the Pope's authority over the King.

One lasting legacy of James I was his commissioning of a new translation of the Bible, which was completed in 1611 and is known as the King James Bible. Efforts to bring the Church of Scotland closer to the Anglican Church in England did not meet with great success, however, and led to continued problems for his son, Charles I, bringing the Covenanters onto the stage of history. James I died in March 1625 and was widely mourned by his subjects.

Kinmont Willie Armstrong

One of the most notorious and best-known of the Border Reivers, Willie Armstrong was known as Kinmont Willie because of the location which he came from, a usual way of defining individuals of the same surname on the Borders (and indeed in Ulster in modern times as well).

Kinmont Willie was at the head of bands of up to 300 reivers and the first raid with which he was associated is recorded as Tynedale in August 1583. During this raid eight villages were attacked, several houses set alight and 800 cattle were stolen. It is also recorded that six men were killed during the raids, 11 were wounded and 30 were taken prisoner by the Armstrongs. It was the first of many raids led by Kinmont Willie.

In 1593 the largest raid involved 1,000 men in Tynedale, and the Armstrongs stole more than 2,000 head of cattle and property valued at £300, quite a sum in those days. Three years later, Armstrong was captured and imprisoned in Carlisle Castle, after having attended one of the unique Borders events, the Truce Day, the purpose of which was to allow complaints from both sides of the frontier to be addressed and justice sought for transgressions. Armstrong should have been safe until sunset the next morning, but the English contingent from Carlisle is reputed to have broken the Truce Day's terms by crossing the Tweed and giving chase, capturing Kinmont Willie and taking him to Carlisle Castle. This outraged Scott of Buccleuch and others on the Scottish side, who mobilised a force and sprung Armstrong from the castle, an event which grew into epic proportions over the years.[26]

Kinmont Willie Armstrong died in the early 1600s, having continued with lower level raids and forays. He had four sons. The Armstrong clan included many members who shortly after settled in Ulster, particularly in counties Fermanagh and Tyrone.

John McKay

In 1834 John Mackay Wilson published the first of his *Tales of the Borders*, recounting the stories of the region and its eventful past. The first tale was published in the *Berwick Advertiser* and was greeted with great interest. The weekly copy of *Tales of the Borders* increased the newspaper's circulation rapidly, from 2,000 to 16,000.[27]

In 1840 the tales were published in book form and went into numerous editions, the latest being published in the early 1990s. Wilson was 28 when he published his first tale and sadly he died a young man. However, his stories and those of fellow contributors helped maintain the identity and folklore of a unique region of the British Isles. The tales date from the thirteenth to the seventeenth centuries. They have been reprinted a number of times and were once widely read in many an Ulster Scots home.

ENDNOTES

1 Johnstone, CL, *The Historical Families of Dumfriesshire and the Border Wars*, Dumfries: 1889

2 Neville, Gwen, K, *The Mother Town. Civic Ritual, Symbol and Experience in the Borders of Scotland*, Oxford: Oxford University Press, 1994, p15–16

3 See, for example, MacDonald Fraser, George, *The Steel Bonnets: The Story of the Anglo-Scottish Border Reivers*, London: Harper Collins, 1989

4 MacDonald Fraser, *op cit*, p1

5 Quoted in MacDonald Fraser, *op cit*, p93

6 See, for example, Fairbairn, Neil, *A Traveller's Guide to the Battlefields of Britain*, London: Evans Brothers Ltd, 1983

7 MacDonald Fraser, *op cit*, p221

8 MacDonald Fraser, *op cit*, p65

9 MacDonald Fraser, *op cit*, p105

10 MacDonald Fraser, *op cit*, p106

11 MacDonald Fraser, *op cit*, p161

12 MacDonald Fraser, *op cit*, p165

13 MacDonald Fraser, *op cit*, p165

14 One of the most prominent East Antrim Mehargs was Matt Meharg, a renowned folklorist from Ballyboley near Ballyclare.

15 This is somewhat similar to the Penal Law in Ireland, which prohibited Roman Catholics from owning a horse valued at over five pounds, since such horses made good cavalry horses and would have therefore been of assistance to any further Jacobite rising.

16 Kermack, WR, *The Scottish Borders to 1603*, Edinburgh: Johnston & Bacon, 1967, p110

17 MacDonald Fraser, *op cit*, p371

18 MacDonald Fraser, *op cit*, p373

19 Cited by MacDonald Fraser in *The Steel Bonnets: The Story of the Anglo-Scottish Border Reivers*, *op cit*, p373

20 Livingstone, Paedar, *The Fermanagh Story, Fourth Edition*, Enniskillen: 1990

21 Livingstone, *op cit*

22 Fitzpatrick, Rory, *God's Frontiersmen: The Scots-Irish Epic*, London: Weidenfeld and Nicolson, 1989

23 Keesing, Rodger, M, *Cultural Anthropology, A Contemporary Perspective*, Orlando: 1981

24 MacDonald Fraser,*op cit*, p47

25 Eddington, Alexander, *Castles and Historic Homes of the Border*, London: Oliver and Boyd, 1949, p37–42, and Bradley, AG, *The Gateway of Scotland*, Boston: 1912, p133–141

26 For a good account of this event see George MacDonald Fraser's *The Steel Bonnets: The Story of the Anglo-Scottish Border Reivers*, *op cit*

27 Brander, Michael, *Tales of the Borders*, Edinburgh: 1991, p9

Chapter Four

PLANTATION AND SETTLEMENT IN ULSTER, 1606–1660

Monea Castle in County Fermanagh is a fine example of Plantation architecture. It was built by Malcolm Hamilton in 1618 and captured by the Maguires during the 1641 Rising. It returned to the Hamilton ownership and was occupied until a fire in 1750.

Upon visiting the Glens of Antrim in the eighteenth century, a French traveller named De Latocnaye reflected:

> "The inhabitants of Cushendall, as well as those of the country in the neighbourhood, are Catholics, and they have this peculiarity, that they do not speak English as do the inhabitants in other parts of the province, who for the most part would not understand Irish … quitting the coast, I had to cross the mountains to get to the interior, and I stopped at Brushin,[1] where most of the inhabitants are Presbyterians. One could hardly imagine that he is among the same people. The way of speaking, and even of dressing, is much more Scotch than Irish."[2]

It is a comment which highlights the population mix of the province at that time and how differences were apparent from one area to another, albeit probably not as exaggerated in some other locations. For example, the 1840s Ordnance Survey Memoir for the Parish of Templecorran stated:

> "In character, habits, customs, and in their accent, idioms and dialect, the inhabitants of this parish as much resemble the Scotch, if not more so, than those of any others in this county. This may be owing to their limited intercourse with strangers, their comparatively retired situation and their equality as to grade and condition. There are not, nor have there been, any others of different extraction residing in the parish, perhaps since its original colonisation by the Scottish settlers of the early part of the seventeenth century."[3]

This was not an uncommon situation in the areas of high Scots settlement. In Antrim and Down there was a considerable English influence prior to the Plantation of the reign of James I. Sir Arthur Chichester, who was Governor of Carrickfergus, would play an important part in ensuring the success of the Plantation scheme which was developed from 1609. Chichester had settlers brought from his native Devon to augment other English settlement in the area around Carrickfergus, but it was the efforts of Hugh Montgomery and Sir James Hamilton which resulted in large numbers of Scots arriving on their lands in County Down and also in County Antrim, providing considerable settlers prior to the official Plantation of Ulster itself.

The factors which promoted a plantation scheme in Ulster related specifically to the politics of what was regarded as a turbulent province. The plantations which occurred effectively opened up Ulster to British influence for the first time, sweeping away the old regime of the Gaelic lords and their subjects. The Elizabethan Wars in Ireland had seen defeat of the native Irish leaders and confiscation of large tracts of lands, including those in Kerry, Cork, Limerick and Tipperary. In Ulster the rebellion by the O'Neill and O'Donnell chiefs saw support from Munster and Connaught as well as Spanish aid. However, defeat at the Battle of Kinsale in 1601 marked the turning point of the war. The eventual defeat and surrender saw the new monarch James I allowing the chieftains regrants of their confiscated estates as freehold estates, but the trend of events weighed against them. Protestant bishops seized the church lands, which were extensive and government officials such as Chichester, continued to harass them. This led to the famous Flight of the Earls in 1607, when Tyrone, Tyrconnell, Maguire and scores of Gaelic sub-chiefs sailed from Lough Swilly to exile in Europe. The background to this event is still debated by historians. Whether Tyrone was guilty of plotting against the Crown or had been the victim of a plot against him by Chichester and others will never be known.[4] Whatever the cause of the Flight of the Earls in 1607, the effect is beyond debate. The estates of the Earls and their followers were forfeited to the Crown. The way was thus open to populate seized lands (the escheated territories) with settlers from England and Scotland, and assert control on Ulster. This would fulfill the ambition of James I, as stated in 1609, "We intend nothing with greater earnestness than the plantation of Ulster with civil men well affected in religion shall be accomplished with zeal and integrity."[5]

The Campbell Plantation House at the Ulster American Folk Park in County Tyrone.

While the government hoped the Plantation would lead to less military expenditure as Ulster became more settled, and that the Reformation would extend and reduce the risk of a Catholic 'Achilles heel' in the event of any European conflict, other more immediate factors were probably important for those who wished to migrate. The settlement was seen by many as an opportunity for commercial expansion. Artisans and tradesmen benefited from the extensive building programme created by the plantation movement.[6] Others found commercial fortunes in the developing settlement and there is evidence of trade from developing towns such as Carrickfergus and the south of England, as archaeological evidence of pottery has helped illustrate. History records that one of the merchants in Carrickfergus, for example, was the unforgettably named Hercules Horseman, whose roots probably lay in the borders region of Scotland.

At the time, England was viewed as overpopulated with increasing numbers of idle poor. The plantation movement provided an outlet for this expanding surplus population. Three quarters of the Plantation settlement were estimated to be tenant farmers or farm labourers. Efforts to encourage development of village settlements around fortified farmhouses or bawns were ultimately unsuccessful. The newcomers wanted to be on their lands and not living several miles from them.[7]

The Plantation scheme operated through three main types of person known as grantees. They were responsible to the King and the authorities for the successful development of the scheme.

One group of grantees was known as Undertakers because, quite literally, they undertook the success of the scheme. This group had chief responsibility for the success of the Plantation. The Scottish Undertakers are probably better known in historical terms and included Michael Balfour of Kinross at Knockninny in Fermanagh; Sir John Home of North Berwick at Magheraboy in Fermanagh; Sir

Edinburgh. Some of the undertakers came from as far east as Haddington, outside the city.

James Douglas and Sir Alexander Hamilton, both of Haddington, given lands in Armagh and Cavan; James Hamilton, Earl of Abercorn, from Renfrew, who was allocated lands at Strabane; and the Duke of Lennox from Stirling, who received lands in Donegal. Families of English extraction which can trace their roots to the Plantation include the Brookes in Fermanagh, whose origins probably lay in Cheshire and who originally had lands in County Donegal; and the Cole family, who also settled in Fermanagh and whose roots lay in Devon but were ultimately of Norman extraction. This latter family would become the Earls of Enniskillen. In total James I awarded grants of 81,000 acres of land to 59 Scottish Undertakers and 81,500 to 51 English Undertakers. By 1621 it was found that 6,520 adult Scots had settled in the six Plantation counties. The following year between four and five thousand men were available to raise as militia in defence, the majority of them also believed to be Scottish. When James I died in 1625, around 15,000 from his native Scotland were believed to be settled in Ulster.[8]

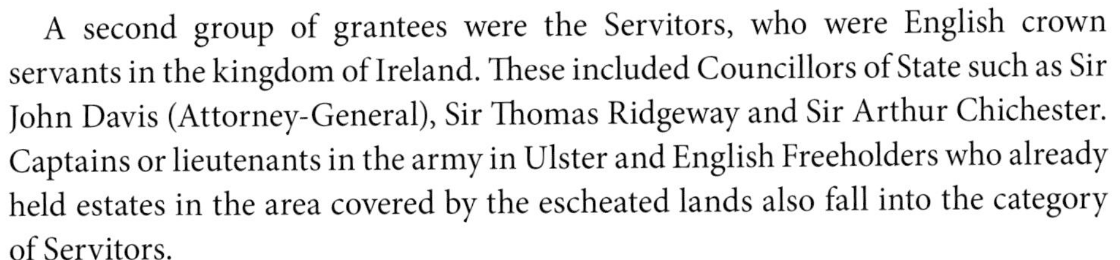

A second group of grantees were the Servitors, who were English crown servants in the kingdom of Ireland. These included Councillors of State such as Sir John Davis (Attorney-General), Sir Thomas Ridgeway and Sir Arthur Chichester. Captains or lieutenants in the army in Ulster and English Freeholders who already held estates in the area covered by the escheated lands also fall into the category of Servitors.

A third group, which is sometimes overlooked in the overall context of the Plantation, was that of native Irish Freeholders. Although the O'Neills who followed the Earl of Tyrone lost out badly, members of the family also received considerable re-grants of land from the King. Among them was Sir Tirlough Henry O'Neill, who received 9,900 acres of land at the Fews in South Armagh. The O'Neills received one third of the 94,013 acres allocated to native Irish landowners, while large land grants also went to the O'Reillys in Cavan, the Maguires in Fermanagh, the O'Cahans in the Roe Valley and the McSweeneys in County Donegal. Irish natives received almost 20% of the escheated lands under the terms of the Plantation. This does not, however, diminish the fact that there were Irish natives who lost lands and who would continue to harbour resentment about the new settlers. An interesting example of this was related at a symposium on the Plantation and personal perspectives, in Omagh in December 2010, at which the author was a panelist. One of the speakers was from a Roman Catholic and nationalist background, and he explained how, during his childhood, he remembered adults referring disparagingly to Protestants as 'planters'. It helped to highlight, if that were needed, that the Plantation was still an important aspect of modern history and that it is still something which everyone has to explore and come to terms with.

In each precinct or barony (a measure of the escheated land), the Chief Undertaker was allowed 3,000 acres of land, but the others were to be allowed no more than 2,000 acres each. From 1614 a rent of £5 6s 8d for every 1,000 areas was to be paid to the King by the Undertaker. Other terms included that produce could be exported for seven years free of tariffs, and necessary articles could be imported free of tariffs for five years. Timber from the King's woods in Ulster could be used for building purposes. This in itself was a lucrative matter. For example, we know that in the Kilrea area of County Londonderry, 50,000 oaks were cut down for the building of the Maiden City, these selling at 10s each. 100,000 ashes where also cut and sold at five shillings each, and 10,000 elms at 6 shillings and 8d each. These lands were held by the Company of Mercers, one of the London companies or Guilds which had been encouraged to become involved in the Plantation. In the North West, the involvement of the London Companies (or Merchant's Guilds) brought economic investment which was highly significant not only in the seventeenth century. For example, in 1828, the Company of Fishmongers erected a new meeting house at Ballykelly for the local Presbyterian congregation in the village, evidence of benevolence continuing from the seventeenth century.[9]

Undertakers of 2,000 acres were expected to build a stone house and bawn (fortified farm dwelling) within three years, those who held 1,500 acres had to build a stone or brick house and bawn, while those holding 1,000 acres were expected to build a bawn. Within three years 24 men aged 18 years or over had to be planted on every 1,000 acres of land, and these had to be English or 'inland' Scots, a term which was intended to ensure that the Scottish settlers were Protestants from the Lowlands and not Roman Catholic Highlanders. These numbers were to represent at least ten families. The Undertakers were also to keep a store of arms and take an Oath of Supremacy, with their undertenants also required to take this oath.

The scheme had measures intended to ensure compliance through the forfeiting of £200 per 1,000 acres grant if the building, planting or residence clauses were not fulfilled within five years. However, although considerable planning undoubtedly went into the aims and objectives of the scheme, there was sometimes a gap between theory and practice, and growth was not always as anticipated. Of settlement land issued to Scots in Fermanagh between 1611–1613, for example, the majority appear not to have been started, went dormant or passed into English hands; marking the failure of the Scots concerned to develop them. In Donegal the figure was eight out of 17, and in Tyrone seven out of 15. It has been demonstrated that the Undertakers who came from the Southwest of Scotland were more successful by far than those from other parts of Lowland Scotland.[10] Whatever the situation, the theory of the conditions had to be relaxed. This was the case, for example, with the time period allowed for building and plantation, and in 1622 another such move was the permitting of Irish to become tenants on one-quarter of the Undertaker's proportions.

The two main groups of settlers came from south west Scotland and the North

West Midlands of England. We can break down the localities from which many of the main Undertakers and undertenants came from, and Dr Philip Robinson did this in the case of Tyrone.[11] There were three main localities in England from which the main landowners came: Devonshire, Staffordshire and Hampshire. Sir Arthur Chichester, who was a native of Devon, introduced families from Devonshire, Lancashire and Cheshire to Carrickfergus. The Scots settlers who came, and were in a majority, not least on account of the close proximity of the Plantation to them, came largely from the south west of Scotland. The majority of Scottish Undertakers came from the central lowland belt, especially the Edinburgh and Haddington area as well as Renfrew and North Ayrshire. The area around Dumfries and Galloway was also important.

A Knox gravestone in the old Raloo cemetery near Larne. The Knox family was one of the Scots families who settled in the area in the seventeenth century.

Although the original Undertaker lands often changed hands, large bodies of Scots still came to inhabit them. In 1635 one account had 10,000 people passing through the port of Irvine in the previous two years to take ship for Ireland. Although probably exaggerated, it does highlight the movement generally. The Borders families also sent representatives, the Humes, Scotts, Armstrongs, Grahams, Kerrs, Johnstones and Maxwells among them. Nine baronies were reserved for Scots specifically, including Mountjoy at Strabane, Magheraboy (Fermanagh) and the Fews (Armagh). Baronies such as Lifford, Clogher and Omagh were reserved exclusively for English settlers, which included families from Norfolk and Suffolk. It is likely that well over half, perhaps two-thirds, of the settler population was Scottish in 1625.[12] In 1630 there were 4,000 to 5,000 adult male Scots in Antrim and Down alone, representing 2,000 families. During the closing decades of the seventeenth century Scots migration was further augmented by the influx of at least 60,000 Scots into Ulster. The area allocated to the various grantee classes included 160,000 acres to 59 Scottish and 51 English Undertakers; 94,000 acres to 280 Irish natives, 26 of the more important Gaelic lords being included; 55,000 acres to Servitors, those who had served the King in Ireland as soldiers of government officials; and 40,000 acres to the London Guilds or Companies. The Church of Ireland received 75,000 acres which had belonged to the pre-Reformation Irish Church, and these were called 'glebe' lands.[13]

The gravestone of John Feer, who died in 1776 at Ballycarry. The family were listed in 1669 at nearby Magheramorne.

The Undertakers and their undertenants had agreed to certain physical commitments when they became part of the Plantation scheme including building stone houses, fortified bawns and settlements, and bringing over tenants. Permanent dwellings of a more sophisticated construction became common and new field patterns were also to be developed, among them the spread of hedged enclosures. This had not been the case prior to the Plantation. An example in the Ordnance Survey Memoir for County Donegal in the 1840s showed that even in the middle of the nineteenth century, areas of

An old postcard by Woolstone Bros, London of Ballygally on the Antrim Coast, which was built by the Shaw family of Greenock in 1625.

the countryside in Donegal were not enclosed, and cattle and sheep were free to wander. [14] As part of the changing landscape of the Plantation, fortified tower houses, which were prevalent in Scotland and the English Border counties, were to be transplanted as an architectural type into Ulster, one of the best remaining examples being Ballygally Castle on the Antrim Coast.

Ballygally was built in 1625 by John, or James, Shaw, who initially settled in County Down and then moved north to the Antrim Coast. He was a native of Greenock, where his ancestors had been the local lairds for generations and their line could be traced back to Macduff, who was Thane of Fife, in AD834.[15] Shaw was, like many of those who came to the Ulster settlements, a younger son and would thus have been unlikely to inherit his father's lands. He appears to have settled in Ulster in 1606, locating firstly in lands belonging to his brother-in-law, Sir Hugh Montgomery of Braidstane in the Ards district of County Down. By 1613 he was listed on a County Antrim jury, and had obtained land grants from the Earl of Antrim. The building that was erected at Ballygally owed much in its architecture to the designs introduced to Scotland by Mary, Queen of Scots, and were common at that time. Features included high walls, a steep roof and turrets at the corners of the building. The walls of the castle, reflecting its defensive purpose, were five feet thick.

In 1619 a government engineer called Nicholas Pynner was sent to conduct a survey on the progress of the Plantation generally and he reported that there had been 107 castles with bawns then built as part of the Plantation; 19 castles without bawns; 42 bawns without castles or homes; and 1897 dwelling houses of stone and timber 'after the English manner'. Some towns were taking shape and we know that by 1659 the main urban settlements, in order of population, were Londonderry, Carrickfergus, Coleraine, and Belfast. In addition, fairs and markets were established, mills erected and the trade of the Ulster ports highlighted economic invigoration.

Historians detail several phases of the Plantation, the first being the years 1610 to 1615, when there was a slow movement of people. Some of the areas which showed greatest concentration of settlers and settlement were not actually part of the official Plantation, such as the North Down area. As is the case with any movement of people, there were those who were wary and awaited news of pioneer settlement before committing themselves. This was reflected in the few years after 1615, when a second and larger wave of settlers made their way to the Plantation counties. For the next few years, although the numbers did not dramatically increase in terms of new settlers, there was considerable movement within the Plantation territory, as settlers moved to what they perceived as better areas or land. Overall, the proximity of Scotland to the Plantation and the encouragement by James I and VI to his Scottish nobles to participate in the scheme, probably assisted in the greater number of Plantation settlers being Scottish. This pattern continued until the outbreak of the 1641 Rising, a turbulent time in Ulster history.

The Rising was spearheaded by the O'Neills and initially those involved were urged not to attack Scots as there was a fear of reprisal from across the North Channel. However, within a short space of time the Rising had degenerated into a general attempt to destroy the Plantation settlement. There are accounts of refugees arriving from Ulster on the west coast of Scotland at ports such as Irvine and Ayr, and having to be assisted by the Scottish Privy Council.[16] Once the dust had cleared over the Rising, and the Cromwellian and Restoration periods, it would appear that the more influential of the settlements was the English one, although the Scots may have remained more numerous. It was generally a time of rebuilding in terms of the Plantation.

A statue of the Scottish Reformer John Knox (c.1514–1572) in Stirling. Knox was the leader of the Scottish Reformation and extended Calvinism from Geneva, having studied there under the Protestant Reformer John Calvin. His influence helped establish Presbyterianism in Scotland and, ultimately, its spread by Scots to other parts of the world.

It has been suggested that the period of the Plantation can be brought to a useful close around 1670, but others such as John Sherry claim that the entire seventeenth century should be taken as the Plantation century in the Ulster context.[17] This is because in the aftermath of the War of the Three Kingdoms and the victory of William III over James II in the struggle for the British throne, there was a massive influx of Scots into Ulster. Factors promoting this included cheap land being available in Ireland and famine taking place in Scotland. The consequence was that between 40,000 and 70,000 Scots crossed the North Channel in search of a better future in the decade of the 1690s. This equated to between 5% and 7% of the overall Scots population of one million at that time, and thus a significant element in the settlement in Ulster. This new injection of Scots was undoubtedly meaningful in the longer term, increasing the gene pool of the settlement and strengthening its numbers to a level which ensured that assimilation was not going to be a factor for the foreseeable future.

In overall terms, the Plantation of Ulster saw the greatest modern input into the history of Ulster from Scotland, and the presence of so many Scots would have long-term social, cultural and political consequences for not only Ulster itself, but also the whole of Ireland. In some sense it was an illustration of the continuity of history, as one author remarked:

> "The north-eastern counties of Down and Antrim received Scots from the same areas to which previously so many from east Ulster had emigrated … It is quite probable that the ancestors of many were indeed of ancient Irish Cruthin or old Ulaid or Dal Riata stock, but they had found a new identity. They did not return as Cruthin or Ulidians, but as canny, hard-headed Scots who became the majority Ulstermen of today – ardent Irishmen at a rugby international but retaining strong ties with Britain." [18]

However, the migration to Ulster was prompted, as had population movements been before and since, by localised factors in terms of time and place. In the Scottish context, there was pressure on the land at home and economic conditions had not progressed in keeping with the expansion of population. Scotsmen established Nova Scotia at the same time, and many also served in the armies of Europe. For example, some suggest that 30,000 Scots were to be found in Poland in 1620. It is estimated that one-tenth of Scotland's population left their homeland for distant and, in the Ulster context, not so far away shores.[19]

The early period of Scottish settlement was not an easy one for many Scots, as in the early 1600s there was a considerable debate within the Church of Scotland, which would continue with devastating effect during the century. At issue was the matter of an attempt by James I to bring the Church of Scotland closer to the Church of England. Although both were Protestant Churches, the Protestant Reformation had come in different ways to the two countries. In England, the Reformation was organised from the top down, that is to say from the King, his nobles and senior clergy. In Scotland, by contrast, the Reformation transformed Scotland from the bottom up, the main impetus being from ordinary people and minor gentry. A major figure was John Knox, who was deeply influenced by the theological thought of John Calvin. Support for Knox and Calvinism rapidly spread throughout the Scots nation.

The grave of Reverend Edward Brice at Ballycarry. Brice was the first Presbyterian minister in Ireland, beginning his ministry there in 1613. Janet Brice Harden from Florida (left), pictured next to the grave in 1986, was one of his direct descendents.

A memorial plaque to Brice on the village green in Ballycarry.

This established the Presbyterian form of church government in Scotland, which was why dissention arose when efforts began to link the Anglican Church and Kirk of Scotland. Central to the argument was the desire by the King to establish Bishops within the Kirk as permanent Moderators. The Presbyterians opposed this, as their church government involved the annual election of Moderators, and those at other levels including the Kirk Sessions. Among those who opposed the plans was

Reverend Edward Brice, minister at Drymen on the shores of Loch Lomond and a member of the Synod of Clydesdale. It is believed that Brice's opposition marked him out with the church authorities, and a charge of impropriety with a female member of his congregation was brought but never proved, suggesting attempts to embarrass the cleric. Brice was friendly with the Edmonstones of Duntreath, and William Edmonstone, now in County Antrim, required a Presbyterian to minister to his family and tenants. Brice took up the opportunity to travel across the North Channel and his arrival and ministry in Ballycarry, as has been noted, afforded him the future place in history as the first Presbyterian minister in Ireland. However, as Reverend Thomas Hamilton points out, Presbyterianism existed in Ireland pre-Plantation, since the first regular Provost of Trinity College, Dublin, and two of its first Fellows, were Presbyterians.[20]

Drymen Church in Scotland. Edward Brice left the congregation of this church, on the shores of Loch Lomond, for Ballycarry in County Antrim.

Edmonstone's land grant included the right to appoint a cleric to the parish church on his estate, and when Brice and others came to be ordained in the Church of Ireland they found a welcoming situation since there were few protestant ministers in the area at that time. One church historian has described the Established Church of the time as being "in a wonderfully comprehensive mood".[21] Although they might have considered potential problems in being ordained from a theological perspective, this turned out not to be the case, as was reflected by Reverend John Livingstone, who detailed his experience when he discussed the matter with Bishop Knox of Raphoe, County Donegal, a fellow Scot:

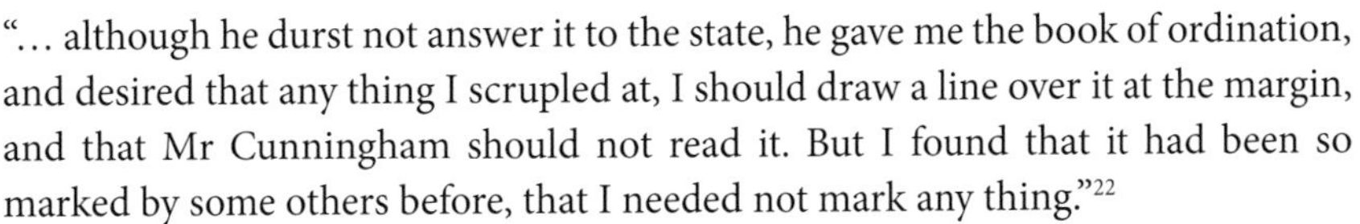

> "... although he durst not answer it to the state, he gave me the book of ordination, and desired that any thing I scrupled at, I should draw a line over it at the margin, and that Mr Cunningham should not read it. But I found that it had been so marked by some others before, that I needed not mark any thing."[22]

It would appear that, to a man, the earliest of the Presbyterian ministers in Ulster were opposed to church reform in Scotland and they brought this strongly held view with them across the North Channel. They included John Livingstone, who had been marked out by the church authorities in Scotland, and who found a congregation in 1630 at Killinchy which appreciated his efforts; Robert Cunningham, who had settled at Holywood in County Down in 1615, where he was ordained by Bishop Echlin, himself a Scot; and George Dunbar, forbidden to preach from his pulpit in Ayr, and transplanted minister to congregations at Ballymena, Larne and Carrickfergus. The most prominent among the early ministers was probably Professor Robert Blair, of Glasgow, who arrived on the

Antrim coast at Glenarm and famously walked to Bangor to take up an appointment there. The Reverend Josiah Welsh, who ministered at Templepatrick, was one with a strong link to the Scottish Protestant Reformation, for his grandfather was none other than John Knox, the great reformer. His mother Elizabeth was Knox's daughter and she had married John Welsh, the couple having three sons.[23]

A grave marker at Castle Upton, Templepatrick, for Reverend Josias Welsh, early Presbyterian minister and grandson of the Scottish reformer, John Knox.

The new ministers co-existed quite happily within the Established Church for a period, but eventually the issues that had been causing controversy in Scotland caught up with them in their new homes. Attempts to make the Church of Ireland closer to the Church of England resulted in new Canon Laws for the church under the Lord Deputy, Thomas Wentworth, in the 1630s, and the Scots felt unable to go along with these plans. The result was dissension and conflict within the church. John Livingstone and Robert Blair, having preached that Christ had "initiated no bishops but presbyters or ministers", were suspended for what was clearly an attack on the Church of Ireland. In 1632, along with Josias Welsh and George Dunbar, they were expelled from their churches. In 1636 the Bishop of Down summoned five ministers, including Edward Brice of Ballycarry and John Ridge of Antrim after they refused to accept a sermon in support of Episcopacy. Following a church court, at which the clerics attempted to defend themselves, the Bishop sentenced them to "perpetual silence within this Diocese", something which robbed them of any official support (but not the support of their congregations, to whom they often continued to preach in the open air or in buildings such as barns) and which was said to have impacted on the aged Brice's death that same year.

The gravestone of Reverend Edward Brice, inside the ruins of Templecorran Church in Ballycarry.

Worse was to follow for Presbyterians. In 1636 Wentworth, the Lord Deputy, authorised the Bishop of Down to arrest and imprison the Presbyterians in his diocese. Some were imprisoned, but many others fled to Scotland. The period of the National Covenant in Scotland extended itself into Ulster, where the Covenant – which as a political mechanism highlighted the concept of conditional loyalty to those who governed – had been subscribed to with enthusiasm among Scots settlers in the east in particular. In Ulster the so-called 'Black Oath' was introduced, which forced Presbyterians to renounce the Covenant and swear unconditional allegiance to King Charles. Those refusing to subscribe were imprisoned. This oath may have helped coin the phrase 'Blackmouths' in relation to Presbyterians. Wentworth, who was demanding the expulsion of all Presbyterians from Ulster, fell foul of the authorities during the period of the English Civil War and was beheaded in May 1641, but his actions had already seen the first attempt at organised emigration by Ulster Scots, and it had been led by two Presbyterian ministers.

Robert Blair, John Livingstone and their congregations embarked on an ambitious attempt to cross the Atlantic in search of religious and social freedoms in the developing American colonies. They commissioned a ship, the *Eagle Wing* (named after a passage in the Book of Exodus which refers to God taking his people as on an eagle's wing to a better future) to be built at Groomsport. The *Eagle Wing* set sail in September 1636, and called for passengers in Loch Ryan on the Scottish coast prior to a perilous voyage into the North Atlantic. Included in her passenger list was the Provost of Ayr, highlighting the close links with Scotland at that time. Beset by winter gales, she almost foundered but for the actions of passengers, one of whom was himself a seafarer. The God-fearing passengers, assembled by their clergy, took the storms as a sign from above that they were not to seek a home in America after all, and, within sight of the distant coastline of Newfoundland, the *Eagle Wing* turned around and set sail back to Belfast Lough, where she arrived in December 1636.

The most turbulent times for the Scots settlers in Ulster were far from over. In 1641 a Rising broke out which threatened the Plantation settlement. Although initially directed against the English settlements, it quickly ceased to make distinction, and before long Scots refugees arrived on the coast at places such as Irvine and Stranraer, their plight causing the Scottish Privy Council to establish a fund to assist them. The arrival of the army of General Robert Monro in Ulster not only saved the Plantation, but also had important religious consequences. Meeting in Carrickfergus in the summer of 1642 the chaplains of the various Scottish regiments stationed there formed the first Presbytery in Ireland, which would answer calls for ministers to Scots congregations. Reverend Robert Cunningham from Ballantrae on the Ayrshire coast was just one of the many ministers appointed to charges by the Army Presbytery as it was known. In 1646 he arrived at Ballycarry to fill the pulpit vacated by his predecessor, Reverend Brice, in 1636, during equally turbulent, if less physically dangerous times.[24]

In the generations and the centuries to come, Presbyterianism would take strong roots in Ulster soil, and, while it was never a smooth passage, it continued to chart a course forward in Ulster and elsewhere, the legacy of which remains to this day.

A memorial in Carrickfergus marks the formation of the first Presbytery in Ireland in June 1642.

HISTORICAL QUOTES

"We had much toil in our preparations and many hindrances in our outsetting, and both sad and glad hearts in taking leave of our friends. At last, about the ninth of September 1636, we loosed from Loch Fergus, but were detained sometime with contrary winds in Loch-Ryan in Scotland, and grounded the ship to search some leaks in the keel of the boat. Yet thereafter we set to sea, and for some space had a fair wind, till we were between three and four hundred leagues from Ireland, and so nearer the banks of Newfoundland than any place of Europe. But if ever the Lord spake by his winds and other dispensations, it was made evident to us, that it was not his will that we should go to New England. For we met with a mighty heavy rain out of the north-west, which did break our rudder, which we got mended (by the skill and courage of captain Andrew Agnew, a godly passenger,) with much of our gallon-head and fore-cross-trees, and tore our foresail, five or six of our champlets, a great beam under the gunner-room door broke. Seas came in over the round-house, and broke a plank or two on the deck, and wet all them that were between the decks. We sprung a leak that gave us seven hundred strokes in two pumps in the half-hour glass. Yet we lay at hull a long time to beat out the storm, till the master and company came one morning, and told us it was impossible to hold out any longer; and although we beat out that storm, yet we might be sure in that season of the year we would foregather with one or two more of that sort before we could reach New England … The next morning, as soon as we saw day, we turned and made good way with a main course and a little of a fore-top sail; and after some tossing, we came at last, on the third of November, to an anchor in Loch-Fergus"

John Livingstone's account of the voyage of the *Eagle Wing* in 1636, taken from Reverend James Seaton Reid's *History of the Irish Presbyterian Church*, vol 1, Edinburgh: Waugh and Innes, 1834.

THE EARLY MINISTERS

Early Presbyterian clergy in Ulster during the Plantation included:

Reverend Edward Brice MA, minister of Drymen in Stirlingshire. At the Synod of Clydesdale in 1607 he had opposed the appointment of Spotiswood, Archbishop of Glasgow, a permanent moderator within the church. This had resulted in him being marked out as a troublemaker. Under pressure from the authorities, he took up an invitation from Sir William Edmonstone to minister in his new settlement at Broadisland, County Antrim, in 1613 and was the first Presbyterian minister in Ireland.

Reverend James Glendinning was a graduate of St Andrew's University and ministered in the Carrickfergus and Carnmoney areas of County Antrim, where he was recorded in 1622.

Reverend Robert Cunningham was chaplain to the Earl of Buccleugh's Scottish regiment in Holland prior to being ordained to the ministry in Ireland by Bishop Echlin. In 1622 he was ministering in Holywood and Craigavad and received a stipend from Sir James Hamilton, one of the two men who spearheaded the plantation settlement in Down prior to the official Plantation of Ulster.

Professor Robert Blair, who was a professor in the College of Glasgow, fell into disputes with the church authorities over prelacy and resigned. He was invited by Sir James Hamilton to come to Ireland and did so in May 1623. Blair was the most eminent of the early ministers.

Unveiling a plaque in honour of the Reverend Edward Brice at Ballycarry in 1993. The clergyman who officiated was Reverend John Hay, then minister at Drymen, Brice's old congregation in Scotland.

Courtesy of Leta Marsden.

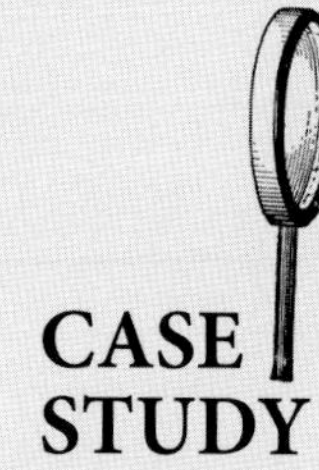

THE BROADISLAND PLANTATION

The settlement of Ballycarry was founded by William Edmonstone of Duntreath in Stirlingshire, who received a land grant of 2,800 acres from John Dalway in 1609. Edmonstone's ancestor, also William, had been given lands at Duntreath in 1445 and another ancestor had been slain at the Battle of Flodden in 1513. William was the eldest son of Sir James Edmonstone and was married to Isobel Haldane of Gleneagles. He first came to the Montgomery lands in Newtownards, County Down in 1607, along with his brother James and Haldane brother-in-law. In 1609 he moved across the lough to the lands at Broadisland, now Ballycarry, while his brother James held 172 acres at Bentra in the same area.

Gravestones of early Scots settlers inside the ruins of Templecorran Church, Ballycarry.

The Edmonstones continued to hold lands in Down for a period as well,[25] but it is clear from records that a nucleus of the family, along with in-laws, were also to be found in the Broadisland settlements. Alexander Edmonstone of Ardfracken townland[26] is mentioned in 1617, James Edmonstone of Broadisland in 1633, and Humphrie Halden of Broadisland and Robert Edmonstone of Aldfraknes townland are mentioned the following year. William Edmonstone died in September 1626 and was succeeded to his lands by his son Archibald, who had four sons. The last of the Edmonstones to live at Redhall, the family home in Antrim, died in 1780, when the estate was bought by the Ker family of County Down. The Scottish branch of the family continues to live at Duntreath Castle near Loch Lomond.

The Hearth Tax was a seventeenth century property tax levied according to the number of fireplaces in a home. The Hearth Rolls included the name and address of each householder, the number of hearths in each house and the tax due. The 1669 Hearth Rolls for County Antrim have survived better than most. The names listed for Ballycarry in that year were Allex Carr, William Steele, James Gamble, Thomas Murray, William Duntan, Widow McClea, David Lapsley, Thomas Stewart, Matthew Loggan, Thomas Donnell, William Dundee, John Armstrong, William Millar, and John McPalliard. Surnames in the parish around the village included Smith, Horsebrooke, Lackey, Ingram, Wilson, Mcffarran, Mcffading, McKenley, Kingingam, Wack, Camell, Hading, Bohanan, Begs, Droman, Peter, Bowman, Clarke, Ashlar, Douglass, Young, Saunderson, Locke, Aclintocke, and Steenson. The spelling of some of these names has changed over the generations. Ashlar, for example, is our modern Esler, and Bohanan would now be Buchanan.

When the Scots moved into the area they had no fortification nearby, apart from the Edmonstone's home at Redhall, which was not suited for defence. John Dalway, an English settler who had come into the area in Elizabethan times, had built a fortified farmhouse or bawn nearer to Carrickfergus. William Edmonstone, as holder of the lands, had entitlement to install a clergyman to the church, which was in a ruinous state, and brought Reverend Edward Brice from Drymen near his home in Stirlingshire. Brice became the first Presbyterian minister in Ireland when he began his ministry in 1613, and the church where he preached was converted by the Scots settlers, who, in building up the walls also located musket loopholes within the walls of the building. These loopholes ringed the building and it would have been impossible to approach from any angle without being detected. Thus the church also served as a fortress for the new Scots settlement.[27]

Redhall House, Ballycarry, home of the Edmonstone family in the seventeenth century.

The history of the Scots Plantation settlement of Broadisland reflects many of the incidents and periods through which the Plantation settlement evolved. The Scots Solemn League and Covenant was subscribed to in the village and in 1641 it was threatened by the Rising of that year. It owed its survival to the proximity of the Scots army based at Carrickfergus, and members of the local community were led by Archibald Edmonstone to support William of Orange in the 1690s. In the eighteenth century the Beggs family, who were believed to be connected to the family of Robert Burns, the Scottish Bard, were among early emigrants to America as part of the westward movement of Ulster Scots. Later in that century the village was a hotbed for the United Irishmen. In the nineteenth century a strong liberal tradition remained which was manifested by support for independent election candidates and Independent Orangeism in the 1900s.

As noted elsewhere in this chapter, the nineteenth century Ordnance Survey Memoir states that "In character, habits, customs, and in their accent, idioms and dialect, the inhabitants of this parish as much resemble the Scotch, if not more so, than those of any others in this county."[28] In modern times the essential cultural legacy of the community has remained and is reflected in the annual Ulster Scots Broadisland Gathering festival, founded in 1993.

CASE STUDY

THE MUNSTER SCHEME

A RETROSPECT OF CONTEMPORARY PLANTATION

Plantation schemes which were contemporary to the Ulster one included those successfully established in Virginia, New England and the West Indies. Earlier Irish settlements which had not proved so successful also obtained a fresh influx of settlers as a result of the Ulster Plantation.

One of the earlier Plantations was that which occurred in Munster in the 1580s. Although it attracted around 4,000 colonists, it disappointed the expectations of its Elizabethan planners. However, by the 1630s the settler population had increased to 22,000, the most successful town being Bandonbridge (Bandon), which was a precisely planned Plantation town. Another was Mallow, which grew up around a settler's castle. The situation in Munster was significantly different from that in Ulster. For example, the natives had already built stone houses and experienced builders were already to be found there. Towns, large buildings, gardens and orchards all existed before the Plantation. In addition much less than half the province had been confiscated for Plantation and the native landowners continued to exert a strong local authority. It has been noted that "The newcomers were forced to compromise to an extent unknown elsewhere",[29] which clearly had an impact on the situation and its development over the generations.

This situation did not occur in Ulster, nor was it intended to. The sixteenth century concept of Plantation was changing and this would have major implications. Concepts of colonial expansion had formerly surrounded the ideas of military conquest followed by absorption of the colony and its native populace into the domestic kingdom.

The concept of Plantation in Ulster was to involve the transfer of an entire package of people, laws and materials into the new territory. In its purest form the territory should, ideally, be almost devoid of native population, as with Virginia in the American colonies. Inherent in this concept would be the complete alteration of the Plantation counties of Ulster, the face of which was to be changed completely ...

HISTORICAL TRAILS
SITES TO VISIT

Monea Castle, County Fermanagh.

Monea Castle, County Fermanagh

Monea Castle in County Fermanagh was the home of Malcolm Hamilton and was completed in 1620. It is one of the best preserved and impressive of Plantation structures and shows design typical to that of Scottish baronial castles of the period. Partially destroyed during the Rising of 1641, it was home to Gustavus Hamilton, defender of Enniskillen against the Jacobites in 1689 and regarded as founder of the famous Inniskilling regiments.

Newtownards, County Down

The Mercat Cross at Newtownards bears the arms of Hugh Montgomery, founder of the settlement, and once had a tall cross on top of the present octagonal structure. It reflects the Scottish tradition of market towns, where business was not only done but also official announcements could be made or posted on the market cross. The octagonal structure was also used to house a watchman and host disorderly persons. Newtownards was in the heart of Hugh Montgomery's settlement of the Ards from 1607 onwards.

Inside the ruins of Templecorran Parish Church in Ballycarry can be found remains of musket loopholes. Even at the Kirk, Scots settlers were conscious of the need to protect themselves if necessary in the early Plantation years.

Templecorran Church Ruins, County Antrim

A musket loophole in the church ruin of the old Templecorran Church at Ballycarry, County Antrim, highlights how the building was utilised by the newly-arrived Scots in the area as not only a church but also a fortress. Further loopholes ringed the building and it would have been impossible to approach from any angle without being detected.

Remains of slates inside the ruin suggest that Templecorran Church's roof was slated, unlike, for example, Sir John Hume's castle at Tully in Fermanagh, which was thatched. This would make the building more defensible and more difficult to burn during attack.

The church structure is medieval in origin. However, we know from old records that in 1622 the walls had been newly erected but not yet roofed. This would suggest that the Scots settlers built up the walls and effectively refurbished the building.

The ruins of Templecorran Church, County Antrim, which was the home of the first Presbyterian congregation in Ireland from 1613.

Edward Brice, the first Presbyterian minister in Ireland, preached at Templecorran, having been installed there in 1613. As part of the terms of his land grant, William Edmonstone had the right to appoint the incumbent for the church and chose Brice, who was minister of Drymen in Stirlingshire, not far from the Edmonstone home at Duntreath.

Hamilton, Scotland

Hamilton in Scotland was founded by Gilbert Hamilton, son of Roger de Hamilton, a Norman who came to Scotland around 1215 and found favour with Alexander II. He was married to the daughter of the Earl of Strathern, thus cementing his position in Scots society. Gilbert Hamilton, who married a niece of King Robert the Bruce, obtained a grant of land in Lanarkshire. The town of Hamilton in Ontario was settled by Lanarkshire Scots in the nineteenth century.

Ballygally is dominated by the seventeenth century castle built by James Shaw of Greenock, which now forms part of a hotel complex.

Ballygally, County Antrim

Ballygally on the County Antrim coast has a fine example of a Plantation castle in Scots architectural style. The castle, which now forms part of Ballygally Castle Hotel, was built by James Shaw, a native of Greenock, where his ancestors had been the local lairds for generations and whose line could be traced back to Macduff, Thane of Fife, in AD834.

The building which was erected at Ballygally owed much in its architecture to the designs introduced to Scotland by Mary, Queen of Scots, and were common at that time. Features included high walls, a steep roof and turrets at the corners of the building. The walls of the castle, reflecting its defensive purpose, were five feet thick.

Above the door of the castle was the date 1625, which probably relates to the date the construction work was completed. One of its former occupants would write:

> "It was built on the model of the French chateau: a style of architecture which had been introduced into Scotland during the reign of Mary, Queen of Scots, who, as the wife of the Dauphin of France, had resided for some time in that country. The characteristic features of this class of buildings are fully exhibited in the high walls, the steep roof, the dormer windows, and the corner turrets … which are still to be seen in Ballygally Castle."[30]

Inside the walled enclosure of the castle was a stream, while the walls ran to the shore. Within the castle complex, which was defended by musket loopholes on the building, were stables, byres, coach houses and other 'office' buildings. The castle was also a focal point within the locality.

In 1641, when rebellion broke out, Ballygally was a sanctuary for the local Scots settlers. The gates were defended against insurgents who had a base in Glenarm, further along the coast, and who harried the locals by incursions on horse, during which several were captured, taken to Glenarm and hanged or drowned. Atrocities were not the preserve of one side or the other, sadly, at this time.

James, or John Shaw, the builder of Ballygally Castle, and others were part of a large wave of settlement. Raymond Gillespie estimates from available statistics that the native population in 1600 was in the region of 2,430 in Counties Antrim and Down.[31] By 1630 the estimate is that there were 3,329 settlers in County Antrim and 6,086 in Down, making a total of 9,415. It was a figure which would not only dominate East Ulster but continued to be of consequence as the later Plantation of Ulster took place.

The last of the Shaws to own Ballygally Castle was William Shaw, the only son of Henry Shaw, who died in 1799. William was a child aged six years at this time and became owner of the castle when he reached adulthood. He was a merchant in Belfast but economic circumstances resulted in his selling Ballygally Castle and estate for £15,400 in 1820 to the Agnew family, who were also prominent in the area and connected to the Shaws through marriage. For some time the castle was also used as a coastguard headquarters, prior to the erection of coastguard cottages nearby.[32] It was also the home of the family of Reverend Classon Porter, a noted local antiquarian, and William Moore, MP for North Armagh, before being taken over as a hotel in the twentieth century.

HISTORICAL QUOTES

Two Hundred Years Ago
***Larne Times and Weekly Telegraph*, 5 October 1912**

"Two hundred years ago, there came from Scotland's storied land
To Carrick's old and fortress town, a Presbyterian band;
They planted on the Castle wall the banner of the blue,
And worshipped God in simple form, as Presbyterians do.
Oh hallowed be their memory, who in our land did sow
The goodly seed of Gospel Truth, two hundred years ago.

Two hundred years ago, our church a little one appeared –
Five ministers, and four elders, the feeble vessel steered.
But now, five hundred pastors, and four thousand elders stand
A host of faithful witnesses within our native land:
Their armour is the Spirit's sword, and onward as they go,
They wave the flag their fathers waved two hundred years ago.

Two hundred years ago, the seed was cast into the ground.
An acorn then – a forest now – its sturdy oaks abound.
Like trees of eastern clime, each branch to earth bows down its head;
And rooted thus, the new-born shoots their forest-foliage spread.
Now shaking fruit of Lebanon upon our mountains grow,
From corn an handful, scattered there two hundred years ago.

Two hundred years ago, the dew of God's refreshing power
On Oldstone and on Antrim fell like Israel's manna shower;
The waters of the six-mile stream flowed rapidly along,
But swifter far the Spirit pass'd o'er the awakened throng.
Where'er the fruitful river went, God's presence seemed to go.
And thus the Spirit blessed our sires, two hundred years ago.

Two hundred years ago was seen the proud and mitred brow
Frowning on Scotland's envied kirk, as it is frowning now

But enemies in Church and State may threaten stern decree
Her Ministers are men of prayer – her people still are free;
Nor threat, nor interdict, nor wile of legislative show,
Shall change the men whose fathers bled, two hundred years ago.

Two hundred years ago, o'er graves the bluebell dropped its head,
The purple heather sadly waved above the honoured dead;
The mist lay heavy on the hill – the lav'rock ceased to soar,
And Scotland mourned her martyr'd sons on mountain and on moor.
And still hers is a mourning Church, but He who made her so
Is nigh to aid her as He was two hundred years ago."

Castle Kennedy on the Ayrshire coast is the ancestral home of the Ulster Kennedy's who crossed the Irish Sea during the Plantation years.

Family Histories

"Thus came several farmers under Mr Montgomery, gentlemen from Scotland, and of the name of the Shaws, Calderwoods, Boyds, of the Keiths from the North. And some foundations are laid for towns, and incorporations, as Newtown, Donaghadee, Comber, Old and New Grey-abbey. Many Hamiltons also followed Sir James, especially his own brethren, all of them worthy men; and other farmers, as the Maxwells, Rosses, Barclays, Moors, Bayleys, and others, whose posterity hold good to this day. He also founded towns and incorporations, viz., Bangor, Holywood, and Killyleagh, where he built a strong castle, and Ballywalter. These foundations being laid, the Scots came hither apace, and became tenants willingly and sub-tenants to their countrymen (whose manner and way they knew), so that in a short time the country began again to be inhabited. The progress of the plantation in the other parts of Ulster was not so rapid as it thus appears to have been in Down and Antrim ..."

Reverend James Seaton Reid in *The History of the Presbyterian Church in Ireland*, Edinburgh: Waugh and Innes, 1834, vol 1

The 1641 Rising

"And theyr principalle design being to march into and besiege Carrickfergus, they judged it unsafe to pass by Lisnegarvey, and therefore resolved to attack it next morning, making little account of the opposition that could be given them by so small a number, not half-armed, and so slenderly provided of ammunition (which they had perfect intelligence of by several Irish that left our party and stole away to them), for that they were so numerous and well provided of ammunition by the fifty barrels of powder they in his Majesty's store, in the castle at Newry, which they surprised the very first night of the rebellion; also, they had got into their hands the arms of all the souldgiers they had murdered in Ulster, and such other arms as they found in the castles and houses they had plundered in and burnt in the whole province. Yet it so pleased God to disappoint their confidence; and that the small garrison they so much slighted was much incouraged by the seasonable arrival of Sir George Rawdon, who, being in London on the 23rd of October, hastened over by ye way of Scotland; and being landed at Bangor, gott to Lisnegarvey, though late, on the 27th November, where these new-raised men and the Lord Conwaye's troope were drawn up in the Market-place, expecting hourly to be assaulted by the rebels; and they stood in that posture all that night, and before sunrise sent some horse to discover their numerous enemy, who were at Mass (it being Sunday); but immediately upon sight of our scouts they quitted their devotions and beat drums, and marched directly to Lisnegarvey; and before ten of ye clock appeared drawn up in battalia in the Waren, not above a muskett shott from the town, and sent out two divisions of about six or seven hundred men apeece to compass the town and plant their field-peeces on the highway to it before their body, and with them their long fowling peeces killed and wounded some of our men as they stood in their ranks in the Market-place; and some of the muskateers were placed in windows to make the like returns of shott to the enemy. And Sir Arthur Terringham (Governor of Newry), who commanded ye garrison, and Sir George Rawdon and the officers, foreseeing if their 2 divisions on both sides of the town should fall in together, that they would overpower our small number. For prevention thereof, a squadron of horse, with some muskateers, was commanded to face one of them yt was marching on ye north side, and to keep ym at a distance as they could; which was so well performed yt the other division, which marched by ye river to ye south side, came in before ye other, time enough to be well beaten back by the horse, and more yn two hundred of ym slain in Bridge Street, and in their retreat as they fled back to their maine body.

After which execution the horse, returning into the Market-place, found ye enemy had forced in our small party on ye north side, and had entered into the towne, and was marching down Castle Street, which our horse so well charged there, yt at least 300 of ye rebells were slain in ye street and in ye meadow behind the houses, through which they did run away to theyre maine body; whereby they were so much discouraged, that almost two hours after, their officers could not get any more parties to adventure a second assault upon us; but in the main space they entertained us with continued shott from theyr body and theyr field-peeces till about one o'clock, that fresh partys were drawn out and beaten back as before, with the loss of theyr men, which they supplied still with others till night; and in the dark they fired all the town, which was in a few hours turned into ashes; and in that confusion and heat of ye fire, the enemy made a fierce assault. But it so pleased God that we were better provided for them than they expected, by a releefe that came to us at nightfall from Belfast …"

Account in the Lisburn Cathedral Vestry Book of the attack on Lisburn during the 1641 Rising, quoted by Reverend James O'Laverty, in his *Historical Account of the Diocese of Down and Connor*, Dublin: 1880

HISTORICAL FIGURES

Hugh Montgomery

Hugh Montgomery was the descendant of a Scots-Norman family which had been present in Ayrshire in Scotland from the twelfth century. He was born in 1560 and was educated in Glasgow before spending some time at the French court and in the army of William I of Orange-Nassau (William III's great grandfather).

Montgomery inherited lands at Braidstane in Ayrshire on the death of his father, and married Elizabeth Shaw, daughter of the Laird of Greenock. He was imprisoned for a time in The Hague after an attack on a member of the Cunningham family with whom he had a vendetta, but later escaped through an intrigue involving a Scottish soldier serving there named Robert Montgomery. Although he was reprimanded by James VI, his relationship with the Scots King and that of his brother George, who was Dean of Norwich, soon saw him back in favour with the King. His influence would be increased when James VI of Scotland also became James I of England in 1603.

When Montgomery obtained his land grants in County Down he did his best to attract wealthy tenants, and a muster roll of 1630 details a high proportion of his tenants had snaphance weapons, a sign that they were men of substance.[33] In 1613 Sir Hugh Montgomery was elected MP for County Down in the Irish Parliament and became an Irish Privy Councillor. It has been claimed that records of taxes which he paid made him the third richest man in Ulster around the same time. In 1622 he was created Viscount Montgomery of the Ards and he also owned lands in Tyrone and Portpatrick. In 1629 his son Sir James Montgomery became a substantial landowner in Greyabbey.

Sir Hugh Montgomery, whose second and less successful marriage was to the Viscountess of Wigton, died in May 1636. He was buried in the parish church in Newtownards the following September, his body having been embalmed and preserved prior to an elaborate mile-long procession into the town which he had largely founded. One chronicler referred to the funeral ceremony as a display "of pomp and heraldry of which Scotsmen of the time were so fond".[34]

The partnership of Montgomery with Sir James Hamilton was to a great extent an alliance of necessity, since Montgomery needed the other to assist in the arrangements which resulted in Con O'Neill being granted a pardon and two-thirds of his lands in County Down being assigned to his Scottish benefactors. Perhaps not surprisingly, both Scots squabbled with each other thereafter, not least over boundaries of their newly acquired lands.

Sir James Hamilton

James Hamilton, one of the two architects of Scots settlement in County Down, was born in 1559 and was the son of Reverend Hans Hamilton, the first Protestant minister in Dunlop, Ayrshire. The family was also linked to the Scottish royal family. James was educated at St Andrew's University and became a teacher, first in Scotland and then in Dublin, where he became Bursar of Trinity College in 1598. He also acted as an agent for James VI, providing the Scots monarch with news of English activities in Ireland prior to being appointed agent to the English Court of Elizabeth I.[35]

Sir James Hamilton had great influence with James VI and I, and used this to good effect in promoting his plans for settlement in East Ulster. Sir Hugh Montgomery came to him in relation to encouraging the King to provide a pardon for Con O'Neill, whose servants had murdered a soldier in Belfast. The price for the pardon effectively was that O'Neill would assign part of his territory to Montgomery.

He and Montgomery did not always see eye to eye, something which probably originated in the fact that Sir James Fullerton, Hamilton's close friend, persuaded the King that the original land grant to Montgomery was too large for one individual.[36]

Hamilton was knighted in 1603 on the accession of James I, and in 1622 he was created Viscount Claneboy. He died at the age of 84 years. His lands in County Down became the subject of family litigation. The town of Hamilton in Scotland is named after the family, having been founded by Gilbert Hamilton, who was married to Isabella, the niece of King Robert the Bruce.

Reverend Patrick Adair

The Adair family came from Galloway or Wigtownshire, the precise location being open to debate. Patrick Adair, whose father was a clergyman, was born between 1625 and 1627, and began his studies in Glasgow College in the winter of 1644. On 7 May 1646, having crossed the North Channel, he was ordained to the parish of Cairncastle, north of Larne in County Antrim. It is believed that he was probably brought to the area by James Shaw of Greenock, who had settled at Ballygally a short distance from Cairncastle.

Adair remained there, but was among the Scots Presbyterians ejected from their pulpits by the authorities in 1661. For a time he was forced to fend for himself, but by the latter part of that decade the situation had become more relaxed and Presbyterian Meeting Houses began to be erected, as at Cairncastle. In 1674 Adair went to Belfast to minister there, and did so at North Street in the city for about 20 years.

A few years before his death, Adair was appointed as a representative of Ulster Presbyterians who met with William of Orange to congratulate him after his arrival in England in November 1688.

Reverend Patrick Adair was one of the early historians of the Irish Presbyterian Church, and his *True Narrative of the Rise and Progress of the Presbyterian Church in Ireland* is a fascinating account of the early years of the Presbyterian community. Adair died in 1694 and was survived by four sons and a daughter. One clergyman, Reverend Dr James Kirkpatrick, said of him that he was:

> "a man of great natural parts and wisdom, eminent piety and exemplary holiness, great ministerial gravity and authority, endowed with savoury and most edifying gifts for his sacred function, wherein he was laborious, painful, and faithful; was a constant, curious, and accurate observer of all public occurrences, and, with all these rare qualities, he had not only the blood and descent, but the spirit and just decorum of a gentleman."[37]

Shields portraying early Scots families are carried at the Broadisland Gathering in 1993 ahead of locals portraying early settlers.

Courtesy of the *Larne Times*.

A Symington family crest on an old gravestone, Templecorran, Ballycarry, Co Antrim. The village of Symington, from which the family takes its name, is in Ayrshire.

ENDNOTES

1 This is believed to refer to Broughshane, County Antrim
2 Stevenson, John, *A Frenchman's Walk through Ireland 1796–7*, Belfast: 1984
3 OS Memoir for Parishes of Glynn, Inver, Kilroot and Templecorran, vol 26, Belfast: Institute of Irish Studies, 1994, p103
4 See, for example, Morgan, Hiram, *Tyrone's Rebellion*, London: Royal Historical Society, 1993
5 Quoted in Fraser, Antonia, *King James VI of Scotland and I of England*, Sphere, 1977, p108
6 Robinson, Philip, *The Plantation of Ulster*, Dublin: Gill and Macmillan, 1984; and Belfast: Ulster Historical Foundation, 1994
7 This was the case with Ballyclough in Clogher, for example, where, in 1619, there were 15 families in a village of nine houses. Three years later most of them lived in the townlands around the former settlement. See Robinson, *op cit*
8 See Sherry, John, *"Weaklynges" sucking at England: A re-assessment of Scottish involvement in the Plantation of Ulster*, Institute of Irish Studies, working papers, vol 1
9 *Belfast News Letter*, 22 February 1828
10 Hill, JM, quoted in Sherry, *op cit*
11 Robinson, *op cit*
12 Stevenson, David, *Scottish Covenanters and Irish Confederates*, Belfast: Ulster Historical Foundation, 1981, p11
13 See the booklet *Plantation of Ulster*, Belfast: Ulster Scots Agency, 2008, or visit the website: www.PlantationofUlster.org
14 See, for example, the OS Memoir for County Donegal, reprinted by the Institute of Irish Studies
15 See, for example, Porter, Classon, *Ballygally Castle*, Ulster Journal of Archaeology, vol VII, April 1901
16 Stevenson, David, *op cit*
17 Sherry, John, *op cit*
18 Hanna, WA, *Celtic Migrations*, Belfast: Pretani Press, 1985, p43
19 Hanna, *op cit*, p43–4
20 Hamilton, Thomas, *History of the Irish Presbyterian Church*, Edinburgh: Undated, p36
21 Hamilton, *op cit*, p38
22 John Livingstone, quoted in *Seaton Reid, James, The History of the Presbyterian Church in Ireland,* vol 1, Edinburgh: 1834, p117–8
23 Josias Welsh, Minister of Templepatrick, County Antrim, in *Ulster Journal of Archaeology*, vol X, 1904, p32
24 Hume, D, and Nelson, JW, *The Templecorran Project*, Larne: 1994
25 *The Montgomery Manuscripts*, p54
26 The correct spelling is Aldfracken, this is the name as spelt in the original record.
27 Hume and Nelson, *op cit*
28 OS Memoir for Parish of Templecorran, Belfast: Institute of Irish Studies, 1994
29 Morragh, Michael, 'The English presence in early Seventeenth century Munster', in Brady and Gillespie, eds, *Natives and Newcomers, The Making of Irish Colonial Society 1534–1641*, Suffolk: 1986
30 See Reverend Classon Porter, Ballygally Castle in the Ulster Journal of Archaeology, April 1901
31 Gillespie, Raymond, *Colonial Ulster: The settlement of East Ulster 1600–1641*, Cork: 1985
32 OS Memoir for the Parish of Carncastle and Killyglen, p11
33 McCavery, Trevor, *Newtown, A History of Newtownards*, Dundonald: 1994, p52
34 Stevenson, John, *Two Centuries of Life in Down*, Dundonald, 1990, p71
35 See, for example, *The Ulster Scot*, January 2006
36 Stevenson, John, *Two Centuries of Life in Down*, Dundonald, 1990, p32
37 Quoted in Killen, WD, ed, Patrick Adair, *Rise and Progress of the Presbyterian Church in Ireland*, Belfast: 1866

Chapter Five

KILLING TIMES:
The story of the Covenanters in Scotland and Ulster

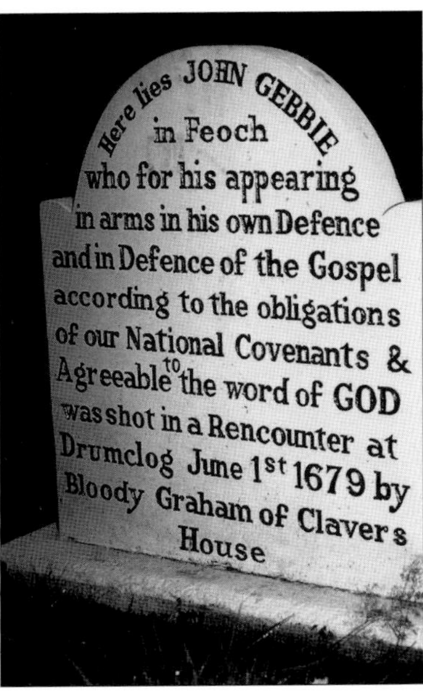

The gravestone of Covenanter John Gebbie at Feoch, Scotland, who was killed at the Battle of Drumclog.

In his work *Old Mortality*, Sir Walter Scott, while not entirely agreeing with the stance of those known in Scottish history as the Covenanters, outlined the burial site of two of their number in the following terms:

> "... upon [their] two stones, which lie beside, may still be read in rude prose, and ruder rhyme, the history of those who sleep beneath them. They belong, we are assured by the epitaph, to the class of persecuted Presbyterians who afforded a melancholy subject for history in the time of Charles II and his successor. In returning from the battle of Pentland Hills a party of the insurgents had been attacked in this glen by a small detachment of the King's troops, and three or four either killed in the skirmish, or shot after being made prisoners, as rebels taken with arms in their hands. The peasantry continued to attach to the tombs of those victims of prelacy an honour which they do not render to more splendid mausoleums; and when they point them out to their sons, and narrate the fate of the sufferers, usually conclude by exorting them to be ready, should times call for it, to resist to the death in the cause of civil and religious liberty, like their brave forefathers ..."[1]

The struggle which Scott refers to had many connections in the north-east of Ireland, for the Covenanters were also to be found in Ulster, where some of them fled for refuge and others settled with Scottish migration.

Among the Scots Covenanters was Colonel James Wallace of Achens, who was Governor of Belfast for a time. He had married into the Edmonstone family of Ballycarry, County Antrim, and spent some time living at their home at Redhall.

He was among those who served with Major General Robert Monro, who was sent to Ulster to quell the Irish rebellion of 1641 and save the Plantation settlement. Wallace had returned to Scotland by 1648, but he was commissioned as Lieutenant Colonel of the Irish Foot by the Committee of Estates on 10 August 1649 and returned to Ulster. It was at this time that Lord Montgomery appointed Wallace the Governor of Belfast, although the pair would later take divergent paths on the Civil War side, the former being a Royalist and the latter strongly in favour of the Covenanter party.

Wallace was to be distinguished for his actions at the Battle of Rullion Green, when the Covenanters were defeated by the authorities as they advanced towards Edinburgh. It was said that Wallace, at this time, was "a true captain … a good man and a skilled soldier ..."[2] He was described as having a rough beard, a long cloak and his huntsman's cap drawn over his brow. To his Royalist prisoners he was always courteous.

We know that despite the adverse weather which they faced, Wallace's soldiers kept unshaken courage, undoubtedly taking example from their commander. As the situation progressed, it became obvious that retreat, if it were possible, was the best option, and Wallace gave an account of leading his men around the eastern front of the Pentland Hills:

> "Being oppressed with multitude we were beaten back, and the enemy came in so full a body, and with so fresh a charge, that, having us once more running, they carried it strongly home, and put us in such confusion that there was no rallying ..."

It was an outcome which spelt disaster for the Covenanter cause and would also see James Wallace bid a final farewell to his native land. He fled to the continent, where he wandered from place to place, supposedly chased by the "vindictive rage" of Charles II's ministers. At the end of 1678, 12 years after he had distinguished himself with valour at Rullion Green, James Wallace died in Rotterdam, much lamented by English and Dutch friends.

What cause encouraged men to brave their lives in rebellion and force some such as Colonel James Wallace into perpetual exile from their homeland? To understand the background we need to know something of not only events but also the religious history of Scotland in the sixteenth and seventeenth centuries.

David Stevenson, in examining the history of the Covenanters, says that their movement was a national one, in that, while support for it was by no means universal, it did attract the participation of the dominant elites in Scottish society, among them nobles and landlords, and also widespread support at the popular level.[3] In a second sense it was also national, as central to the movement was the idea of the preservation of Scotland's national identity.

Part of that identity was tied up in the religious affiliations of Scotland and some of the threat to this identity lay in the Union of the Crowns of England and Scotland in 1603. The Scottish Reformation of 1560 had a strong national element to it, in that part of the Protestant Reformation was the rejection of the Pope as having international authority in religion. While Scots Protestants would initially have seen themselves as a province of the universal true church of God, the reality was that this did not develop, and their own General Assembly remained their highest earthly religious authority.

The idea came about through this circumstance that the Church of Scotland was favoured and indeed special, despite the small size of Scotland herself. The idea of a nation with a special covenanted relationship with God thus developed. Into this situation had come the Union of the Crowns. To understand the differing emphasis on the church in both England and Scotland it is worth bearing in mind Stevenson's comment:

> "The different forms of Protestantism which were to prevail in England and Scotland can be linked closely with the very different ways in which Reformation had come about in the two countries. In England Reformation and [briefly, under Mary Tudor in the 1500s] Counter Reformation were imposed from above by royal dictat. The result was in some senses a 'conservative' Reformation. The new Church of England recognised the monarch as its supreme head on earth, royal power being exercised through powerful bishops acting as the crown's agents. In church structure, beliefs and worship, many features inherited from the Catholic past were retained which were rejected by more radical Protestant churches. Among the latter was the Reformed Church of Scotland, born not by royal decree but through armed rebellion against royal authority [Mary Queen of Scots] ..."[4]

A memorial to Covenanters who were killed by the authorities in Greyfriars churchyard, Edinburgh.

The Scottish Church was born in rebellion, says Stevenson, and established traditions of autonomy. However, religion was too important a force for autonomy to be acceptable to the state, and the Union of the Crowns would see attempts to bring the Church of Scotland closer into line with that of England. Initially, the Scots did not expect such a move and believed that James VI of Scotland's becoming

James I of England boded well for Scotland, which was a small nation compared to England. However, when James moved south to administer his kingdom from London he sent a metaphorical message to his subjects north of the border. It was added to when he declared in 1607, "when I have two Nations under my government, can you imagine I will respect the lesser, and neglect the greater?"

James' monarchy was not only an absentee one, but also an anglicising one. He lured some of the leading Presbyterian ministers to London and had them imprisoned and began to restore Bishops to many of their pre-Reformation powers. An act of supremacy claimed royal power over the church. There was, however, what was known as a 'working compromise' in that no attempts were made to outrightly abolish the Presbyterian hierarchy of courts from Kirk session in the parish through to General Assembly for the nation. The church had all but ceased to be Presbyterian by definition as autonomous with parity of ministers, and dedicated Presbyterians within were leaderless, isolated and aging.

There was some opposition to what was going on, and it came to the surface over reform of worship. Whereas changes in structure had only affected a minority within the Church, change in worship affected all. James I attempted to introduce what were called the Five Articles of Perth reforming worship, but opposition led to him wisely deciding not to implement them. They had given rise to some meeting at conventicles or prayer meetings, and these people would form the nucleus of the movement which was to emerge 20 years later.

Charles I, having succeeded his father, precipitated the crisis which produced the Covenanting movement. He came to the throne in 1625 with a major series of policy initiatives aimed at limiting the power of the nobility, reforming the administration and anglicising worship. While his father had known his limitations in these regards, Charles I decided that he had absolute power and should be obeyed, and the end result was chaos. In 1636 Charles introduced a new Book of Canons or Code of Regulations for the Church of Scotland, which was largely a reprint of the English Book of Canons. He also introduced a new Scottish Book of Prayer, again based on its English counterpart. These were introduced without any consultation with the General Assembly, and thus combined disquiet over the manner of their attempted imposition with a feeling of national grievance.

Tensions over the Roman Catholic threat in Europe added to the situation, as did the suppression of Scots Protestant dissidents in the north of Ireland. Thus the introduction of the new prayer book came at a time when it was least advisable. On Sunday, 23 July 1637, the prayer book was to be introduced in Edinburgh, with the aim of having the city provide an example for the entire country. The example which followed, however, was not the one which Charles wanted to see. In St Giles Cathedral rioting began as soon as the Dean began to read from the new liturgy, and the Dean was forced to lock himself in the steeple for the day as it spread outside. The minister of Greyfriars had to flee from his church while in the Trinity Church in the city the minister waited to hear what was happening elsewhere and prudently returned to his traditional service.

Whatever the true story of the riots – and it would appear there were significant figures directing them and awaiting developments before publicly associating themselves with the new movement – the stage was now set for confrontation.

Charles did not handle the tense situation very well. He blamed a radical minority for the trouble, and rejected a Supplication and Complaint presented to the Scottish Council on 18 October 1637, blaming the Bishops for the trouble and claiming that the prayer book was unconstitutional. Charles ordered the chief supplicants arrested and he took full responsibility for the prayer book. Instead of now obeying their King, however, two men, Archibald Johnston and Alexander Henderson, drafted the National Covenant.

The Grassmarket at Edinburgh, where many Covenanters were executed, from a sketch in John Howie's *Scot Worthies* (1870).

The Covenant reaffirmed James VI's pledge to defend the Protestant Church, and suggested that legislation relating to episcopacy within the Church of Scotland might have been unconstitutional. On 28 February 1638, the Covenant was signed by nobles and lairds who gathered at St Giles in Edinburgh, and it thence travelled across the city, being most famously signed at Greyfriars, and across the country.

A General Assembly was called and ratified the Covenant, also disestablishing the episcopacy which had been set up in Scotland. The Marquis of Hamilton and the King continued talks with the Covenanters, but prepared for war. In March 1639 the Covenanters seized Edinburgh Castle and other venues, and two months later Charles had an army on the Scottish borders, while the Earl of Huntley seized Aberdeen for the King. At the Battle of the Bridge o' Dee on 19 June 1639, the Earl of Montrose defeated Huntley in a crushing victory for the Covenanters. After a few more skirmishes, the Pacification of Berwick saw both armies being stood down, but little had been resolved. Charles did not accept the position of the Covenanters and mustered his forces in the north of England. However, the Covenanters came to him and defeated his army at the Battle of Newburn on 28 August 1640, imposing terms of surrender on the King which included that he end attempts to interfere with the Kirk. Over the next year the revolutionary aspects of the movement saw the roles of the monarch and executive reduced, which led to Montrose, as a moderate, siding with the King. However, any thoughts that Charles had about arresting the Covenanter leaders and defeating their movement were distracted by events in England and Ireland at this tense political time.

The Bass Rock off North Berwick, once a prison for Covenanters including the famous Alexander Peden, from a sketch in John Howie's *Scot Worthies* (1870).

Events across the British Isles assumed the nature of civil war. In September 1645 the Royalist force of Montrose was utterly defeated at Philliphaugh by David Leslie, and 6,000 men returned from the north of England. It was the end of hopes for a Royalist Scotland. The presence of the Army of the Solemn League and Covenant in England was also an effort to preserve the Covenant in Scotland. The Covenanters had obtained an agreement to provide military help for the English parliamentarians in return for acceptance of the New Covenant. They also assisted by sending a 10,000 strong army into Ulster.

Something of the Covenanters' thinking can be understood by examining the New Covenant. The rights of parliaments and liberties of the kingdoms of England and Scotland were to be upheld, religious uniformity on the lines of Scottish Presbyterianism was to be established, and there was to be a federal relationship with England and Scotland as equal partners. The Covenanters were exporting their revolution to try and preserve it.

In October 1641, meanwhile, a rising had broken out, targeted against the British settlements in Ulster. It was led by the O'Neills. Contemporary accounts of the loss of life that occurred and who was responsible have varied depending on those telling or retelling them. Historians differ over the basis of the Rising, but there can certainly be little doubt that it resulted in a traumatic period in history.

Initially, when the 1641 rebellion broke out, the rebels were said to have had orders not to attack Scottish settlers in Ulster. The reasons for this may have been fear of the consequences of attack from Scotland, where Covenanter armies had been victorious, or belief that an alliance might be forged with the Scots. However, within two weeks the orders, irrespective of why they had been issued, were being ignored. Scots and English settlers alike became targets and the swift success of the rebellion in Tyrone spread panic in the official and unofficial Plantation settlements across Ulster. There were massacres of Protestant settlers by the rebels, notably at Clough, Portglenone, Portadown, Loughgall and other areas, and there was at least one prominent massacre of Roman Catholics in Islandmagee by Scots. The Islandmagee massacre was probably retaliation for a massacre of Protestants on the Bann at Portglenone. It is believed to have included soldiers who had fled from North Antrim to the relative safety of Carrickfergus, although the testimony of one survivor, Brian Magee, in May 1653, suggests that several of the neighbours of the Magees were involved. He named Robert and James Browne, William Gillis, William Boyd, James Boyd, Alexander McAlister, John McMaster and his son, also John, and John Nelson as having stormed into their house with murderous intent. The slaughter in the Magee house included his mother, brother, three sisters and another woman. A further ten people were said to have been killed that night by the raiding party. Magee, his father and his brothers who had escaped from the house, went the next day to Carrickfergus to seek assistance from the authorities, but the soldiers whom they met murdered the party apart from Bryan Magee, who escaped. He survived to give his account of the incidents from a new home at Leggycorry, County Down, in 1653. Although the numbers murdered in the

Islandmagee massacre were exaggerated in later years, neighbour had turned against neighbour, and it was not one of the more glorious episodes in Ulster Scots history.[5]

When the Rising broke out, it was not long before refugees began arriving at the Scottish ports. The situation in Ulster had, since the inception of the Rising, an impact on Scotland, for refugees had fled there and reports from Bute, Ayr, Irvine, Portpatrick and Stranraer suggest a constant stream in the December of 1641.[6] In Coleraine, which may have been a typical example, the men remained to fight, but the women and children were shipped across to Scotland for safety. Such were the numbers of destitute Ulster Scots refugees in Scotland that in February 1642 the Scottish Privy Council ordered a collection throughout the country for them.[7]

In January 1642, arms worth over 14,500 Pounds Scottish were handed over by the Scottish Privy Council to James Edmonstone, who had been sent across by Chichester on behalf of English officers in County Down. Hundreds of volunteers were also arriving in Ireland from Scotland (men who had been disbanded from the Covenanter armies) and King Charles I also signed commissions raising regiments with Ulster commanders and dispatching around 1,500 men to Ireland.

The largest force to arrive was dispatched under General Robert Monro and arrived in Carrickfergus in April 1642. The importance of the garrison town was acknowledged by the rebels, who had hoped to take the castle but been prevented by defeat in battle at Lisburn. Had the O'Neillite forces succeeded, the surrounding Scottish settlements would undoubtedly have been abandoned by their inhabitants, and given that refugees from as far away as North Antrim streamed into Carrick for safety, the future of the entire East Ulster plantation would undoubtedly have been under serious threat. As fate had it, however, the army which arrived to occupy Carrickfergus in 1642 was not that of the Irish forces, but of the Scots.

In April 1642 Major General Robert Monro arrived at Carrickfergus at the head of an army comprising ten regiments and at least 2,500 troops. The regiments included those under the Earl of Glencairn, General Monro, the Earl of Lothian, the Marquis of Argyll and Colonel Robert Home.[8]

The effectiveness of this force did not take long to materialise. The first sortie resulted in defeat for the rebels at Lisburn. About 150 Irish were killed while Monro lost only two of his men. At Loughbrickland the rebel garrison refused to surrender, and, as was the military practice, was put to the sword, while Newry, perhaps mindful of this example, surrendered to the Scots and their English allies. Atrocities which had been carried out by the rebels in the early stages of the Rising were now repaid by the new force. Further developments included the capture of Dunluce Castle from the MacDonnells – it was handed over to a Campbell commander – and an effective presence along the Bann. The Earl of Antrim, who had offered his assistance in maintaining the peace of the country, was arrested and imprisoned at Carrick on the basis that some of his tenants were in revolt.

While the Dublin government under Ormonde came out in support of the King during the great parliamentary/monarchy debate in England in 1643, the Scots army continued to support parliament. However, there was considerable strain in 1644 because some of the regiments wanted to return to Scotland to join the Covenanter armies raised there against the Royalist forces. Three regiments left, while the remainder stayed, and there were fears that Monro would seek to move on Dublin. He did capture Belfast, forcing Sir Arthur Chichester to withdraw to England, but a stalemate developed between English Royalist and Plantation interests and Covenanter ones.

By April 1644, 1,400 men had been sent back to Scotland, where they served under Colonel Robert Hume. Meanwhile, Hume's lieutenant, Colonel John Maxwell, took charge of the New Scots regiment in Ulster. From the following autumn the English parliament was demanding that the Scots give up Belfast and Monro's position as Commander in Chief of all the forces was revoked. The high point of the Scots army had been reached. At Benburb, in June 1646, plans to sweep O'Neill's forces out of Ulster in the combined assault of the forces of Monro and Lord Clandeboye failed to materialise. This was a result of the defeat of Monro's force by Owen Roe O'Neill, which saw the Scots play little active part in further confrontation with the Irish, while the latter did not seek to push further into Ulster.

A portrayal of Covenanters at prayer from Robert Pollok's book *Tales of the Covenanters* (1858).

Political divisions within the Scots would lead to the downfall of Monro; indeed tensions surfaced as early as 1642. When some of the Scots signed an Engagement with the King – a secret agreement which it was hoped would serve both interests – there was an intrigue with the so-called Anti-Engagers, who seized control after the defeat of the Engagers at Preston in August 1648. George Monck and others, including Glencairn's Regiment, seized Carrickfergus. As events unfolded Monck was to fall from favour and a rising in Ulster, royalist in tone and Presbyterian in ethos, resulted in him being dislodged after the execution of Charles I. Belfast was seized and Lieutenant Colonel James Wallace, who had intermarried with the Edmonstone family of Redhall, County Antrim, was appointed Governor.

As the course of the English Civil War continued to dominate Irish affairs, Oliver Cromwell arrived in 1649 with a large English army and quelled Ireland. The English Commonwealth, not surprisingly, was suspicions of the Ulster Presbyterian settlement, which had condemned the execution of the King, and was hostile to the Ulster Scots. This was underlined by an undeveloped scheme to transport them from Antrim and Down to Tipperary. Eventually moderation prevailed and the authorities felt it was better to win the Ulster Scots over rather than transport them, disgruntled and resentful, into another part of Ireland.

The 1641 Rising, which was led by Sir Phelim O'Neill and other leading Ulster Gaelic chieftains, centred on the pre-plantation heartland of South East Tyrone and quickly spread. Castles were captured and most of the plantation settlements were attacked. Settlers were massacred, although most suffered through loss of property and dispossession. There were a number of massacres on both sides during the turbulent years of 1641 and 1642, but more settlers probably died through being deprived of clothing and food in that unforgiving winter. The presence of the Scots Covenanter army saved the Plantation in the east and established Presbyterianism as an administrative body in Ulster. The chaplains of the Army met to form the first Presbytery in Ireland in 1642. The Presbyterian Church in Ireland can trace its structural and organisational roots to this event in Carrickfergus.

The consequences of 1641 included the Commonwealth seizing all or most Roman Catholic lands in West Ulster and Antrim and Down. Although not initially taken up, more Scots and English settlers did arrive to settle, particularly in the last decades of the seventeenth century, thus extending the Ulster Plantation.

The 1641 Rising had a major impact on the Plantation settlement and on seventeenth century Ulster. It was not the impact which Sir Phelim O'Neill had hoped for or anticipated:

> "The effect of the army's years in Ulster remained, however. The Irish confederates had been prevented from conquering Ulster. The Scots-dominated Ulster plantation had survived. And presbyterianism had been firmly established in Ulster. They were all, obviously, of immense importance in the development of Ireland in the centuries ahead." [9]

In the context of the Scots Covenanters, the same author adds:

> "In Scotland since the sixteenth century two great popular historical mythologies have emerged, often rivals but sometimes intertwined. One has concentrated on her royal dynasty and its sufferings, forming itself round the dethronement and ultimate execution of Mary, Queen of Scots, the martyrdom of Charles I and his Scottish representative the Marquis of Montrose, the unjust expulsion of James VII and the death at Killiecrankie of Graham of Claverhouse as a sacrificial offering, the Jacobite risings and Bonnie Prince Charlie, loyal Highlanders and tartan trappings, romanticism and nostalgia. The other is the Presbyterian/Covenanting tradition of struggle for religious and other freedoms, of the rights of the people and the individual conscience, of the fight against the oppressive and corrupt rulers of the land (typified by the Stuart dynasty), of poor folk hunted across the moors by brutal troopers. The original 'Nobleman's Covenant' had thus evolved into the people's Covenants, creating a tradition that has fed into working class and democratic movements."[10]

Robert Burns (1759–1796) in one of his poems remarks:

> "The Solemn League and Covenant
> Now brings a smile, now brings a fear.
> But sacred Freedom, too, was theirs:
> If thou'rt a slave, indulge thy sneer."[11]

The great Ulster poet Sir Samuel Ferguson also captured something of the Covenanter experience in Scotland and Ulster in the Ballad of Willie Gilliland, formerly of Carrick in Ayrshire and latterly of Glenwherry, in which he effectively sums up the Covenanter cause in the memorable lines:

> "Upon the mountain solitude and in a rebel ring
> He has worshipped God upon the hill, in spite of church and king."

Another Covenanter who found refuge in Antrim was David Houston of Paisley, who was associated with James Renwick and fought at the Battle of Bothwell Bridge, in June 1679. He was captured in 1688 and was sent to Edinburgh to stand trial by the Privy Council, but escaped and returned back to County Antrim, where he had been a field preacher. In his history of the Kellswater Reformed Presbyterian Church, the late Superintendent Robert Buchanan relates:

> "It is reliably reported that he took ill in the vicinity of a barn owned by a family called Sloan at Carncomb, above Connor, and crawled inside. The family heard the man and was concerned, not knowing whether he was a criminal or otherwise. When they heard him praying, however, they realised that he was a man of God and brought him into their house."[12]

David Houston died in December 1696 and was one of the many Covenanting legacies which we share with Scotland and America. It was from the Kellswater area that many Covenanting Presbyterians emigrated to America and played a part in the Revolutionary War. Another of the lasting legacies of the Covenanter period was provided by one Richard Cameron, who took charge of sentinels who guarded the Presbyterians during their conventicles on the moors. These sentinels were armed and would alert the worshippers if the military were sighted. Cameron's sentinels became raised as a Covenanter regiment, the Cameronians, which continued to exist as a Scottish regiment and a Territorial Army regiment until the late 1960s. The regiment had the distinction of being the only regiment of the British Army which was allowed to parade to church service with fixed bayonets, in recognition of the service they had given to the Covenanters on the moors in seventeenth century Scotland.

HISTORICAL TRAILS
SITES TO VISIT

The late David Roy (left) and John Reardon (right), Scottish Covenanter Memorials Association members, during a visit to the Peden Memorial at Glenwherry, County Antrim. Alexander Peden is known as the Prophet of the Covenanters. An annual conventicle (outdoor worship) is still held there.

The Wigtown Memorial to the Covenanter Martyrs who drowned on the incoming tide rather than recant the National Covenant.

Peden memorial stone at Glenwherry

Sited on the Douglas Road and within sight of Slemish mountain, is the farm where the Prophet of the Covenant, Alexander Peden (1626–1686), once laboured and lived. Each year a traditional conventicle is held there by the Reformed Presbyterian Church, the ecclesiastical heirs of the Covenanters. Legend has it that nearby, during the time of persecution, Covenanters were surrounded by soldiers as they worshipped, but that a mist came down and they were able to escape through it. The story is that the stream which flows in the area has been called the Misty Burn since that occasion.

The Wigtown Martyrs Memorial

There is an impressive memorial just outside the village of Wigtown, on what would have been the shores of the Solway. It marks the site where, in May 1685,

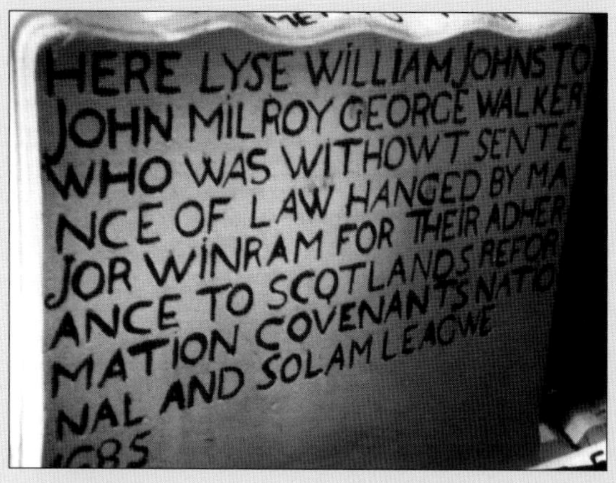

A gravestone at Wigtown in Scotland commemorating Covenanters William Johnston, John Milroy and George Walker, who were hanged "without sentence of law" in 1685.

two Covenanters, Margaret Wilson and Margaret McLauchlan, were tied to stakes in the Solway Firth and threatened with drowning if they did not recant the Covenant. Neither of the women recanted, saying that Christ was the only head of the church. This was a central issue with the Covenanters, as they opposed Charles I's attempts to be head of the church. The Covenanter motto was "For Christ's Crown and Covenant". There are headstones in the Wigtown churchyard for several Covenanters, including Margaret McLauchlan, Margaret Wilson, William Johnston, John Milroy and George Walker (the latter three were hanged). Margaret Wilson's family included emigrants to Ulster, one of whose descendants was US President Woodrow Wilson.

St Nicholas Church, Carrickfergus

In 1642 the chaplains of the Covenanter Army, which was stationed in Carrickfergus, assembled for the purpose of forming a Presbytery of the Kirk. The administrative history of the Presbyterian Church in Ireland can be traced to this event, since prior to this ministers had operated under the terms of the Anglican Establishment and through its church structure.

The Army Presbytery soon found itself receiving calls to assist congregations which had been affected by the loss of clergy and appointed ministers accordingly. For example, the Army Presbytery appointed the Reverend Robert Cunningham, who was the second minister in Ballycarry, County Antrim and the first Presbyterian minister in Ireland. Cunningham came from Ballantrae on the west coast of Scotland and ministered in Ulster until his death in 1697.

A memorial in Carrickfergus commemorates the first Presbytery in 1642 and takes the form of a burning bush, the Presbyterian symbol. It is believed that the Presbytery first met in St Nicholas' Church, which is a beautiful Norman building with much of historical interest among its stained glass windows and memorials. The presence of Major General Robert Monro's Scottish army helped secure Plantation settlements, particularly in the east of Ulster, during the period of the 1641 Rising.

Reverend Robert Hanna, Reformed Presbyterian Minister of Kellswater, with American historian Sam Thomas during a visit to the site associated with David Houston of Paisley.

Kells, County Antrim

Kellswater Reformed Presbyterian Church is located in the townland of Carnaughts near Kells in County Antrim, and close to the Kells Water. It is a tranquil and peaceful spot.

A plaque and lecture hall in honour and memory of David Houston, a prominent Covenanter who preached in the area and the wider Glens of Antrim, is located in the grounds of Kellswater Reformed Presbyterian Church.

Houston, who died in December 1696, was active in the area for many years. He was among those associated with James Renwick and fought at the Battle of Bothwell Bridge in June 1679. He was captured in May 1688 and sent from Ulster to stand trial in Edinburgh, but escaped and returned to County Antrim.

The Lecture Hall at Kellswater Reformed Presbyterian Church was erected by Henry H Houston, a descendant of Reverend Houston, from Philadelphia in the United States.

The Kellswater congregation was one of those ministered to at a later period by Reverend William Martin, who was ordained at the Vow in County Antrim in 1757 and was effectively the first minister of Kellswater. In 1772 Reverend Martin led a migration to America from the North Antrim area, with five shiploads of his congregation and their neighbours settling in the Piedmont region of the Carolinas. James McKinney, who also ministered at Kellswater, later emigrated to America, where, in common with the Reformed Presbyterian Church movement, he became a bitter opponent of slavery.[13]

The Covenanters prison inside the Greyfriars churchyard in Edinburgh. Many of those imprisoned here later drowned when the ship taking them to servitude in the West Indies was lost off Orkney.

Greyfriars Churchyard, Edinburgh

Greyfriars is a most famous site in the context of the Covenanting period, for it was here, in 1638, that the original Solemn League and Covenant was signed. The churchyard was to have other elements which have been inextricably associated with the Covenanters. There is a

Covenanter memorial commemorating all those Covenanter adherents who lost their lives during the so-called 'Killing Times', while within the grounds of the cemetery is an area where Covenanter prisoners were held in appalling conditions.

A short distance away at the Grassmarket is the spot where many Covenanters were hanged for their loyalty to their cause, the spot where the gallows once stood is now marked by a memorial in the form of a Scottish saltire.

A modern Covenanter Memorial at St John's Town of Dalry.

St John's Town of Dalry

St John's Town of Dalry in Kirkcudbrightshire (on the A713 from Castle Douglas to Ayr) was the site of the starting point of the Pentland Rising of 1666. In 2004 a member of the Scottish Covenanter Memorials Association, Bill Dunnigan, who was manager of Mayflower Engineering of Sheffield, donated a steel sculpture in memory of the Covenanters. The sculpture is based on the burning bush of Exodus, chapter three, and is five metres in height. It weighs three tons.

On some of the leaves are the names of prominent Covenanters including Margaret McLauchlin and Margaret Wilson, the Wigtown Martyrs, Richard Cameron, Reverend James Renwick and Reverend Alexander Peden.

Dalry, located in the picturesque Dumfries and Galloway region, was the site of strong support for the Covenanters, and at least one local man, James MacGeachan, was banished to Carolina as a slave in June 1684 on account of his adherence to the Covenanter cause. The church at Dalry was used by Robert Grierson of Lag, one of the major persecutors of the Covenanters in Galloway, as a stable for his horses. On 13 November 1666, soldiers from the garrison at Dalry mistreated an old man named Grier in the village. They were about to brand him with a hot iron for failing to pay a fine, when the villagers rose up against them, freeing the old man and later killing one of the soldiers. Over 200 Covenanters then made their way to attack Dumfries. The group was among the 900 who were defeated by a force of around 3,000 soldiers in the Pentland Hills on 28 November 1666. Around 100 Covenanters were killed and many more were later executed. A number of men from Dalry were hanged in Ayr for their part in the Rising.[14]

St Giles Cathedral, Edinburgh

An extremely historic building, the cathedral's foundation lies in the twelfth century, but it was only accorded cathedral status in 1633, following the Protestant Reformation. A stained glass window and a statue depict the Reformer John Knox, who was appointed minister in 1559.

In 1637 riots took place in and outside the cathedral, after attempts to introduce the Scottish Prayer Book. In a famous incident said to have precipitated the rioting, Jenny Geddis is reputed to have thrown her stool at the clergyman attempting to read from the prayer book and shouted "Wha dare say mass in my lug?". However, it appears that Jenny's protest is more likely to have occurred in 1660 at the time of Charles II's restoration.[15] There is a memorial stool in the cathedral which reminds us of the dramatic event.

St Giles is a fascinating and very atmospheric building, which includes a memorial to the founder of the Boy's Brigade, a bronze relief memorial to the writer Robert Louis Stevenson, and also the Thistle Chapel, which was built between 1909 and 1911 and is the home to Scotland's historic order of chivalry.

HISTORICAL QUOTES

"In obedience to the Commandment of God, conforme to the practice of the godly in former times, and according to the laudable example of our Worthy and Religious Progenitors, & of many yet living amongst us, which was warranted also by act of Councill, commanding a generall band to be made and subscribed by his Majesty's subjects, of all ranks, for two causes: One was, For defending the true Religion, as it was then reformed, and is expressed in the Confession of Faith above written, and a former large Confession established by sundry acts of lawful generall assemblies, & of Parliament, unto which it hath relation, set down in publick Catechismes, and which had been for many years with a blessing from Heaven preached, and professed in this Kirk and Kingdome, as Gods undoubted truth, grounded only upon his written Word. The other cause was, for maintaining the King's Majesty, his Person, and Estate: the true worship of God and the King's authority, being so straitly joined, as that they had the same friends, and common enemies, and did stand and fall together. And finally, being convinced in our mindes, and confessing with our mouthes, that the present and succeeding generations in this land, are bound to keep the fore said nationall Oath and Subscription inviolable, Wee should be We Noblemen, Barons, Gentlemen, Burgesses, Ministers & Commons under subscribing, considering divers times before & especially at this time, the danger of the true reformed Religion, of the King's honour, and of the publick peace of the Kingdome: By the manifold innovation and evills generally contained, and particularely mentioned in our late supplications, complaints, and protestations, Do hereby profess, and before God, his Angels, and the World solemnly declare, That with our whole hearts we agree and resolve, all the days of our life, constantly to adhere unto, and to defend the foresaid true Religion ..."

The Text of the National Covenant, Greyfriars Kirk, 28 February 1638

An old postcard of the memorial at the battlefield of Bothwell Bridge, where Covenanters suffered defeat.

The following was written by James Renwick, Covenanter Minister and Martyr, the day before his execution at the Grassmarket in Edinburgh on 17 February 1688. He was born on 15 February 1662, at Moniaive, in the parish of Glencairn, Dumfriesshire, the son of a weaver. He learned to read the Bible at the age of six years and would be the last of the Covenanter Martyrs of Scotland.

"Now, my dear friends in precious Christ, I think I need not tell you that, as I have lived, so I die, in the same persuasion with the true reformed and covenanted Presbyterian Church of Scotland. I adhere to the testimony of the day, as it is held forth in our Informatory Vindication, and in the testimony against the present toleration; and that I own, and seal with my blood, all the precious truths, even the controverted truths, that I have taught. So I would exhort every one of you to make sure your personal reconciliation with God in Christ, for I fear many of you have that yet to do; and when you come where I am, to look pale death in the face, ye will not be a little shaken and terrified if ye have not laid hold on eternal life. I would exhort you to much diligence in the use of means; to be careful in keeping your societies; to be frequent and fervent in secret prayer; to read much the written Word of God, and to examine yourselves by it.

Do not weary to maintain, in your places and stations, the present testimony; for when Christ goeth forth to defeat antichrist, with that name written on His vesture and on His thigh, KING OF KINGS, AND LORD OF LORDS, He will make it glorious in the earth. And if you can but transmit it to posterity, ye may count it a great generation work. But beware of the ministers that have accepted this toleration, and all others that bend that way; and follow them not, for the sun hath gone down on them. Do not fear that the Lord will cast off Scotland; for He will certainly return, and show Himself glorious in our land. But watch and pray, for He is bringing on a sad overthrowing stroke, which shall make many say that they have easily got through that have got a scaffold for Christ; and do not regard the sufferings of this present world, for they are not worthy to be compared to the glory that shall be revealed.

I may say, to His praise, that I have found His cross sweet and lovely unto me; for I have had many joyful hours, and not a fearful thought since I came to prison. He hath strengthened me to outbrave man and outface death; and I am now longing for the joyful hour of my dissolution; and there is nothing in the world I am sorry to leave but you; but I go unto better company, and so I must take my leave of you all.

Farewell beloved sufferers, and followers of the Lamb. Farewell Christian intimates. Farewell Christian and comfortable mother and sisters. Farewell sweet societies. Farewell desirable general meetings. Farewell night wanderings, cold and weariness for Christ. Farewell sweet Bible, and preaching of the Gospel. Farewell sun, moon, and stars, and all sublunary things. Farewell conflicts with a body of death. Welcome scaffold for precious Christ. Welcome heavenly Jerusalem. Welcome innumerable company of angels. Welcome General Assembly and Church of the first-born. Welcome, crown of glory, white robes, and song of Moses and the Lamb. And, above all, welcome, O thou blessed Trinity and One God! O Eternal One, I commit my soul into Thy eternal rest!"

Standard of the Covenant

"While stepping over the bleak hills of Lanarkshire the other day, a gentleman happened to call at a remote farm house, in a parish which lies on its north east corner. The conversation naturally turning on the Catholic bill,[16] to which such isolated men may be excused from being so tenacious in their prejudices, the farmer, now a very venerable personage, said his father had fought at Bothwell-bridge, of which he still had some relics. These heirlooms had descended and were preserved in the family with zealous care. They consisted of a genuine Ferara, sheep headed and of formidable dimensions, which hung suspended over the brace: and what was more of interest, and kept securely locked up in an ancient chest, one of the identical standards which had floated above the ranks of the Covenanters. This is of fine linen, about five feet square. At the top, in one corner, is an open Bible, the writing, seemingly in Hebrew, however, has nearly gone, except Verbum Dei, in large English letters. In the other corner is the Scottish thistle, surmounted with a crown, and the following inscription occupies the body of the standard in capital letters of a blood red colour – "For this parish of Shotts, for Reformation in church and State, according to the Word of God, and our Covenants."

'A Standard of the Covenant', *Belfast News Letter,* 5 May 1829

The Cameronian Regiment memorial in Glasgow. The regiment owed its origins to sentinels who guarded the Conventicles in the seventeenth century.

HISTORICAL FIGURES

Major General Sir Robert Monro

Robert Monro came from a family with a strong tradition of military service and had served on the continent between 1628 and 1636 in the payroll of the Swedish army. He took part in the Thirty Year's War. By 1638 he had come home to Scotland and was involved in the service of the Scottish Covenanters. His military capabilities were clear through his successful capture of several castles, including Spynie Palace, fortified home of the Bishops of Moray, Drum Castle, the seat of the Clan Irvine, and Huntly Castle, seat of another loyalist clan, the Gordons.

Monro received the commission to raise a regiment in March 1640 and did so across a large area of Eastern Scotland. This regiment would also see service in Ulster a few years later, serving there until 1648 with the garrison town of Carrickfergus being its base.

In 1642 Monro had been sent to Ulster as second-in-command of a Covenanter Army headed by Alexander Leslie. Monro, however, was in effect the overall commander and his presence in Ulster was to preserve the British Plantation settlement there. His troops quickly moved to secure their base at Carrickfergus and then took on the O'Neills elsewhere, an early success being the capture of Newry in April 1642. In April 1644 Monro was placed in overall command of all English and Scots forces in Ulster by the English parliament.

His efforts in Ulster were not always successful, and attempts to seize Dundalk and Drogheda proved too ambitious. The need for troops to be sent to Scotland to defend against the Royalists led to the depletion and weakening of Monro's force, and in June 1646 his force was routed by Owen Roe O'Neill, when over 2,000 Scots were killed at the Battle of Benburb. Monro withdrew to Carrickfergus, although O'Neill did not follow up the advantage.

Internal division was to affect Monro, and men under his command refused to consider a truce with the English parliament, as had occurred in Scotland. George Monck was appointed overall commander and Monro was captured with the town of Carrickfergus in September 1648. He spent five years in the Tower of London and was released by Oliver Cromwell in 1654. He returned to Ulster, where he had estates in the Ardes, his wife being the Widow of Viscount Montgomery. Monro is believed to have died around 1680 at Comber. One of his descendants was Henry Munro, a Lisburn draper who was leader of the Down United Irishmen in 1798 and was executed for his part in the Rising that year.

The memorial at Douglas Road, Glenwherry, commemorating Alexander Peden, the Scottish Covenanter.

Alexander Peden, Prophet of the Covenant

One of the most prominent Covenanters of the seventeenth century was Reverend Alexander Peden, who was born in 1626 near Cumnock in Ayrshire.

He had been a schoolmaster and then became minister for New Luce in Galloway in 1658. Two years later, as a result of the Restoration of Charles II and persecution of non-conformists, he was ejected from his pulpit and entered a new phase of his life. He drew himself to the attention of the authorities by holding conventicles and a proclamation was issued against him in 1666. Peden spent part of his time evading the authorities across the North Channel in Ulster, and it is his time at Glenwherry in County Antrim that is still recalled today by an annual conventicle organised by Reformed Presbyterians, the descendants of the Covenanters.

In 1673, Peden was arrested at Knockdow near Ballantrae on the coast of Ayrshire where he had been conducting an illegal conventicle, and taken prisoner to Edinburgh, subsequently being confined on the Bass Rock off the Scottish coast, a famous and bleak prison for the Covenanters. He was sentenced to banishment in America but was released, along with others, by an American ship's captain in London who found out why his reluctant passengers had been placed on the ship. Alexander Peden again began a wandering lifestyle as a covenanter preacher in both Scotland and Ulster, continually on the run from the authorities.

Eventually, he went back to his native parish of Sorn in Ayrshire, where a cave was dug for him beside the River Lugar, as he did not dare to stay in the home of his brother who lived at Auchinleck. Peden knew that he was nearing his end and requested to be buried at Airdsmoss, close to the resting place of another prominent Covenanter, Richard Cameron. He was, however, buried in Auchinleck churchyard when he died in January 1686. Several weeks later dragoons from Sorn castle disinterred his corpse with the intention of hanging it from the Cumnock Gallows, but William Crichton, who was the Second Earl of Dumfries, intervened, concerned that the action would provoke a rebellion in the strongly Covenanter countryside around. Instead the troops buried Peden at the foot of the gallows as a mark of disrespect. In 1891 a memorial was erected to mark the site, which had become a cemetery surrounding Peden's grave.

During his lifetime, Peden was accredited with prophetic statements. For example, when being put onto the ship which was to take him to the West Indies, he was said to have remarked that the ship was not yet built that would take him there. He was also said to have prayed for deliverance at one point while he and others were being pursued by dragoons, and, as if in answer to his prayer, a mist came down and allowed them to escape. A similar story is told in Glenwherry, County Antrim, where a mist is said to have come and allowed covenanters to escape the authorities. Not surprisingly, Peden assumed considerable status as "the prophet of the Covenanters".

Colonel James Wallace

Colonel James Wallace of Achens was among the army officers who were sent to Ulster in 1642 with Major General Robert Monro. Six years later he had returned to Scotland but was commissioned Lieutenant Colonel of the Irish Foot, which comprised soldiers who had served in Ulster under Monro. Wallace came back to Ulster and served for a year.

In 1650 he married Helen Edmonstone, widow of John Dalway of Carrickfergus, and lived for a time at the seat of the Edmonstone family, Redhall House, in Ballycarry, County Antrim. He would later be involved in the Pentland Rising of 1666 and was among those Covenanters defeated at Rullion Green near Edinburgh. Wallace was said to have always been courteous to the Royalist prisoners which his men captured, but victory was not to lie with the Covenanters at Rullion Green, and he gave an account of the battle:

> "Being oppressed with multitude we were beaten back, and the enemy came in so full a body, and with so fresh a charge that, having us once more running, they carried it strongly home, and put us in such confusion that there was no rallying ..."

The defeat at Rullion Green saw the end of the last of the Covenanter Risings of the seventeenth century.

James Wallace was forced to flee to the Continent, where he moved from place to place to evade the attention of the agents of Charles II. He died in 1678 in Rotterdam and was said to have been much lamented by his English and Dutch friends there.

One writer, Robert McWard, provided a suitable epitaph for Colonel Wallace:

> "... if the cause for which he had suffered was mentioned, when it was scarce believed he understood or could speak, there was a sunshine of supreme joy looked out of his countenance, and a raising of hands on high to receive the confessor's crown, together with a lifting up of the voice ... as to sing the conqueror's song of victory. It was the crossing of a true knight, for whom all the trumpets sounded on either side ..."[17]

An old postcard of the memorial at Stirling to the Wigtown Martyrs, who were drowned in the Solway Firth rather than renounce the Covenant.

Margaret Wilson

The Covenanter cause was very strong in southwest Scotland and one of the most famous and horrific incidents there was the drowning of the Wigtown Martyrs, two women who refused to renounce the Covenanter cause.

One was Margaret McLauchlan, who was in her sixties. She was already imprisoned in Wigtown when Margaret Wilson and her younger sister were arrested. All were tried together and sentenced to be drowned.

Margaret Wilson was the daughter of a farmer named Gilbert Wilson of Glenvernoch, who had conformed to Episcopacy, and who paid a bond of £100 for the freedom of his younger daughter, Agnes, who was around thirteen years of age. His older daughter, who was 18 years old, refused to renounce the Covenant and she and Margaret McLauchlan were tied to stakes at the mouth of the Bladnoch River, to await the rising tide on 11 May 1685. The older woman was tied further out in an effort to encourage the younger to recant when she saw her friend drowning in front of her.

However, despite all efforts to get her to renounce the Covenant and express the four words which would have freed her – "God Save the King" – Margaret Wilson would only say, "God save him, if he will, for it is his salvation I desire." However, when the officer in charge, Major Windram, ordered her to swear an oath on the matter, she demanded to be returned to the waters.

Local history states that Margaret Wilson met her fate that day singing the twenty-fifth Psalm and reciting from the Book of Romans. Both she and the second Margaret would be known in history as The Wigtown Martyrs. There is an impressive memorial to them in Stirling cemetery, while at Wigtown today a representation of a stake is a stark reminder of their fate.

Reverend CH Dick, writing of Galloway history in 1916, would relate that a man named Patrick Stuart, with whom the Wilsons were friendly, had betrayed them to the authorities, leading to the tragic sequence of events. Descendants of Gilbert Wilson later settled in Ulster, and among their line is the Presbyterian President of the United States, Woodrow Wilson.

Richard Cameron

Nicknamed 'the Lion of the Covenant', Richard Cameron was born at Falkland in Fife in or around 1648. He had been a school teacher before he became a Covenanter preacher. As a consequence of his religious activity he spent some time in exile in the Netherlands, returning to his native land in 1680 when he and others issued what is known as the 'Sanquhar Declaration', which called for open rebellion against the King, Charles II. He predicted that the Stuart line would fall for, among other things, "usurping the royal prerogatives of King Jesus."

The followers of Richard took the name of Cameronians, and they were used to guard and protect the illegal conventicles on moors and hillsides. This group provided the beginnings of a famous Scottish regiment, the Cameronians, who were the only British line regiment permitted to carry fixed bayonets on church parades as a reflection of their formative years.

In 1680, the Lion of the Covenant was killed in a skirmish on 22 July 1680, with the King's troops at Ayrsmoss near Cumnock. He had been surrounded and decided to fight to the death, issuing a famous prayer which is still recalled by Covenanters, "Lord, spare the green and take the ripe".

As was the gruesome common practice at the time, Cameron's head and hands were cut off and displayed on an Edinburgh gate by the authorities to dissuade their opponents.

Although he did not live to see it, the success of William III, Prince of Orange, would lead to a pardon for his followers and their incorporation into the British Army as the Cameronian Regiment. It also partially confirmed his prophecy on the end of the Stuart line. They would never rule in Britain after James II lost the throne, although Mary, wife of the Prince of Orange, was daughter of James II and did jointly rule with William until her death.

ENDNOTES

1 Scott, Walter, *Old Mortality*, Koln: 1999 edition, p23–24
2 See Roy, David, *Broadisland Journal*, Ballycarry, County Antrim, vol 7, 2001
3 Stevenson, David, *The National Covenant and Scotland*, Edinburgh: 1988, p6
4 Stevenson, *The National Covenant and Scotland, op cit*, p6
5 Magee's testimony is detailed in O'Laverty, James, *Historical Account of the Diocese of Down and Connor, Ancient and Modern*, Dublin: 1880, reprinted Ballynahinch: 1981
6 Stevenson, David, *Scottish Covenanters and Irish Confederates*, Belfast: 1981, p53
7 Stevenson, *Scottish Covenanters and Irish Confederates, op cit*, p53
8 For a detailed account of the army and its various regiments see Furgol, Edward, M, *A Regimental History of the Covenanting Armies 1639–1651*, Edinburgh: 1990
9 Stevenson, *Scottish Covenanters and Irish Confederates, op cit*, p313
10 Stevenson, *Scottish Covenanters and Irish Confederates, op cit*, p83–84
11 Burns, Robert, *The Solemn League and Covenant*, 1795
12 Buchanan, Robert, *Kellswater Reformed Presbyterian Church. A Short History*, Kellswater: 1989, p19
13 Buchanan, *op cit*, p23
14 Information from literature on the Covenanters in Dalry, published by Dumfries and Galloway Council, in association with the Scottish Covenanter Memorials Association.
15 *St Giles' Cathedral*, Pitkin: 1994, p13
16 The term 'Catholic Bill' relates to the Catholic Emancipation Bill.
17 Roy, *op cit*, p20–21

Chapter Six

WILLIAMITES AND JACOBITES ON BOTH SIDES OF THE NORTH CHANNEL

Re-enactors' portrayal of the Battle of the Boyne at Cookstown, County Tyrone, in 1990.

Both sides of the North Channel were closely intertwined with each other's history during the period of the Williamite and Jacobite Wars, and the sea channel between them may have helped shape the future development of the islands. At one point in the stirring events of the period, James II hoped to lead an army from Lough Foyle to Scotland, where they would link up with the forces of the Jacobite commander in Scotland, James Graham of Claverhouse, known variously in Scottish history, depending on your viewpoint, as Bonnie Dundee or Bloody Clavers. However, the Siege at Londonderry tied up James II's army and made it impossible for the movement of troops to pass unhindered. By the time the siege ended, the prospect of Jacobite movement to Scotland had become impractical as pressure mounted from the Williamites. Just before the lifting of the seige, Graham lost his life in the Battle of Killiecrankie which was, ironically, a Jacobite victory.

Many people associate the Jacobite rebellion in Scotland primarily with the arrival of Bonnie Prince Charlie, but its roots go back to the period of the English Civil War in the years 1642–49. The first Jacobite Uprising took place 30 years before he was born.

The walls of Londonderry. The city withstood the longest seige in British military history.

The tensions of the period owed much to the ascent to the throne of James II of England and VII of Scotland, brother of Charles II. James was a devout Roman Catholic and came to the throne of a nation which was by then firmly anti-Catholic. His subjects were deeply concerned that James would attempt to re-establish the Roman Catholic faith as the official religion. The King's desire to maintain a large standing army also caused great concern. Sir Walter Scott gave his verdict:

> "Any prince less obstinate and bigoted than James might easily have seen that the army would not become his instrument in altering the laws and religion of the country. But he proceeded to provoke a struggle, which it was plain must be maintained against the universal sentiments of his subjects. He had the folly not only to set up Catholic worship in his royal chapel, with the greatest pomp and publicity, but to send an ambassador, Lord Castlemaine, to the Pope to invite His Holiness to countenance his proceedings by sending him a nuncio (envoy) from the See of Rome. Such a communication was, by the law of England, an act of high treason, and excited the deepest resentment."

James made no secret of his wish "that all the people of our dominions were members of the Catholic Church ..."[1] He tempered this, however, with promises that he wished to establish his government on a basis which would make his subjects happy, but his actions were having the opposite effect.

James continued in such a vein, resulting in even Louis XIV of France remarking that the monarch was "more likely to distance Protestants from our religion than to attract them to it ..."[2] (and Louis was hardly perfectly liberal in his treatment of French Protestants). This, combined with the prospect of an absolute monarch backed by a standing army caused great concern. The birth of a male heir to the throne to his second wife Mary of Modena galvanised this concern, for it meant that the throne would remain Roman Catholic. Up to that point it was hoped that James' Protestant daughter Mary, wife of William, Prince of Orange, would succeed her father to the throne. On 10 June 1688, the diarist John Evelyn noted, therefore, "A young Prince born, which will cause dispute ..."[3]

In the Spring of 1688 the increasing concerns had led to two prominent men – Admiral Edward Russell and Rear Admiral Arthur Herbert – travelling to Holland and taking a message from 'men of power and influence'. This asked William, the Prince of Orange, James' Protestant son-in-law, what might be expected of him amidst discontent of Protestants in England. Although William appeared reticent at first, by November 1688, John Evelyn, was writing of preparations by the Dutch to invade England. It was a celebrated 'Protestant wind' which brought the invading fleet to the coast of Devon. William landed at Brixham and moved troops quickly towards London, James fled to France, and parliament offered the throne to William and Mary, in what is known in England as 'the Glorious Revolution'.

In Ireland different circumstances prevailed, where Richard Talbot, the Earl of Tyrconnell, was determined to hold the island for James. He had already removed Protestants from positions of influence and officers from army positions, leading to many of the latter going to Holland to join the army of the Prince of Orange. In the middle of the turmoil created by 'Lying Dick Talbot', as he was known to his enemies, rumour spread around the north of Ireland that massacre of the Protestants there was planned on a grand scale. This supposed warning was contained in a document found in the street of the village of Comber, County Down, and it was never discovered who wrote this letter or whether it was a hoax. The letter warned of the massacre breaking out on 9 December 1688 and when Lord Antrim's Redshanks arrived outside the walled city of Londonderry just before this date, those inside feared the massacre was to start there. Amid deliberations by the city fathers over what to do, the gates were closed by young apprentices in the face of James' troops, and soon hundreds and thousands of Protestant refugees came to Londonderry for shelter. Among the first of them, history records, was a John Cowan and his infantry company from St Johnston in County Donegal. They and others defied the King and his army and survived the longest siege in British military history – 105 days of misery, courage, and tenacity.

A Williamite officer, from a cigarette card produced by Cope Brothers of Liverpool.

In Ulster, Protestant gentlemen had established the Council of the North, and militias were formed to oppose the Jacobites. In the west the Protestant citizens of Enniskillen raised a regiment – Colonel Tiffin's Regiment – that eventually developed into the Inniskillings, one of the famous Irish regiments, whose descendant regiments included the Royal Ulster Rifles, the Royal Irish Rangers and the Royal Irish Regiment.

The Apprentice Boys of Derry is a Protestant fraternity established to commemorate the siege and relief of the city during the Williamite campaign. The siege, which Protestant inhabitants in the city withstood through considerable hardship and deprivation from 1688 to 1689, was the longest in British military history. The organisation claims that the first club was formed in 1714.

Plaque at Groomsport commemorating the landing in 1689 of Schomberg, William of Orange's commander.

The arrival of the Duke of Schomberg on the coast of County Down, on 20 August 1689, with a strong force of Williamite troops, saw a different type of turning point for Protestants in Ireland. Sir Patrick Dunn, writing from Chester to James Hamilton of Bangor, detailed:

> "Seaventy saile of the Ships that went with the Duk of Schonberg's army returned last night being Munday, they bring the news that the Duk of Schonberg landed all his men on Tuesday was seavan night before sun set at Bangor: att their landing the Irish fled but the protestants came flocking in to him ..."[4]

Carrickfergus Castle, the chief Jacobite garrison in Antrim, was besieged and fell after a week of fighting. East Ulster confirmed its Williamite strength, and, as the Jacobites marched from the walls of Derry, more and more of the province came again into the control of those loyal to King William of England, who was soon to be monarch of Ireland too.

The decisive actions that followed the arrival of William at Carrickfergus, in June 1690, saw Williamite victory at the Battle of the Boyne on 1 July. William was wounded prior to the Battle, as he reviewed Jacobite positions from the banks of the river on 30 June, and a rumour went around that he had been killed. His loss would undoubtedly have reversed the cause and been a crucial factor in the future history of Ireland, if not these islands. The Prince of Orange was only wounded, however, and the next day was in the fray of the battle. James, sensing defeat, fled the field, his army said to have displayed inexpertise brought about by Tyrconnell's purge of Protestant officers. The Protestants of the south, who had suffered atrocities at the hands of Lord Garmoyle's Dragoons and others, now saw relief as the Williamite army marched on Sligo, Athlone and other towns. James, who had come to Ireland from France in the hope of securing the island, left Kinsale for France with his hopes shattered. At Aughrim in County Galway, two European commanders, St Ruth and Ginkel, met on 12 July 1691 and the Jacobites were dealt a fatal blow. There followed the Siege and Treaty of Limerick and the end of the War. In subsequent generations Protestants and Roman Catholics in Ireland would look on the period in different ways. For the former, William of Orange, Marshal Schomberg, Reverend George Walker and others would assume great status, while for the latter it was not so much James, as figures such as Sarsfield who would be revered. The Flight of the Wild Geese after the war – Jacobite officers and troops who remained loyal to James and went to exile in Europe, serving with distinction on many battlefields – became legendary in Irish history.

In Scotland, meanwhile, the memory of the Jacobite cause in Scotland was to assume similar proportions to the cherished position of William III among Irish Protestants. Sir Walter Scott, in his famous song *Bonnie Dundee*, epitomised the meeting of the Scottish Parliament at which James Graham of Claverhouse urged the members to fight for James after he had fled to France in 1688:

"To the Lords of Convention twas Clavourhouse spoke,
Ere the King's crown go down there are crowns to be broke,
So each Cavalier who loves honour and me
Let him follow the bonnets of Bonnie Dundee

Then awa to the hills, to the lea, to the rocks,
Ere I own a usurper I'll crouch wi' the fox,
And tremble false Whigs in the midst of your glee
You've no seen the last of my bonnets and me" [5]

The Scottish parliament, which was divided on the issue, finally came down on the side of William. Graham was summoned to appear to answer his position over an intercepted letter showing his loyalty to James. He fled to the Highlands with his supporters and had soon rallied some of the Clans, under himself as Lieutenant-General of King James. Those who joined him included MacDonald of Sleat, MacLean of Dowart, Stewart of Appin, Cameron of Lochiel, MacDonald of Keppoch, MacNeill of Barra and MacDonald of Glencoe.

These Highland chiefs had a pragmatic reason for their support of James, for they feared the loss of lands given to them when he was Commissioner for Scotland during the reign of Charles II (1660–1685). Much of this land had once been part of the estates of the Duke of Argyll, chief of the Clan Campbell, a Clan which was Presbyterian and had supported Oliver Cromwell during the Civil War. There was, to put it mildly, 'bad blood' between the Campbells and MacDonalds. This would later become clear through the horrific agency of the 1692 Glencoe Massacre, when Campbell troops were quartered with MacDonald families and set upon the latter during the night, with murderous intent and effect.

Major-General Hugh McKay, one of William's best officers, was given the task of suppressing the Highlanders, and the two armies met in north-west Perthshire, on the field of Killiecrankie. McKay had about 3,000 foot soldiers and some horse, which were of little consequence on the rough terrain, while Dundee had between 2,000 and 3,000 men, including 300 men from Ireland. The Highlanders charged from their hillside and had overtaken the Williamite lines before bayonets could be fixed, leaving McKay's force broken and in disarray.

Scottish historian, P Hume-Brown, records:

> "Two circumstances saved McKay from utter ruin. True to their inveterate habit, the Highlanders no sooner saw themselves masters of the field than they fell upon the spoils; and under cover of night McKay was able to cross the Garry with the feeble remnant of his host. Still more fortunately for the defeated commander, his victorious antagonist fell in the first onset of the battle, and his death turned a brilliant advantage into a fatal disaster."[6]

It was said after the battle that Claverhouse, who had been a fierce opponent of the Covenanters during Charles II's reign, had fallen at Killiecrankie by the hand of his servant, a Covenanter from Lanarkshire whose kin had been killed by Dundee. The legend grew that this man, in order to exact revenge, had volunteered for service and was employed as a groom. He had waited for an opportunity, which came at Killiecrankie. He shot Claverhouse with a silver bullet, because of the popular superstition that he belonged to the Devil and was unlikely to be affected by lead. Whether any element of this fanciful tale was true or not, the death of Dundee had occurred and the Highlanders were no longer the formidable force they had been.

Although there was an effort to regroup, on 1 May 1690, a detachment of William's army surprised the Jacobites at Cromdale on the banks of the River Spey and scattered them. The defeat at the Boyne for James a few weeks later, followed by the battle of Aughrim and the Treaty of Limerick ended the campaigns. The cause, however, continued to flourish in Scotland.

This situation was assisted by the massacre of Glencoe. The government had set aside £12,000 to ensure a promise from the Highland chieftains of their loyalty. This may not have been distributed very fairly by the Earl of Breadalbane, a Campbell, but was in any case followed up by a proclamation of allegiance which had to be signed by 1 January 1692. The chiefs all took the oath of allegiance, but through a mix-up MacIan, chief of the Clan MacDonald of Glencoe, failed to do so by the time stated. Although it was accepted by the officers in authority that MacDonald had made a mistake by presenting himself with the military authority in Fort William rather than the civil officer, the Sheriff of Argyllshire in Inveraray, and had complied with the spirit of the proclamation, it was decided at a higher level that an example should be made of the MacDonalds. What occurred was that 120 troops, many of them Highlanders, were sent to Glencoe to be quartered with the MacDonalds from the end of January 1692. The troops, who were Campbells, the hereditary enemies of the MacDonalds, received orders to put to the sword all MacDonalds under the age of seventy years and in the early hours of the morning of 14 February the order was carried out, the unsuspecting families being butchered, including a boy of about six years old, and several aged and bedridden. Although an inquiry would be held into the incident, no one was ever brought to trial. Around 150 of the MacDonalds had managed to escape, while the Glencoe Massacre would stir the flames of Jacobism and be long remembered for generations to come.

The issue at the centre of the Glorious Revolution (or War of the Three Kingdoms), meanwhile, was one of succession to the throne, and it was carried beyond the two men whose dispute occasioned the issue having arisen. On 6 September 1701, James II died in exile in France at the age of 67. William, his son-in-law, died at the age of 51 of pneumonia on 8 March 1702, his wife Mary having died seven years before. William was succeeded by Anne, Mary's younger sister and the daughter of James II from his first marriage. On the principle of male succession, however, her half-brother James – the son of Mary of Modena – had a prior claim on the throne. He was just 13 when she came to the throne, and would be known in later history as the 'Old Pretender', while his son, Charles, would be referred to as the 'Young Pretender'. Many regarded James as rightful monarch, and his term 'Pretender' should be explained to derive from the French word *pretendant*, meaning claimant, although opponents undoubtedly used it in a different context.

Events in Britain entered a new historical chapter with the Act of Union of 1707, which occasioned considerable debate in Scotland. The measure was an unpopular one in Scotland, and the Duke of Hamilton was prompted to ask in Parliament:

> "Are one of the descendants here of those worthy patriots who defended the liberty of their country against all invaders, who assisted the great King Robert Bruce to restore the constitution and avenge the falsehood of England?"[7]

It is likely that, as was the case with the Irish Parliament a century later, considerable bribes were used to obtain the measure the government in London wanted. On 6 March 1707, Queen Anne gave her assent to the Treaty of Union. Sir Walter Scott said that:

> "The detestation of the Treaty being for the present the ruling passion of the times, all other distinctions of party, and even of religious opinion in Scotland, were laid aside ... A singular coalition took place, in which Episcopalians, Presbyterians, Cavaliers and many friends of the Revolution drowned all hostility. Even the Cameronians, who now formed a powerful body in the state, retained the same zeal against the Union when established, which had induced them to rise in arms in support of it while it was in progress ..."[8]

The Union in fact provided the spark for Jacobite rising, since many believed Scotland should have her own monarch, and eyes turned towards the exiled house of Stuart. Presbyterians did not at that point mind that James Stuart would be a Roman Catholic, believing that he might be converted or have Protestant children. Louis XIV was aware of these sentiments and sent the young James to Scotland with an invasion fleet of 5,000 men to help him win back the British throne. The expedition was initially met with poor winds, but sailed from Dunkirk on 17 March 1708, reaching the east coast of Scotland and dropping anchor off Crail, a fishing village on the Fife coast. James wanted to be put ashore at Wemyss Castle, seat of the Earl of Wemyss whose family had long backed the Stuart cause. Admiral Forbin, who was in charge of the expedition, however, recounts that all was not going well:

> "In vain we made signals, lit fires and fired our cannon. Nobody appeared … At daybreak we discovered the English fleet had anchored at four leagues distance

from us, and the sight of them caused me considerable uneasiness. We were shut in a sort of bay, with a cape to be doubled before we could gain the open sea."[9]

In reply to James' demands that they be put ashore, he was quite firm:

"Sire, by the orders of my royal master, I am directed to take the same precautions for the safety of your august person as for His Majesty's own. This must be my chief care. You are at present in safety, and I will never consent to your being exposed in a ruinous chateau in an open country, where a few hours might put you in the hands of your enemies ..." [10]

The expedition ended, and the ships sailed for the open sea. Ironically, the mood in Scotland had been one of strong support for James, with the Jacobites mustering support and sympathy. The government forces were not in a good position, the Earl of Leven only able to raise two or three regiments and recording that the Jacobites in Edinburgh were "in such numbers and show themselves so elated that I dare scarce look them in the face as I walk the streets."

The 1715 Rising

Despite the strong support in Scotland, Admiral Forbin's decision had resulted in the failure of the attempts to restore a Stuart to the throne of Scotland. A second rebellion in favour of James took place after the death of Queen Anne and the ascension to the throne of George I, Elector of Hanover. The Earl of Mar raised the standard of the Old Pretender on 6 September 1715 and his forces were to occupy Perth, while a number of skirmishes took place, the most significant of which was at Sheriffmuir, a moorland near Dunblane in Perthshire, on 13 November 1715. Mar had at least 8,000 men in his army, the Duke of Argyll, his opponent, had 3,500. Both armies retreated from each other, concluding an indecisive battle, but both claimed the victory. Mar, however, abandoned all thoughts of movement westward.

Although the Rising had been overshadowed by the death of Louis XIV five days before, James set foot on Scottish soil on 22 December that year, having come from France on a fishing vessel to evade the English navy. Things were not going well, for he realised Sheriffmuir had been indecisive while a Jacobite detachment at Preston had been forced to surrender. Disillusionment would follow on both sides. Hume-Brown notes:

"Instead of the hero-king of their imagination, the Highlanders saw an unimpassioned and stately person well fitted to play a part in a Court ceremony, but neither by his physical nor his mental qualities capable of inspiring enthusiasm or leading a desperate cause ..." "Nor was the disenchantment of the Prince less grievous than their own. He had expected to find an imposing host which only required his presence to lead it to certain victory: what he saw was a motley band of 4,000 foot and 500 horse, whose sorry army presented a strange contrast to that of the disciplined troops of France in whose ranks he had served as a volunteer."[11]

There was some desperate skirmishing by the Highlanders, but they were eventually forced into the mountains and James sailed back to France from Montrose on 4 February 1715, along with the Earl of Mar, Lord Drummond and others. The 1715 Rising had seen division among the Scots themselves, one example being Sir Thomas Kennedy, who had been Lord Provost of Edinburgh between 1685 and 1686. He had seven sons. Two of them, David and Francis, were active Jacobites in 1715; another, Magnus, was a Jacobite sympathiser; and the others ranged from being moderately to militantly Whig. David Kennedy would go into exile in the Netherlands, where he died in 1723; Thomas became a judge in the Scottish Exchequer Court; and William, was a commissioned officer who fought against the Jacobites in 1715. In the Borders region, the Maxwells and Johnstones were opposed to each other over the landing of James. Lord Nithsdale, who was a Maxwell, led the local Jacobites and consequently lost his title, and the Marquis of Annandale, a Johnstone, who was Lord Lieutenant of the County, rallied militia on behalf of George I.[12]

The 1719 Attempt

Four years later there was an uprising again. A fleet under the Duke of Ormonde set sail from Spain, but was badly damaged by storms off Cape Finisterre. Two ships with 300 regular soldiers were despatched to the Isle of Lewis and were met by the Earl of Seaforth and the Marquis of Tullibardine, two Jacobite sympathisers. At Glenshiel a battle was fought with a government force of 1,100 men including Whig clans of the northern highlands, among them Rosses and Munros. Neither side gained a clear victory although Seaforth was badly wounded. On the advice of the Jacobite leaders, the Spanish soldiers laid down their weapons and the Highlanders dispersed.

Although pockets of sympathy remained for the Jacobite cause, James was not the kind of man to inspire great personal affection. It was to be very different in the case of his son, Bonnie Prince Charlie.

Bonnie Prince Charlie and the last attempt

Charles Edward Louis Philip Sylvester Casimer Maria Stuart was the elder son of James, the Old Pretender, and was born on 31 December 1720 in Rome. His home was the Palazzo Muti, a splendid residence which Pope Clement had given his royal parents on their wedding day. Charles was an active boy and had a love of music which was already developed by the age of four. By six and a half he could speak fluently in French, Italian and English; indeed, during 1745–46 he learned enough Gaelic to hold a conversation with his Highlanders.

Sir Walter Scott describes Charles as a young man:

> "Prince Charles Edward, styling himself Prince of Wales, was a youth of tall stature and fair complexion. His features were of a noble and elevated cast, but tinged with an expression of melancholy. His manners were courteous, his temper apparently good, his courage of a nature fit for the most desperate undertakings, his strength of constitution admirable and his knowledge of manly exercises and accomplishments perfect."

The events which led to Charles' arrival in Scotland surrounded the War of the Austrian Succession. In this war, Louis XV was concerned that the Dutch would join forces with England and Austria against France, Prussia and Spain, and he decided that a diversionary invasion of England on behalf of the Stuarts would protect his army in Flanders. Plans for invasion were formulated and came to a sad end when the French fleet was severely damaged by storms off the coast of Torbay in 1744. Although most of them managed to get back to France, Louis abandoned the idea of invasion because of the damage which had been caused to his fleet. Charles returned crestfallen to Paris, but in August that same year, an emissary informed him that if he could persuade the French government to grant him an army of 6,000 and 10,000 arms, he could count on the support of his Scottish friends.

Charles was fed up waiting on the French by now, and determined to arrive in Scotland himself, he secured a man-of-war, the *Elizabeth*, a brig and a transport vessel from the French. He sailed from Nantes on 5 July 1745 and was confident of his cause, as George II's army had been defeated at Fontenoy a few weeks before, by many Jacobite exiles from Ireland among others.

The other ships had to put back following an engagement and flight from British warships respectively. However, one vessel, *La Doutelle*, carried on with Charles on board and reached Eriskay. The Marquis of Tullibardine saw symbolism in the day, and, having witnessed a golden eagle hovering over the ship, is reported to have said to the prince: "The king of birds is come to welcome Your Royal Highness upon your arrival in Scotland."[13]

For Charles the first sight he got of his intended kingdom was a wind-swept and rainy coast. A local fisherman carried him to the shore on his back, and provided him with a meal of fish and a bed for the night. His welcome was warmer than that from the head of one of the MacDonald clans, who advised him to return home without delay. Charles replied that he had come home and believed that his faithful Highlanders would stand by him. Such was the case with Cameron of Lochgiel, who was at first reticent but then pledged himself to stand by Charles over his "rash undertaking". At Glenfinnan on 19 August 1745, clans including the Camerons, MacDonalds, McLeods and others assembled. The Marquis of Tullibardine, aging and arthritic, unfurled the Prince's red, white and blue standard, and Charles told them that he would shed the last drop of his blood in the cause. The uprising had begun.

The Government, meanwhile, offered a reward of £30,000 for anyone who would seize and secure the Young Pretender, something which Charles later matched in relation to George II. However, Sir John Cope, Commander of the Forces in Scotland, realised that the terrain was not suitable for battle in Perthshire and marched his troops to Inverness, leaving the road to Perth open to the Prince. Bonnie Prince Charlie entered the city on 4 September and by 15 September the Jacobites were on the outskirts of the Scottish capital, Edinburgh. Charles men swept through the city and tens of thousands greeted the Prince as he rode in triumph at the head of his troops.

However, all was not completely going Charles' way, for he had failed to conquer the castle and Cope had sailed his army from Inverness to Dunbar, 30 miles from the capital, where they were joined by various Lowland families, helping provide a force of 3,000.

On 21 September 1745, both forces met at the Battle of Prestonpans, the English army being routed after a surprise attack, when a local man led the Scots along a secret path through a marsh in the dead of night. It took about 15 minutes to result in a rout for the government force, with Cope and the survivors fleeing to Berwick-on-Tweed.

Charles would write of the battle (known to the Jacobites as Gladsmuir):

> "... we gained a complete victory over General Cope who commanded 3,000 fut and to regiments of ye best Dragoons in ye island, he being advantageously posted with also baterys of cannon and morters, wee having neither hors nor artillery with us, and being to attack them in their position, and being obliged to pas before their noses in a defile and Bog."
>
> "Only our first line had occasion to engaje, for actually in five minutes ye field was clired of ye Enemy, all ye fut killed, wounded or taken prisoner; and of ye horse only to hundred escaped like rabets, one by one; on our side, we only losed a hundred men between killed and wounded, and ye army afterwards had a fine plunder." [14]

Charles had several options now, including staying in Scotland and strengthening his position there. He held court in Edinburgh for six weeks and then determined to march in to England. This was not a decision supported widely among his officers and men, 1,000 of whom deserted prior to his crossing the border. Superstitious clansmen were also dismayed when Lochgiel, unsheathing his sword as they crossed the border, cut his hand in the process.

John Murray of Boughton noted the symbolism involved in the event: "It was a remarkable thing that this, being the first time they had entered England, the

Highlanders, without any orders given, all drew their swords with one consent upon entering the River Tweed, and every man as he landed on t'other side wheel'd about to the left and faced Scotland again."[15]

There was early triumph, with Carlisle falling to the Scots and Charles riding into the city on a white stallion with a procession of 100 pipers in attendance. But the hopes of thousands of recruits to the Jacobite cause in such places as Preston and Manchester proved in vain. In the former, three recruits joined the army and two of them were Welsh, At Manchester, where 1,500 recruits had been hoped for, only 200 'common fellows' were persuaded to join the ranks.

The interior of St Ann's Church in Manchester, which was built as a response to the fact that the Collegiege Church in the city (now the cathedral) had become the centre of Jacobite sympathy in the city. It was consecrated in July 1712.

The Jacobite Manchester Regiment was raised in support of Bonnie Prince Charlie, many of them being abandoned to their fate at Carlisle in the face of Cumberland's advance.

As Charles headed via Manchester, Stockport, Macclesfield, Ashbourne and Leek to Derby, the garrison at Edinburgh was reinforced and was able to plunder and wreck the homes of prominent Jacobites and attack wounded Highlanders in the hospital. Charles would not be dissuaded from heading south by this news, and his progress caused general panic, even though there were two government armies seeking him and an army of 70,000 men of all sorts began to assemble in London itself. People began withdrawing money from banks, and the Royal Yacht prepared to take George II and his family to safety.

However, Charles' chiefs were concerned about the situation, knowing that they faced not one but two superior armies, and that there had been no Jacobite rising in England or French diversionary invasion as expected. They therefore advised Charles to return to his heartland, where support was secure and they would not be isolated. Charles had to accept the logic of this, and on 6 December (Black Friday as it was known in Jacobite circles) they began the march north. It was a dispirited army that headed towards home, although yet undefeated. When Cumberland engaged the rear of the retreating columns he was defeated and did not engage them again.

When they reached Carlisle, Charles left a garrison of 400 men of the Jacobite Manchester Regiment, but it was an idle gesture and meant certain death for the soldiers when they were, inevitably, forced to surrender the garrison to Cumberland on 30 December. Although there was a lukewarm welcome for the Prince and his army in Glasgow, victory was won over government forces at Falkirk. Following the victory, however, Charles continued with the siege of Stirling Castle, something which was alien to the Highland method of fighting, and nearly half of his army deserted him. Some were sick, some went because they had not seen their families for six months and others did not want to spend the Scottish winter attempting to capture fort after fort. It was against this background that, while resting at Nairn on the Moray Firth in north-east Scotland, Charles had to decide whether to meet the Duke of Cumberland in open battle or retreat into the mountains and harass Cumberland's army with guerrilla warfare. He chose the former and on 16 April 1746, at Culloden Moor the two armies would meet.

Charles went into battle with division among his officers, the Irish Jacobites wanting to meet Cumberland on open battlefield there and then, while his Highland chiefs were more reticent. Charles did not have his full army of 9,000, which would have been equal to Cumberland's, because half had deserted up to that point. A tactical error led to the army being exhausted. It was intended to attack Cumberland's army at dead of night, but the 12 mile march would not have resulted in the Scots reaching Cumberland before daybreak. The expedition, tired and hungry, marched back to Culloden moor, where they threw themselves down into an exhausted sleep.

The next day the action began about one in the afternoon and the Highlanders received an artillery exchange that badly impacted on them. A charge also proved costly, even though it did breach the first line of two regiments, as Cumberland had anticipated the move and had strengthened his second line, which decimated the Clans as they charged. Only the MacDonalds could possibly have saved the day but they seemed to lose heart and retreated in good order, leaving disaster in their wake. Dragoons now charged and a full flight occurred. Some were lucky to escape, but Chevalier Johnstone recounted the cold-blooded killings that so punctuated the battle and forever blackened the name of Cumberland:

> "The road from Culloden to Inverness was everywhere strewed with dead bodies. The Duke of Cumberland had the cruelty to allow our wounded to remain amongst the dead on the field of battle, stripped of their clothes, from Wednesday, the day of our unfortunate engagement, till three o'clock in the afternoon of Friday, when he sent detachments to kill all those who were still in life ... He ordered a barn which contained many of the wounded Highlanders to be set on fire; and having stationed soldiers round it, they with fixed bayonets drove back the unfortunate men who attempted to save themselves."[16]

It was a Scottish version of the massacre at Scullabogue during the later United Irish Rising in Wexford in 1798, when Protestants suffered a similar fate.

Although some officers acted honourably, Major James Wolfe among them (refusing to shoot a wounded Jacobite commander), Cumberland acted with the greatest callous disregard for the honourable conduct of war. Charles for his part, meanwhile, appears to have lost courage in the heat of the battle, and in later life he said he should have died with his men at Culloden. He instead fled to safety in the Highlands and it was a measure of the regard with which the now persecuted Highlanders retained for him that they did not betray him for the £30,000 price on his head. Devotion ran deep, and when Roderick MacKenzie, an ex-Jacobite officer, was shot and fatally wounded by English troops, he proclaimed to them that they had shot their prince. His head was cut off and sent to London, in the belief that it was that of Charles, leading to the relaxation in the search for him for a time.

Towards the end of June 1746, Bonnie Prince Charlie, disguised as a maidservant, was accompanied to Skye by Flora Macdonald, whose stepfather was commander of the government militia on Skye. He spent time in caves, protected by his most loyal band, the Seven Men of Glenmoriston, who had fought with him since the beginning. In September two French frigates arrived and Charles and a few close friends boarded the ships for safety.

Many officers and men were not so lucky, being tried in England for fear that Scottish juries would not convict them. Lots were drawn and one in 20 were picked to face the courts. In all 120 were hanged, among them Lord Balmarino, who, in his last testament, made plain his view that William of Orange was "a vile, unnatural usurper" and that Queen Anne similarly had no right to the throne.

In France two of those who fled with Charles – Lochiel and Lord Ogilvie – were made lieutenant-colonels in the French army. However, Charles' military expedition was well and truly over, and he increasingly turned to drink and a succession of women. He died in Rome on 31 January 1788 at the age of 68 years. His daughter Charlotte died two years later and his brother, Henry Stuart (or Cardinal York), the last directly in line, died in 1807.

Jacobite sympathy remained as a sentimental force in Britain for decades afterwards. A Jacobite Club in Manchester, known as John Shaw's Club, continued to exist until 1892. At Traquair House, near Edinburgh, the wrought iron gates which were closed behind the Prince when he left the estate were to be reopened only when a Stuart was again on the throne. They remain firmly closed today.

The poets and songwriters have also handed much down that relates to the Jacobite period. For example, one of the famous Scottish songs is *Will ye no come back again*:

Bonnie Charlie's noo awa,
Safely owre the friendly main;
Mony a heart will break in twa,
Should he ne'er come back again.

Will ye no come back again?
Will ye no come back again?
Better lo'ed ye canna be,
Will ye no come back again?

Ye trusted in your Hieland men,
They trusted you, dear Charlie;
They kent you hiding in the glen,
Your cleadin' was but barely.
English bribes were a' in vain,
An e'en tho' puirer we may be;
Siller canna buy the heart
That beats aye for thine and thee.

Will ye no come back again?
Will ye no come back again?
Better lo'ed ye canna be,
Will ye no come back again?

The Williamite and Jacobite wars acted in a curiously paradoxical way to emphasise the links and the divisions that existed between Ulster and Scotland. On one hand, Protestant refuges were sent to the west coast of Scotland from the north of Ireland as Jacobite pressure continued there. On the other, the Jacobites also looked to Scotland, to James Graham and his Highland army, for support. In subsequent years the Jacobite cause would not be exclusively Roman Catholic, as Presbyterians would also be among those supporting Bonnie Prince Charlie. To some extent, however, those divisions between support for the Jacobites and the Williamites in Scotland can perhaps be mirrored by support for the two main soccer teams of Glasgow Rangers and Glasgow Celtic today. Friendly rivalry on the football pitch, and, sometimes, not so friendly rivalry between some fans, has generally replaced the high drama and the deadly fighting of an earlier period. Given the context of support for the 'Old Firm' teams, it should be no surprise that Orange and Green Ulster soccer fans are among the stalwarts supporters of both sides and regularly travel to watch them play.

Portadown, County Armagh, 1985.

The events of the 1680s and 1690s in the British Isles are remembered by the Orange Institution, which holds parades in England, Scotland and Ireland to mark the occasion of William's victory over James at the Boyne. Orangeism spread from Ireland to the north of England and Scotland after members of militia regiments,

This statue of William III, Prince of Orange, at Carrickfergus, County Antrim, commemorates his landing at the pier in June 1690. William swiftly made his way toward the Boyne, where he defeated his rival and father-in-law James II in battle.

sent to quell the United Irish Rising in 1798, became Orangemen and formed lodges, transferring them to civilian lodges when they returned to areas such as Manchester, Bolton and Ayrshire. The Order looks back to the events of the 1680s and 1690s as its formative years, and in the aftermath of the events Orange Societies and Clubs were formed to commemorate the victory. It was not until 1795 and the Battle of the Diamond in Loughgall, County Armagh, however, that Orangeism would be structured and organised in such a way that it would continue to be a major component in the social life of many Protestants, and the political and cultural life of Irish, and, to a lesser extent, British society.

History is often full of irony. Ironically, given the support of Flora MacDonald for Bonnie Prince Charlie in the eighteenth century, when she and her husband emigrated to the American colonies and settled in North Carolina with other Highlanders, they remained loyal to the throne and George III during the American Revolution. There is one famous battle, that of Moore's Creek Bridge, where the proponents were virtually all from Ulster or Scotland. On one side, defending the King, were MacDonalds from the Scottish Highlands, and on the opposing side were Ulster Presbyterians who were in rebellion against the Crown. The latter won the battle as the American cause would win the war. Ironically, the MacDonalds ended up on the losing causes on both sides of the Atlantic.[17]

HISTORICAL QUOTES

An account from a Williamite officer of the progress of the Prince of Orange, June 1690. Detailed in O'Laverty, *Historical Account of the Diocese of Down and Connor*, Dublin: 1880

"We stayed there [Belfast] two days and three nights, and we went thence on Tuesday … to Lisbourne, where there is a great house and good gardens belonging now to my Lady Mulgrave; it was left her, with the whole estate, which is worth £14,000 per annum, by my Ld Conaway; the house is out of repair. There's a market kept there that day. Wednesday the 24th we set forth betimes in ye morning resolved to join our army which was then encamped at Loughbrickland. We passed by Hillsborough [Fort] a great house, belonging to the King, standing on a hill on the left hand of the road."

THE BATTLE AT THE BOYNE

Extract from Woodburn, James, B, *The Ulster Scot*, London: 1912

"Everywhere he [William] was received with shouts of joy, and on the night he arrived bonfires were lighted on all the hills of Antrim and Down. These announced to the people that 'the Protestant King' had arrived. A deputation of Presbyterian ministers, headed by the aged Patrick Adair, waited upon him in Belfast, and he received them most graciously. A day or two later at Hillsborough he ordered the Collector of Customs at Belfast to pay £1,200 every year to trustees for the Presbyterian ministers of Ulster because of the losses they had sustained through loyalty to himself. Thus the ministers received again their Regium Donum which had not been paid to them since 1682.

William reviewed his troops at Loughbrickland, and found that he had an army of 36,000 men, composed of regiments from every Protestant nation in Europe. Half of them were English. There was also a Scotch regiment, a regiment from Finland, and one from Brandenburg, troops of horse and a fine regiment from Holland, a brigade of Danes, a body of French Huguenots, some troops from Switzerland, and the boldest defenders of Derry and Enniskillen. They were all Protestants except the Dutch Blue Guards, who were for the most part Catholics, but who fought for love of William.

He reached the Boyne two miles above Drogheda on June 30th. James' army was drawn up on the other side of the river. The latter had the stronger position, and nearly as many men as William, but he had a poorer force, as he was badly provided with artillery. His army was composed of 7,000 French veterans: the remainder were Irish. Each of his soldiers wore a white badge on his hat, while the Protestant forces donned a green sprig …"

Re-enactors of the Battle of the Boyne, Cookstown, 1990.

Local Volunteers Corps, eighteenth century
***Belfast Weekly Telegraph*, 5 February 1910**

"In 1708 an invasion of this country was threatened by the adherents of James, commonly known as the Old Pretender. It was decided to embody the militia, and the officials appointed to array Belfast and district met for that purpose on the 20th of May in that year, when ninety men were enrolled, under the command of the Sovereign of the town.

The oath was tendered to the company, and was refused by twenty-six privates of the Presbyterian persuasion, but this opposition arose solely from their being unacquainted with the nature and extent of the oath, and not from any attachment to the Pretender.

… On the 28th of October 1745, two Belfast corps, numbering about 220 men, marched to Carrickfergus by direction of the late Lord Antrim, then Lord Lieutenant of the County, on an alarm spread that a large body of Highland rebels had collected a number of fishing boats on the West Coast of Scotland with intention to land in our bay.

The two companies remained in that garrison ten days, and performed the duty of regulars with great military order. Both were uniformly well armed, clothed and disciplined at their own expense. Besides which there were under arms in this town one company called invalids, uniformly clothed, and two companies of militia …"

Andrew Morrow JP

HISTORICAL TRAILS
SITES TO VISIT

St Columb's Cathedral in Londonderry

Londonderry

Scene of the longest siege in British military history, Londonderry was developed by the London Guilds or Companies who invested in the walled city during the Plantation of Ulster in the early 1600s. In December 1688, a new garrison was dispatched to the Protestant citadel and Lord Antrim's Redshanks, comprising of Roman Catholic soldiers from the Glens of Antrim and west of Scotland, made their way towards the city. However, fears of a massacre inside resulted in the gates of the city being closed to the military, a direct act of defiance against James II, who was still technically King of Ireland. The siege and its outcome earned Londonderry the title of 'the Maiden City.'

Today the walls give an immediate and physical impression of the extent of the city in 1688, when the siege started and when 20,000 are estimated to have sought shelter inside its walls. There is a museum at both the Apprentice Boys Memorial Hall and St Columb's Cathedral, and a memorial mound to the Apprentice Boys is also located in the grounds of the cathedral. Each August and December the Apprentice Boys of Derry organisation commemorates the events of 1688–1689.

Groomsport, County Down

Groomsport, County Down

The small fishing port of Groomsport outside Bangor in County Down was the site for the landing of Marshall Schomberg, William of Orange's trusted general, in 1689. Schomberg arrived on the coast of Down as a vanguard for William, and he moved around the coast of Belfast Lough to successfully lay siege to Carrickfergus, which was then a Jacobite garrison.

Prior to his arrival off the County Down coast, Williamite forces centred on Enniskillen had defeated James' troops, which were under the command of Justin McCarthy, at the Battle of Newtownbutler in August 1689. This and the failure to capture Londonderry, and the subsequent relief of the city, led to the Jacobites being in no position to oppose the arrival of Schomberg's army at Groomsport.

Groomsport, which saw the arrival of the Williamites, was also the site in 1636 of the departure of the emigrant ship *Eagle Wing*, which was ultimately unsuccessful in taking two congregations of Ulster Presbyterians to America.

Oldbridge, Boyne Valley

The Williamite army camped north of the River Boyne in June 1690, and crossed the river at a number of points on the morning of 1 July, some at Rosnaree, most at Oldbridge and some on a location closer to the town of Drogheda. There was a memorial obelisk erected in the 1730s at the site where the Oldbridge crossing took place, but this was blown up in the 1920s during Troubles in Ireland, and now only the iron bridge across the river gives an indication of where it was located.

Archaeology has provided some idea of the village of Oldbridge and the site of the buildings has been recreated on the 500 acre site on the southern side of the Boyne, owned by the Government of the Republic of Ireland. Developments there also include an interpretative centre and walkways around the site of what was a major European battle. The interpretive centre helps set the story of the battle in context and also highlights the European import to the events of the Williamite Wars.

Glenfinnan and Loch Shiel

It was at Glenfinnan, which is almost 20 miles west of Fort William in the Scottish Highlands that Bonnie Prince Charlie raised his standard, proclaimed his father King James III of England, and signaled the beginning of the Jacobite uprising of 1745. Only 200 Highlanders were with him at the time, but he was eventually joined by Cameron of Loch Shiel and 800 men. They marched south, gathering numbers on the journey and would eventually cross the Tweed into England. There was panic in London, but the Prince had overstretched himself in moving into England, and the promise of Jacobite support in English cities did not materialise to any great or meaningful degree. The Rising was brought to an end eight months later at Culloden.

Glenfinnan has a spectacular column featuring a clansman in full battle dress, and this was erected by Alexander MacDonald of Glenaladale in 1815. There is also a visitor centre which tells the story of the '45. Glenfinnan is a scenic and poignant place, resonant with the stirring history of the eighteenth century and the Jacobite rising.

Culloden

The battle site at Culloden lies five miles east of Inverness. It was here that Stuart hopes of regaining the throne of the United Kingdom were finally defeated. The last ever battle to be fought on British soil, it took place on 16 April 1746. The second Jacobite rebellion began on 19 August 1745, with the raising of the Stuart's standard at Glenfinnan on the west coast, and soon clans were rallying to Bonnie Prince Charlie. But the excursion of the Scots across the Tweed into England proved too ambitious and the Jacobite army began a retreat north, pursued by the Duke of Cumberland. At Culloden the Jacobites made a tactical error in staging a night march which exhausted the men and achieved little. The moor at Culloden was also unsuited for the Highlanders' mode of battle, which tended to be undisciplined and was benefited by terrain which gave cover. The King's troops, on the other hand, outnumbered and outmatched their opponents. Around 1,500 Highlanders were slaughtered, many as they lay wounded on the battlefield, and Bonnie Prince Charlie fled to the hills and offshore islands, where loyal Highlanders prevented his capture, despite a price being put on his head.

He eventually fled back to France, from whence he came, and took with him all hopes of the restoration of the Stuart monarchy.

In Scotland, the effect of the defeat of the Rising was the suppression of the Clan system, along with the prohibition of tartan and playing the bagpipes.

HISTORICAL FIGURES

Charles Edward Stuart (Bonnie Prince Charlie).

Bonnie Prince Charlie

The grandson of James II, Charles Edward Stuart is more commonly known in British history as 'Bonnie Prince Charlie'. He was born in Rome on 31 December 1720, the son of James Francis Edward Stuart and his Polish wife Maria.

In December 1743, James named Charles Prince Regent, giving him full authority to act in his name, and eighteen months later he led a rising aimed at restoring his father – and the Stuarts – to the thrones of the United Kingdom. He fitted out two ships, the *Elizabeth* and the *Doutelle*, and they arrived at Eriskay on 23 July 1745, Charles stepping ashore with seven staunch supporters.

Members of the Highland Clans, both Presbyterian and Roman Catholic, gave their support to Charles as a representative of the Stuart dynasty, and he rallied an army which crossed the Tweed and marched southward towards London. But promised Jacobite support in England failed to materialise, and the Scots decided to return home, pursued by the King's troops, including the Duke of Cumberland. The two forces would meet up at Culloden, where the Jacobites were decisively defeated and The Young Pretender, as Charles was known, was forced into hiding, being sheltered by Flora MacDonald among others, and being disguised at one point as her Irish maidservant, Betty Burke. He returned safely to France, but did not give up the idea of the throne of England, making it known that he would be prepared to become a Protestant in order to have the Stuarts restored.

Charles's domestic life was not a happy one. He had numerous affairs, and he increasingly turned to alcohol. When his father died in 1766, Charles' anticipation that the Pope would recognise him as Charles III was to result in disappointment. His marriage to Princess Louise of Stolberg-Gedern ended after eight years and followed on from a relationship of several years with Clementina Walkinshaw, who bore him a daughter, Charlotte. In 1774 Charles and Princess Louise moved to Florence, where the Prince adopted the title Duke of Albany, giving his daughter Charlotte the title Duchess of Albany. Creation of titles could not restore the throne to the Stuarts, however, and Charles died in Rome on 31 January 1788. He was initially buried in the Cathedral of Frascati, where his bother Henry Benedict Stuart was bishop. In 1807 his remains were removed and located in the crypt of Saint Peter's Basilica in the Vatican, where his father and brother are also buried. A small urn at Frascati contains the heart of Charles and is buried underneath his monument in the cathedral.

A man of many names, he was referred to as Charles III by his Jacobite supporters, his opponents called him The Young Pretender and history generally records him as Bonnie Prince Charlie.

Archibald Edmonstone

Archibald Edmonstone was grandson of William Edmonstone of Duntreath in Stirlingshire and Ballycarry, and lived at Redhall, near Carrickfergus in County Antrim. In the Williamite period in Ireland, he became one of the Council of Protestant Gentlemen of the North, who opposed James II. When it became clear that a new Jacobite regiment was to be located at Carrickfergus, Edmonstone and others were greatly concerned. In January 1689 he was involved with unsuccessful plans to seize Carrickfergus. In a letter to his son-in-law, James Montgomery of Rosemount, Greyabbey, he highlighted that he had 1,000 men in eight companies. Although they did not seize Carrickfergus, they did seize a boat belonging to the Jacobite forces.

On 20 February 1689, Colonel Cormac O'Neill, commander of the Jacobite garrison, was so concerned with the size of Williamite forces attempting to gain entry to the town that he reached an agreement with them that effectively meant that the existing garrison was confined to barracks. However, following the Break of Dromore, on 14 March 1689, this situation changed and the Williamites were in retreat.

Edmonstone was appointed Lieutenant Colonel of Sir Robert Adair's Ballymena Regiment, and was involved in a courageous but unsuccessful attempt to prevent the Jacobites crossing the Bann at Portglenone. The Williamites continued to retreat towards Londonderry, however, and at the age of 63 years Edmonstone was one of the defenders of the fort at Culmore, just as the siege of Londonderry was starting. History records that Edmonstone died there on 14 April 1689, of "over fatigue", not a surprising end to the life of an elderly gentleman soldier more used to the comforts of home than the transformation to living – and fighting – in the field.

James MacKinlay

A Scottish soldier in the army of William of Orange, James MacKinlay, was among those who fought at the Battle of the Boyne in July 1690. After the victory of the Williamites in Ireland, MacKinlay remained and founded the Ulster branch of the family tree. History records little of him thereafter, other than the fact that

An old postcard of the McKinley farmstead in County Antrim. The Ulster ancestor of President William McKinley was James MacKinlay, who fought for William of Orange at the Battle of the Boyne.

Reproduced by kind permission of the Lawrence Collection, National Library of Ireland.

he was the Ulster ancestor of President William McKinley. In the early eighteenth century one member of the family, David, emigrated to America, settling in Pennsylvania and changing the spelling of the surname to McKinley. History often provides ironies, and another is that while James MacKinlay fought for William of Orange, some of his descendants were 'out' in 1798 with the rebellion against the authorities of the day.[18]

ENDNOTES

1 van der Zee, Henri and Barbara, *1688 Revolution in the family*, London: 1988, p143
2 van der Zee, *op cit*, p22
3 Bowle, John, ed, *The Diary of John Evelyn*, Oxford: 1983, p358
4 O'Laverty, J, *An Historical Account of the Diocese of Down and Connor, Ancient and Modern*, originally published in 1880, reprinted Ballynahinch: 1981, vol II, p382
5 I have met people in Scotland from the Covenanter tradition who have objections to this song being sung or played.
6 Quoted in McKinnon, Robert, *The Jacobite Rebellions*, London: 1973, p21
7 Quoted in Daiches, David, Scotland and the Union, London: 1977, p164
8 McKinnon, Robert, *The Jacobite Rebellions*, London: 1973, p41
9 McKinnon, *op cit,* p44
10 McKinnon, *op cit,*, p44
11 McKinnon, *op cit,*, p54
12 Johnstone, CL, *The Historical Families of Dumfriesshire and the Border Wars*, Dumfries: 1889
13 Sinclair-Stevenson, Christopher, *Inglorious Rebellion. The Jacobite Risings of 1708, 1715 and 1719*, Hamish Hamilton, London: 1971, p191
14 McKinnon, *op cit,* p82
15 Quoted in McKinnon, *op cit*, p85
16 Quoted in McKinnon, *op cit*, p103
17 See, for example, Douglas, Hugh, *Flora MacDonald, The Most Loyal Rebel*, Stroud: 1993
18 See, for example, Wayne Morgan, H, *William McKinley and his America*, Syracuse: 1963

Chapter Seven

CROSS CURRENTS: radicalism in the Ulster Scots community

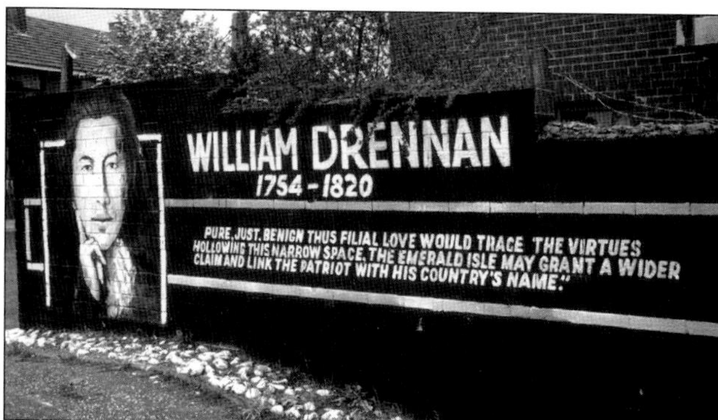

A mural in nationalist North Belfast commemorates the Presbyterian radical Dr William Drennan, a United Irish leader in the 1790s.

One of the cross-currents which flow from Scotland to Ulster through the Ulster Scots community is a strong radicalism. Owing something to the Covenanter opposition to authority and a similar and equally robust disrespect for the establishment from the Borderers, this radicalism has been expressed time and again by Ulster Scots. Fed by treatment of Presbyterians in the 1630s, resentment continued into the next century and was epitomised in the east at any rate in the 1770s. Agitation at that time surrounded the raising of rents on many farms, particularly in County Antrim. The agitation was flamed by economic recession, which affected farmer-weavers. This group was more independent than tenant farmers, had a steady income, and usually long-term (three-life) leases off their land. Known elsewhere as the Hearts of Oak, and in Antrim as the Hearts of Steel or Steelboys, they violently opposed rent increases, and collection of county cess and taxes. Their traditional forms of opposition included cattle maiming, burning of hay ricks, and attacks on persons and property.

At one stage the Hearts of Steel were so strong that they were able to march into Belfast to free members of their organisation imprisoned in the town, while at other times troops had to be sent from Dublin to help protect Big Houses, and landlords had to fortify their homes. A letter from Mrs Eliza O'Neill of Flowerfield, Portstewart, described an attack on her Uncle Daniel's home, which had been surrounded by around 200 men, and a barn and stable burnt. Although the occupants inside were armed and had soldiers with them, such a fire was kept up from the Steelboys that they could effect little: "There is melancholy accounts of them every day, and although there is a deal of army come yet they can't find them out. It is as bad as the Irish rebellion [of 1641]. They are all Presbyterians ..." she said.[1]

In the beginning of 1770, the Steelboys made their presence felt through attacks and a crude blackmail attempt. In March that year a house belonging to Edward Brice in the North East Division of Carrickfergus was burned, and threatening letters were afterwards sent into the town demanding a specific sum of money in return for not burning the town. As a consequence, several of them were captured at the Commons, outside Carrick, but were "allowed to escape",[2] perhaps because two of them were nephews of one of the respectable inhabitants of the town.

Others were not to be so lucky, for several were hanged in the town, with George McKeown, John Campbell, John Clark and James McNeilly listed as being among them. On 9 May 1772, the last of them were hanged for burning a house belonging to Marriott Dalway in Middle Division.[3] Others followed the same fate, while many fled to America just prior to the main agitation there for independence from Britain. Unfortunately, but not surprisingly, no one publicised their membership of the Hearts of Steel at the time, so it is impossible to directly link the movement and its radicalism with areas where agitation against George III was strong. However, it seems more than a coincidence that their arrival occurred just at a time when agitation became rife in America. They did not start the revolutionary fire, but there could be little doubt that those supportive of the movement would not have doused it in America.

While the Steelboys were a more lower class or lower middle class phenomenon, the Irish Volunteers were much more middle class and genteel about their radicalism and political demands. The Irish Volunteers were a largely middle class body formed to resist the threat of French invasion after troops were sent to America to help quell the rebellion there. As such, they were welcome to the authorities, but it soon became clear that the movement, particularly in Ulster, was rather more radical than the establishment would have wanted.

From the onset of the movement, it remained independent of the government, and this was highlighted by a statement from the Belfast Volunteer Company issued on 17 March 1778, asserting its independence from government control.[4] Enough companies followed this lead for Volunteering to assume a philosophy and mantle of independent armed service. There were, however, conflicting ideas about the proper role that an armed force should assume in politics, and the Volunteers did manage to help establish a Free Trade measure from the government in 1779. In December 1779 the Newry Volunteers asserted that Ireland needed legislative independence in order to protect the commercial concessions wrung from the British authorities,[5] and this was a forerunner of events to come.

At a famous Convention held by the Volunteers at Dungannon, in February 1782, resolutions approved there were also soon adopted by county grand juries and constituency assemblies, adding to the weight of demand for legislative independence. Britain was forced to concede the Constitution of 1782 as a consequence, but the Volunteers were unhappy, demanding that the British Parliament pass an act renouncing the right to legislate in Ireland.

The high point of the Volunteers had passed and divisions emerged within. The 1783 provincial assembly in Ulster showed how radical the province's Volunteers had become, with demands for annual parliaments, elections by secret ballot, and extension of the franchise among them. Both Ulster and Connaught bodies also supported Catholic Emancipation, but there was a division on this issue with those in Munster and Leinster. By the summer of 1784 the increasing radicalism had caused the more cautious to put a distance between themselves and the Volunteers, and many men of influence had left, with the movement attempting to win back influence by recruiting greater numbers. By 1785 the Dublin Parliament had moved to erode the Volunteer base by voting 139 to 63 to establish a new militia. That it did not come into being until 1793 probably highlighted how weak the Volunteers had become.

Historian PDH Smyth asserts that the Volunteers had always suffered from divided loyalties, but that one of the negative aspects of the movement was that it brought the gun into Irish politics.[6] There could be no doubt that, in the short-term at any rate, the training many had in the Volunteer movement was put to use in 1798, when physical rather than political rebellion broke out in Ireland.

The Rising of 1798

The Ballynure, County Antrim, weaver poet James Campbell (1758–1818) was among those who witnessed the stirring events of 1798. He was a Presbyterian – like the majority of those who joined in open rebellion against the authorities and turned up at the Battles of Antrim, Ballynahinch and elsewhere in Ulster – and reflected on their behalf in the aftermath of the ill-fated rebellion:

"In Ninety Eight we armed again." wrote Campbell,
"To right some things that we thought wrong,
We got sae little for our pains
It's no worth minding in a song"[7]

That attitude was to be a widespread one of disillusionment in the aftermath of the Rising in Antrim and subsequent defeat also at Ballynahinch. In Ballycarry, County Antrim, something of that sense is underlined by the fact that the grave of a 16 year old hanged for his part in the Rising was forgotten for many years while that of another of the insurgents, James Orr, the village bard, had a fine and large monument erected by his fellow Freemasons. The difference was that William Nelson had

The Battle of Ballynahinch, June 1798, depicted on an old postcard. Defeat of the insurgents there signaled the end of Presbyterian hopes that the Rising in Ulster would succeed.

died as a rebel on the village Main Street, with all the political baggage that would carry in later decades, while Orr escaped and came back from America to live a life beyond the 1798 Rising.

Defeat of the United Irishmen in 1798 came as the climax to a century of turbulence and radicalism in Ireland, Europe and America. There were undoubtedly close links between the radicals of the period, for example, there are accounts of United Irish corps marching under Irish Volunteer banners to battle in 1798. In one famous incident, at Templepatrick in County Antrim, a cannon which had been retained from the Volunteer days was hidden in the local Presbyterian Church the night before the Battle of Antrim and then taken with the rebels into the town, where it was said to have fired only a couple of times before the carriage on which it rested collapsed· The effectiveness of the Templepatrick cannon may have been questionable, but the link with the Volunteer movement in terms of radical ideas and physical weaponry was not. Jemmy Hope, the weaver and farm labourer born in Templepatrick and of Highland Covenanter stock, outlined the connection which he had with the Volunteers and United Irishmen, becoming a member of the Roughfort Corps of the Irish Volunteer movement, and being thereafter recruited into the United Irishmen: "A deputation from Belfast formed the Molusk society, of which I became a member, the Hightown society having been that in which I was initiated, and composed of the men I had first joined in arms as a Volunteer".[8]

In October 1791, at a meeting off Crown Entry in Belfast, the Society of United Irishmen was formed. The aims of this Society, which was to operate openly and constitutionally until 1794, were to unite Protestant (ie Anglican), Catholic and Dissenter in the common name of Irishman. The original declaration stated, among other things, that:

> "In the present great era of reform, when unjust governments are falling in every quarter of Europe ... when all government is acknowledged to originate from the people, and to be so far only obligatory as it protects their rights and promotes their welfare; we think it our duty, as Irishmen, to come forward and state what we feel to be our heavy grievance, and what we know to be its effectual remedy." [9]

McArt's Fort on Belfast's Cave Hill, where Presbyterian United Irishmen secretly met and pledged to overthrow the authorities, precipitating the 1798 rebellion.

This grievance, essentially, was that "we are ruled by Englishmen, and the servants of Englishmen, whose object is the interest of another country ..." and the remedy was a national parliament elected by an equal representation of the people. The sentiments, and indeed other matters pertaining to the United Irishmen, relate closely to those of the Irish Volunteer movement. The year that the Volunteers were disbanded also saw suppression of the United Irish newspaper the *Northern Star*, and the United Irishmen began to go underground. A complication to the political map came in 1795 when, after a battle between Protestants and Roman Catholic 'Defenders' (an agrarian secret society) at Loughgall, County Armagh, the Orange Institution had been formed.[10] Initially largely Anglican in nature and membership, many of its members joined the yeomanry in 1798 and helped to crush the East Ulster Presbyterians.

James Orr's cottage, Ballycarry, from an old postcard. Orr was the foremost of the Ulster Weaver poets and a radical weaver born in 1770.

In 1798 the United Irishmen are estimated to have had a force of some 500,000, about half of whom were armed, and of these almost 70,000 were Ulster Presbyterians and just over 30,000 were Ulster Catholics. The movement was doomed from the start in that a system of informers had seen the arrests of major leaders even before the rebellion broke out. Hostilities in the south started on 24 May, but it was to be the following month before the rebellion occurred in Ulster.

On 7 June 1798, the order for the Presbyterian radicals in Antrim to *'turn oot'*, as it was referred to in Ulster Scots, was greeted with a variety of responses. James Orr the Ballycarry poet noted how while some prepared to go to battle, others hid in the corners of byres. Some, as at Ballynure in County Antrim, were said to have complained of a remarkable incidence of bowel complaints and sprained ankles. But there were also those who set out for the rendezvous point at Donegore Hill near Antrim town. Antrim was a strategic point militarily, commanding the main road from Belfast to Derry. Under the command of Henry Joy McCracken, the United Army of Ulster gathered at least 3,000 strong, with others arriving by the hour at Donegore. At Randalstown the market house had been burned and the town captured by the rebels under Samuel Orr, and Larne and other towns had been taken. Ballymena suffered a similar fate and by the evening much of County Antrim was in the control of rebel hands. However, it was only to be for a short time.

An old postcard depicting the Battle of Antrim, 7 June 1798, in which the insurgent United Army of Ulster was defeated.

For at 2pm that afternoon Samuel Orr and his Randalstown contingent had made a mistake of grave dimension and had effectively lost the Battle of Antrim. Mistaking a cavalry retreat for an attack they, coming over the bridge to the town, had scattered and their action had spread panic across the board. The military immediately took up on the unexpected advantage, scattering the insurgents further. Only a small number, including the famous 'Spartan Band' of about 50 men, were regrouped. They included James Hope and James Orr. McCracken was forced in tactical retreat to Slemish mountain, but was informed by the military that his whereabouts were known. He tried to cross into County Down, but quickly realised this was impossible. Observing a picket line at the Collin mountain near Ballyclare, McCracken is said to have seen men who had a few days earlier stood with him at the Battle of Antrim. He was later captured in disguise on the Commons above Carrickfergus, his aim having been to board a ship in the port and make his getaway.

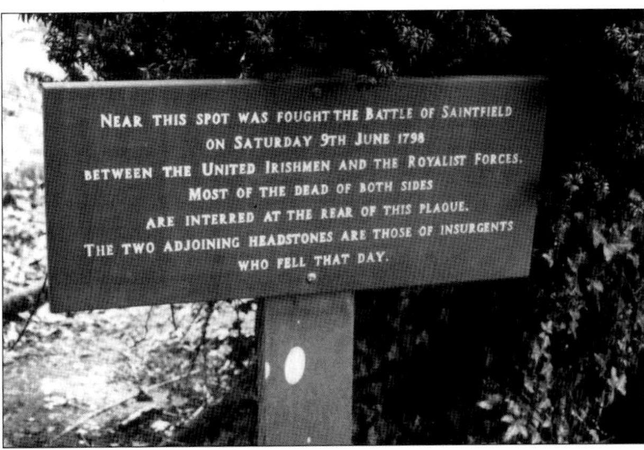

A plaque in Saintfield, County Down, commemorating the battle there during the United Irish Rising.

Two days after the defeat at Antrim, the County Down rebels had staged their own rebellion. Despite a shaky start, not least because of the arrest of most of the Down High Command, the rebels, under Lisburn draper Henry Munro, captured Newtownards, Saintfield and Ballynahinch. However, the arrests of the officers had had a detrimental effect. One of the leaders is said to have complained that the forces met rather by accident than design, and were in no better order than a country mob. At Ballynahinch, as the army arrived to do battle, hundreds of men left in the night, apparently including some 2,000 Catholic Defenders from Loughinisland. The Battle of Ballynahinch was as successful for the insurgents as the Battle of Antrim. Perhaps matters might have been different had Munro bowed to his soldiers' wishes for a night attack on the British regiments there, who were apparently suffering from consumption of too much liquor, but he did not. Instead Munro led his troops from Edenvaddy Hill into Ballynahinch on 13 June, winning ground as they did so. However, again a retreat by the enemy was mistaken for an advance and the rebels fled at a crucial moment. The battle was lost, and a general retreat by way of Edenvaddy Hill took place, with men falling all along the way. There were not only men who died, for among those who fell following the Battle of Ballynahinch was a young girl named Betsy Gray, who would become famous, cut down with her brother and sweetheart by the yeomanry outside the town.[11]

Antrim High Street, County Antrim, site of the main fighting during the Battle of Antrim.

Many thousands of others followed the fate of Betsy Gray, and in County Antrim, 16 year old Willie Nelson became her young counterpart. At Greyabbey in County Down, Presbyterian minister Reverend James Porter was hanged at his church gates, while in the fields around Ballynahinch and Antrim men were hunted down in retribution for their part in the Rising. The Presbyterian General Synod of Ulster, meeting shortly after the Rising, appealed to the King to overlook "the madness of the multitude".[12] Individual congregations such as that at Ballycarry sent their own loyal addresses, in their case to Lord Castlereagh, while villages and communities followed suit. The Presbyterians, sullen no doubt, largely turned their backs on the rebellion, as some of their number had done on the day they were called to battle. A few years later, during Emmett's Revolt, attempts by Thomas Russell (known in later history as 'The Man from God Knows Where') to raise the Hearts of Down and the other radicals of the Ninety Eight proved less successful than Henry Joy McCracken's order to the United Army of Ulster that 7 June.

The turnaround from radical revolutionaries (if such they really were) to peaceable supporters of the link with Britain is seen as something of an astonishing phenomenon. James Orr, Bard of Ballycarry, is a case in point. Fleeing with a price on his head, he later returned under amnesty and applied to join the local yeomanry. He was turned down for the militia, but became prominent in his community nevertheless. While the Presbyterians might accept the Act of Union as a more just settlement than they had previously had – it swept away the corrupt Dublin parliament which they opposed – it would prove impossible to completely cover the strain of radicalism which characterised them as a community.

Reformism under the Union

The Union, however, was welcomed, by, among others, some of the very men who had been leading lights in the Rising. This was because the Act of Union was seen as a great Act of Reform. The Dublin Parliament was removed and that old corrupt Ascendancy legislature swept away. This emphasis on reformism was to be important in terms of Presbyterianism during the nineteenth century. The view of those such as the great liberal Church leader Henry Montgomery was that Ireland's ills could be remedied through reform of the structure of Irish society. This was evidenced through Presbyterian support for Catholic Emancipation (the right for Roman Catholics to sit in parliament) when Daniel O'Connell took up this cause in the first decades of the century and the Union.

Presbyterian support for Catholic Emancipation was nothing novel; it had been evident during the era of the Irish Volunteer movement, as well as that of the United Irishmen. O'Connell was appreciative of the support of Montgomery, as a prominent representative of northern Protestants at the time. However, his relationship with the Presbyterian leader of the so-called 'New Light' wing within the Ulster Scots religious community became more stormy when Montgomery made clear that he could not and would not support O'Connell's second great campaign, that of Repeal of the Union. Montgomery made plain that while Presbyterians could be happy that Roman Catholics, through O'Connell's successful campaign, had won the right to sit in Parliament, they could not support the cutting of the links with Britain.[13]

The radical strain within the Ulster Scots tradition became clear in the nineteenth century through voting patterns. Presbyterians, particularly in the eastern coastal counties and in an area including parts of Londonderry and East Donegal, tended to vote for the Liberal Party.[14] This voting pattern also saw Church of Ireland members often voting Conservative, while Roman Catholics tended to be in the same camp as the Presbyterians. Often this situation led to bitter disputes. For example, in 1869, when local landlord Marriott Dalway supported the Liberal Captain Hugh Seymour against the Conservative candidate Sir Shafto Adair, he was eventually expelled from his membership of the Orange Order and went on to form a short-lived Grand Orange Lodge of Carrickfergus.[15] In the early 1900s independent candidates standing against Conservatives often found ready support among radical Presbyterian communities.

Independent Orangemen at Magheramorne, County Antrim, c.1905. The Independent Orange Order espoused radical unionist politics during the period, appearing to support the prospect of Home Rule for Ireland for a time, at least at leadership level.

Probably the clearest example of this is the situation which in turn led to the formation of the Independent Orange Institution. The Orange Order was, at the turn of the nineteenth century, seen by radical Protestants as being dominated by landlords. This conservative domination of the Order caused political problems. Colonel Edward Saunderson, the Grand Master of the Belfast Grand Lodge and leader of the Irish Unionist Party, was heckled over his voting record in the House of Commons at the Twelfth of July platform in 1902. A central figure in this episode was Thomas Sloan, who was an Orangeman and very active in the Belfast Protestant Association. Sloan was later summoned to appear before the Grand Lodge to account for his actions, but of more significant import was the fact that five days after the Twelfth the prominent Orange MP William Johnston of Ballykilbeg, who represented South Belfast, died. Johnston had been a radical in his own right, making some within the Orange establishment uncomfortable from time to time, not least when he led an illegal parade to assert the rights of Orangemen to march in 1867. His action may not at the time have appealed to the Orange leadership, but it did appeal to those on the lower levels of the social ladder, who were increasingly being given voting rights in society. In 1868 Johnston was elected as an MP, following a short prison term for his defiance of the Party Processions Act. Later offered a government position, he was subsequently dropped, owing to partisan comments and was elected MP for South Belfast.

The Conservatives nominated a County Down landlord for the seat, but the Belfast Protestant Association put forward Sloan, and he won the electoral contest. However, the rift within the Orange Order was a major one. Sloan was suspended for his protest at the Twelfth of July, as were three lodges that supported his candidature. Those involved decided to form an Independent Order, which they said would be free of political domination. They held their first demonstration in July 1903, and had two main heartlands, in Belfast and County Antrim. The Independent Order proved radical indeed. The most famous policy document issued from its ranks was the 1905 Magheramorne Manifesto, which appeared to offer at least the possibility of devolution (Home Rule) for Ireland, a nationalist demand. In 1907 the movement was also very supportive of striking dockers in Belfast. The divisions created by the Orange split remained strong, and in Belfast and elsewhere it was not just lodges that were divided but also families. In Magheramorne, County Antrim, the Independent Lodge was stoned on the Twelfth of July by supporters of the established lodges in the area.[16] By the time of the height of the Third Home Rule crisis, Independent Orangeism in the area had been subsumed in the established lodges, as Protestants generally banded together in the face of a formidable nationalist political machine. However, it would continue to be strong in North Antrim particularly.

At the centre of the Independent Orange split was probably the old radicalism of the Ulster Scots, which almost seems based on the perpetuality of dissent. Working class Protestants in Belfast and tenant farmers in the countryside rejected the Conservative landlords, and not only in terms of the Orange Order of 1902 and 1903. Electoral trends reflect that Presbyterians tended to vote for Liberal candidates in a large area of Ulster, stretching into East Donegal, until Gladstone's conversion to Home Rule, after which political blocs began to solidify between Orange and Green.[17] It is interesting that at the time of the Signing of the Ulster Covenant of 1912, in the east Antrim village of Ballycarry the Covenant was not signed in churches as it had been elsewhere, but on the estate of landlord WJ Porritt, perhaps a sign that the radical element within local Presbyterianism was of sufficient strength to effectively prevent the churches being made available for this purpose.[18]

Whatever the localised political mechanisms, the radicalism of the Ulster Scots community is essentially based on a distrust of centralised authority. The idea of a social contract between those who govern and their subjects was espoused by John Locke in the 1680s, and helped to justify the Williamite claim to the throne of England on the basis that James II had broken the contract with his subjects.[19] The County Down born philosopher, Francis Hutchinson, born in 1690, also suggested that it was acceptable for tenants to resist greedy landlords. This was translated into the context of wider society and it was viewed permissible to oppose a ruler or government if they were deemed to have exceeded themselves in terms of how they dealt with their people.[20] This sense of contract would later be expounded in a very conservative way in 1912. As Ulster Unionists in particular argued vehemently against Home Rule for Ireland, Thomas Sinclair, an Ulster Scot of the liberal tradition, designed the Ulster Covenant, which was signed by 471,414 men and women, who pledged to stand by one another to oppose Home Rule.

At the base of the original Scots Covenant of the 1630s was a contract between the King and his subjects and that of 1912 also had similar connotations. It suggested that if the authorities went against the wishes of the people, then the people would band together to appoint new authority.[21] At Gardenmore Presbyterian Church in

Larne, Reverend DH Hanson told a congregation including members of the Ulster Volunteers, the private army established by Sir Edward Carson and Sir James Craig, that "It was said to them, as it was said to Athanasius – 'All the world is against you' and they replied as he did 'Then we are against the world'..."[22] This viewpoint of Ulster Scots in the political sense in Northern Ireland has led to some becoming confused over where loyalties lie. One commentator, David Miller, suggested that Ulster's loyalist community, were "Queen's Rebels",[23] an accurate enough title based on their historical ethos of a contract with those who rule, which, if broken, they were not obliged to maintain. This outworking of seventeenth century philosophy has often taken modern observers by surprise. It should not necessarily do so, given the strong influence of Calvinism, Covenanters and Reivers on the Protestant community in the Ulster counties. It is, however, a curious variant of radicalism. While at some points in history it has sought to establish something new, as in 1798, there is also the curious circumstance that at other times, as in 1912, it was also a radicalism which was determinedly conservative in ethos and tone, wishing to preserve something which existed and was perceived to be under threat, as opposed to bringing forward something new.

The radicalism which was evidenced in Ulster in the eighteenth, nineteenth and twentieth centuries probably related considerably to the cultural experience of the Ulster Scots community. Looking back is nothing new to those from Scotland, indeed it has been pointed out how long Borderers are capable of nursing a grudge for – some suggest decades.[24] Thus many Presbyterians looked back to times of suppression and repression for their cultural community in the seventeenth century. In 1704 the Test Act prevented all non-conformists from playing a part in local government of their own community and area, and this contributed to the emigration of many to the United States, although other factors were involved. It was no coincidence, however, that the area which was hit hard by the Test Act regulations, Londonderry and its hinterland, would also provide the first organised emigration in 1718 from Ulster – five ships taking several hundred emigrants from Coleraine, Macosquin, Aghadowey and Londonderry to a new life in New Londonderry and New Hampshire. This emigration was led by their local Presbyterian minister, Reverend James McGregor. They would be followed by many tens of thousands of others. This emigration also means that the 1798 Rising cannot be taken in isolation from the Ulster Scots perspective.

There had been revolutions in America and France. In America at least 250,000 Ulster emigrants, possibly as many as 300,000,[25] had found a home and many had played a leading role in the war against King George. The first declarations of independence, for example, were issued by Ulster Presbyterian settlements at Hanna's Town, Pine Creek, (Pennsylvania) and Mecklenburg (North Carolina). The news from America must have been filtering back to the kith and kin on the other side of the Atlantic and, given the bitterness felt by the Presbyterians towards the authorities, they would not have been averse to a repeat of the American events in Ireland. News also reached Belfast through ship captains and their crews (Henry Joy McCracken's father was captain on a ship plying between Belfast and the Americas, for example). The French Revolution was also widely welcomed by the Presbyterians. They celebrated the Fall of the Bastille in Belfast, planted Liberty Trees, wore their hair short like French Revolutionaries (earning the title for some of 'Croppies') and, eventually, the more radical of them looked for French help in their rebellion. We must not discount the 'domino effect' in history.

Ever since the arrival of Presbyterian Lowlanders in Antrim and Down in the early 1600s, they had faced persecution from the authorities. In 1636, for example, two congregations left Groomsport in County Down bound for America, on the ship *Eagle Wing*, eventually having to turn back. In 1636 a number of Presbyterian ministers were forbidden to preach and worse was to follow. Many were expelled from their churches, which were technically Anglican and under the control of the Church of Ireland. The first Presbyterian minister in Ireland, Reverend Edward Brice of Ballycarry, County Antrim, was said to have died of a broken heart after he was forbidden to minister to his people, all of them settled from Scotland. Only a common threat to the Protestants of Ulster, as in 1641 and 1688–90 united them, but at other times the Anglicans and Presbyterians were often in opposite camps.

A park ranger outlines the story of the Battle of Kings Mountain to an official delegation from Larne in 1998. The battle helped pave the way for American victory during the War of Independence.

The era which brought the American and French revolutions was known as the Era of Enlightenment, and this was a period which also had influence in Scotland. The ideas of men such as Thomas Paine, that all men were created equal with equal rights, were widely disseminated. Wolfe Tone referred to Paine's book *The Rights of Man* as being the Koran of the Belfast Presbyterians. In addition, the Presbyterians founded reading clubs or reading societies, which met to discuss the modern ideas and their implications (and perhaps their applications). The view the authorities had of these reading clubs is underlined by the raid on the premises of the Doagh club, in County Antrim, when the furniture and books were burnt in the main street after the building had been ransacked by the yeomanry.[26]

In Scotland there was also radicalism and in July 1792 a group was formed in Edinburgh, calling itself the Associated Friends of the People. Consisting of radical gentlemen and middle class reformers, it won the support of radicals among the lower classes in Scotland. However, United Irish hopes of allying with the cross-channel movement and receiving support from it appear to have foundered in 1792 and 1793, when addresses from the Dublin and Belfast United Irishmen were met with, at best, a lukewarm response.[27] Promised support for the 1798 Rising of between 100,000 and 200,000 United Scotsmen never materialised, and it was clear that the idea of a republic was not shared by the majority of radicals in Scotland or, if it was, not sufficiently to merit physical support. It was clearly the case that the radical leaders in Scotland felt, despite promises of support for the United

Irishmen, that little could be achieved by localised risings in parts of Scotland, which would quickly bring down the wrath of the authorities.

All these and some other strands have to be woven into the single fabric of radicalism within the Ulster Scots community. That is not to say, however, that all those who were Ulster Scots were radicals. James Wilson, one of the founding leaders of the Orange Order in 1795, for example, was a Presbyterian farmer,[28] while General Knox, who was in the command of the west of the province of Ulster in 1798, was confident enough to state that he could rest its safety on the Presbyterians there who were loyal to the King.[29] Alexander Chesney, from Ballymena, was one of the prominent loyalists during the American Revolution, losing his lands and having to return as a Customs officer to Ulster as a result.[30] Generally, however, radicalism was a cloak which would not only fit but also be well worn in Ulster Scots communities. They were, to paraphrase US Senator James Webb, "Born Fighting" and if they felt the cause was right, they would never surrender.[31]

HISTORICAL TRAILS
SITES TO VISIT

Antrim town, County Antrim

The United Army of Ulster was led into Antrim town on 7 June 1798 by Henry Joy McCracken, a member of a prominent Belfast merchant family. As they approached the town through the Scotch Quarter, they found that many of the thatched weaver's cottages had been torched by the authorities, correctly believing that the occupants were not there because they had joined the insurgents.

The main focus of the battle took place in Antrim High Street, between the courthouse and the Church of Ireland and adjoining cemetery. Although the battle initially went well for the United Irishmen, a tactical mistake resulted in the authorities gaining the day. Only a small group of around 50 men, known as the Spartan Band, remained with McCracken and tried to ensure an orderly retreat and escape. The Spartan Band hid out for a time on Slemish Mountain, but McCracken was later captured.

Donegore Hill outside Antrim was the main rendezvous point for the United Army, and after the battle the Ballycarry poet James Orr highlighted seeing frantic activity there, as well as the discarding of property, ammunition and weapons when the insurgents tried to make hasty and disorganised retreat.

In the Old Presbyterian cemetery off Antrim's High Street is the gravestone of a man who innocently came out after the battle to congratulate the victorious troops of the Monaghan militia, only to be shot, mistaken as an attacker. Ironically, given the later context of Irish history, Presbyterian rebels in Antrim were quelled by the Monaghan militia, which was comprised largely of Roman Catholics who were loyal to the Crown.

Ballynahinch, County Down

The Battle of Ballynahinch on 9 June 1798 saw insurgents move from their camp at Edenvaddy Hill outside the town and clash with government troops in the centre of Ballynahinch. The commander of the insurgents was Henry Munro, a Lisburn draper who had hastily taken command of the rebels. The evening of 8 June saw the troops in an inebriated state after they raided spirit grocers in the town, but Munro would not yield to the suggestions of some of his officers that they should attack at that point. His chivalry cost him dearly, for despite early advances his force was defeated due to a tactical error in the midst of the battle, and a rout occurred across the countryside.

Just outside the town Betsy Gray, a young girl who had been drawn to the gathering of the insurgents and probably gotten carried away in the atmosphere, was cut down by yeomanry, who also killed her brother and her sweetheart. Gray became a martyr, her name long remembered in the area.

Kings Mountain historical site marker.

Memorial plaque at Kings Mountain, South Carolina.

Kings Mountain, South Carolina

Located in the Piedmont region of the Carolinas, Kings Mountain was the site of a pivotal battle in the American Revolution in October 1780. The British commander, Patrick Ferguson, had brought his forces into the region to quell the rebellion and encourage those loyal to the King to rally to the flag. He threatened those in the mountains of the consequences of disloyalty, but had no impact. Instead, the Over Mountain Men assembled at Sycamore Shoals in Tennessee and marched across the mountains, many of them being first generation settlers from Ballymena,

Ballymoney and surrounding areas. They were adept hunters in the forests of Appalachia, and the redcoat's bayonet charges were no match for men who did not abide by the normal conventions of battle. The British force, which had assembled on the top of Kings Mountain, was defeated, and Ferguson was killed.

The battle was followed by another at Hanna's Cowpens in January 1781 (where the American commander was General Daniel Morgan from Draperstown), and proved a turning point in the Revolution. Unable to capture the south, Lord Cornwallis accepted that he could not subjugate the Americans. Kings Mountain and Cowpens led to the British surrender at Yorktown in October 1781.

The national park at Kings Mountain gives an excellent interpretation of the battle, and visitors can also walk to the two memorials at the top of the mountain and view where various incidents during the battle occurred.

Muck Island off Islandmagee in County Antrim. Presbyterian rebel William McClelland hid out here after the defeat of the United Irishmen in June 1798.

Portmuck, County Antrim

The McClelland family, who lived at Portmuck in Islandmagee in 1798, was deeply involved in the stirring events of the period. The family farm occupied a prominent headland and William McClelland would become one of the leaders of the United Irishmen in Islandmagee. He led his colleagues on 7 June 1798, when the Rising, or Turn Out, took place in County Antrim, and later had a price put on his head by the authorities.

During the Rising Islandmagee insurgents appeared on the hills at the north of the island, where they were watched anxiously by loyalists in Larne opposed to the Rising. McClelland and his men later crossed the causeway further south and rendezvoused with the insurgents from Ballycarry.

Local legend tells us that, after the failure of the 1798 Rising, William McClelland hid out in a cave on Muck Island, adjacent to the coast, while the word was put out that he had fled. His wife was supposed to have been taken to the Maidens Islands off the Antrim coast for safety, returning to Portmuck to give birth to a child who was said to have been the last born there for nearly 150 years. The McClellands were a Scottish family who had settled in Islandmagee at the end of the seventeenth century.

HISTORICAL QUOTES

Letter dated 27 March 1772, from Mrs Eliza O'Neill, Flowerfield, near Portstewart, County Londonderry to her mother, Mrs Elizabeth Tobin, Gorey, County Wexford. It describes an attack on a 'big house' by the Presbyterian Hearts of Steel. Featured in *Aspects of Irish Social History*, edited by WH Crawford and Brian Trainor, Belfast: 1984, the original is held by the Public Record Office of Northern Ireland.

"... All the discourse of this country is about the Hearts of Steel. You see in Faulkner's paper their proceedings at Mr Johnston's in the County Down, which lies not far this side of Newry, but he has since taken up near sixty of them by the assistance of the army. Captain Rankin I am well acquainted with: 'twas he quelled the Oak Boys formerly, and he is indefatigable in pursuit of the Steel Boys, but by their stirring only in the night they battle the army and all the schemes of magistrates. Rankin had one engagement with them in the County Derry about ten miles from Coleraine; he killed four, but they escaped from him being a dark night. He had thirty soldiers, they two thousand men – (perhaps this is tedious to you, but your neighbours will be apt to ask questions).

Last Friday night two hundred of them came again to my Uncle Daniel's about twelve o'clock at night. They first set fire to his barn and stable which were in a row, and his hay stack and a quantity of straw in another stack. They sheltered themselves behind and at the corners of the outhouses, and haggard wall, and fired constantly and smartly on the front and end of the house. The young men and soldiers although they fired out could never get one shot at them. It was moonlight and they could not even see them, but knew by the firing they were numerous nor could they venture out as the others were so posted as to have them in their view before they could reach them. Their loss consists of a large quantity of oats, some wheat, a good deal of timber they had in the stable, and almost all their fodder which is not to be bought for money, and all their windows broke, but their horses were saved. The Steel Boys ordered them to leave the place or they would come again and burn their house about their ears, for one of them had been killed when they were there before, and they swore they would be revenged.

There is melancholy accounts of them every day, and although there is a deal of army come yet they can't find them out. It is as bad as the Irish rebellion. They are all Presbyterians. They are not yet nearer us than five or six miles and I hope the short nights or the assizes will stop their progress. In summer they can't stir much and next winter I expect to be in Dublin. The Mayor of Coleraine has taken four last week. ...

P.S.-We have bags of sand nailed up in most of our windows to keep out their balls, and plenty of charges ready made in paper, to charge the faster, and six guns always ready."

An account from the *Belfast News Letter*, 21 March 1780, highlighting the mix of conservatism and radicalism which attended the Belfast Volunteers and the Presbyterian community, who filled the majority of the ranks.

"BELFAST

The 17th, 1778, being the day on which the Belfaft Firft Volunteer Company affociated – that corps paraded on Friday laft, (St Patrick's Day) and fired three vollies; after which a number of the members dined together at the Donegall Arms, and were honoured with the prefence of feveral Gentlemen who were Volunteers in the year 1745.

The following, with many other patriotic toafts, were drunk:
The King and Constitution
The Queen and Royal Family
Profperity to Ireland
The friends of Ireland in the Britifh Parliament
The majority of the Houfe of Commons of Ireland on a late conftitutional divifion
Unanimity and profperity to the Volunteers of Ireland
The Earl of Donegall, Colonel of the Belfaft United Companies
The Earl of Charlemont, and the Volunteer Officers now affembled in this town
The Old Volunteers of the town of Belfaft
An honourable and lafting peace with America
Conftitutional fecurity to the Free Trade of Ireland, and wifdom to make a proper ufe of it
A happy completion of the good work fo well begun in eftablishing the rights of this kingdom
Liberty to those who dare to contend for it ..."

The Dying Declaration of William Orr of Farranshane, Antrim, Presbyterian United Irish martyr, 5 October 1797. Orr was tried for administering a United Irish oath and, amid controversy, found guilty and sentenced to be hanged. His execution at Carrickfergus excited much bitterness and resentment among the Presbyterian community in County Antrim. When the United Irishmen attacked Antrim on 7 June 1798, it was to the battle cry of "Remember Orr!"

"TO THE PUBLICK.

My Friends and Fellow Countrymen,

The grave of William Orr of Farranshane, Antrim, Presbyterian martyr of the United Irish period, who was hanged in 1797.

IN the Thirty-first Year of my Life, I have been sentenced to die upon the Gallows, and this Sentence has been in Pursuance of a Verdict of Twelve Men, who should have been indifferently and impartially chosen; how far they have been so, I leave to that Country from which they have been chosen, to determine; and how far they have discharged their Duty, I leave to their God and to themselves. ___ They have in pronouncing their Verdict, thought proper to recommend me as an Object of humane Mercy; in Return, I pray to God, if they have erred, to have Mercy upon them. The Judge, who condemned me, humanely shed Tears in uttering my Sentence, but whether he did wisely in so highly commending the wretched Informer, who swore away my Life, I leave to his own cool reflection, solemnly assuring him and all the World, with my dying Breath, that that Informer was foresworn. The Law under which I suffer, is surely a severe one; may the Makers and Promoters of it be justified in the Integrity of their Motives and the Purity of their own Lives __ by that Law, I am stamped a Felon, but my heart disdains the Imputation. My comfortable Lot and industrious Course of Life, best refute the Charge of being an Adventurer for Plunder; but if to have loved my Country, to have known its wrongs, to have felt the Injuries of the persecuted Catholic, and to have united with them and all other Religious Persuasions in the most orderly and least sanguinary Means of procuring Redress:- If those be Felonies, I am a Felon, but not otherwise. Had my Councils (for whose honourable Exertions I am indebted) prevailed in their Motion to have me tried for High Treason, rather than under the Insurrection Law, I should have been entitled then to a full Defence and my Actions and Intentions have been better vindicated, but that was refused, and I must now submit to what has passed.

To the generous Protection of my Country, I leave a beloved Wife, who has been constant and true to me, and whose Grief for my Fate has already nearly occasioned her Death. I leave five living Children, who have been my Delight – may they love their Country as I have done, and die for it, if needful …

WILLIAM ORR,
Carrickfergus Gaol,
October 5, 1797."

This Address suggests that the congregation may have been removed from those who had taken part in the Rising, or wished to prevent the wrath of the authorities descending on the area, which had been a hotbed of the Rebellion.

Ballycarry Declaration of Loyalty, 1798

"At a numerous meeting of the Congregation of Broadisland, in the County of Antrim (the earliest Presbyterian settlement in the Kingdom) on Sunday 29th Inst. the following Loyal and Constitutional sentiments were unanimously declared.

Deeply impressed with the dreadful calamities occasioned by the late madness of insurrection; and feeling the strongest predilection for the Constitution of this country by King, Lords, and Commons; and being, as our Ancestors were, warmly attached to the principles of the Hanoverian Succession; we do now formally declare that we will according to our respective stations, and agreeable to our Prayers every Lord's Day, support that form of Government in His Majesty's illustrious House for ourselves; and endeavour to hand it down to our children unimpaired.

And we do further declare our gratitude to Divine Providence excited, and our hope therefore animated, by the total disappearance of every symptom of Rebellion in this neighbourhood; by the King's Message of Mercy to the country, as well as by seeing a Nobleman of Lord Cornwallis's abilities, character and experience at the head of its administration."

Signed by John Bankhead, and transmitted to Lord Castlereagh by Mr Ker of Red Hall.

James Orr's poem, *The Wanderer,* may have been inspired by his experience at Slemish with the Spartan Band, led by McCracken and seeking to evade the authorities and cross into County Down to join insurgents there. It tells the story of a fugitive being given shelter for the night by a kind hearted friend.

The Memorial to weaver poet James Orr in the Templecorran cemetery, Ballycarry.

THE WANDERER
Tune – Mary's Dream,

"Wha's there?" she ax't. The wan'rers rap
Against the pane the lassie scaur'd:
The blast that bray'd on *Slimiss* tap
Wad hardly let a haet be heard.
"A frien," he cried, "for common crimes
"Tost thro' the country fore and aft"–
"Mair lown," quo' she – thir's woefu' times! –
"The herd's aboon me on the laft."

"I call'd," he whisper'd, "wi' a wight
'Wham aft I've help'd han' an' purse;
"He wadna let me stay a' night –
"Weel! sic a heart's a greater curse:
"But Leezie's gentler. Hark that hail!
"This piercin' night is rougher far" –
"Come roun," she said, "an' shun the gale,
"I'm gaun to slip aside the bar."

Waes me! how wat ye're? Gie's your hat,
An' dry your face wi' something – hae.
In sic a takin' wee I wat;
I wad preserve my greatest fae:
We'll mak' nae fire; the *picquet* bauld
Might see the light, an' may be stap;
But I'll sit up: my bed's no cauld,
Gae till't awee an' tak' a nap

HISTORICAL FIGURES

William Orr. Sketch by Chris H Ashworth.

William Orr of Farranshane

William Orr was a well-to-do Presbyterian farmer from Farranshane (now Crosskennan) near Antrim town. He was arrested in 1796 on a charge of having administered the illegal United Irish oath to two army deserters. During his imprisonment, hundreds of his neighbours harvested the crops from his farm, a common way of ordinary people showing solidarity with those imprisoned as United Irishmen. Orr was tried the following year, 1797, and, amid allegations surrounding bribery and intimidation of the jury, was found guilty and sentenced to death.

The 31 year old issued a Dying Declaration prior to his execution, and was accompanied to the gallows by two Presbyterian ministers, Reverend William Stavely of Knockbracken and Reverend Adam Hill of Ballynure. The 31 year old declared:

"… if to have loved my country, to have known its wrongs, to have felt the Injuries of the persecuted Catholic [a reference to the Penal Laws] and to have united with them and all other Religious Persuasions in the most orderly and least sanguinary means of procuring redress – if these be felonies, I am a felon, but not otherwise."

It was said that most of the townspeople left Carrickfergus that day rather than be present for the execution. Orr's body was taken to the village of Ballynure after the hanging, and was guarded by members of the local Masonic lodge; Orr, like many others of the Presbyterian radicals, having been a Freemason. His body was interred at Castle Upton, Templepatrick.

Secret service payment books from Dublin Castle in the 1790s have revealed that one of the army deserters who gave evidence against Orr was in the pay of the authorities at Dublin Castle. The sense of injustice which attended Orr's trial and execution led to the battle cry of the United Irishmen being "Remember Orr" when they stormed Antrim town on 7 June 1798, during the United Irish Rising.

The grave of Reverend James Porter, hanged by the authorities outside his church in the aftermath of the United Irish rebellion.

Reverend James Porter of Greyabbey

A native of County Donegal, he was born in 1753, one of a family of eight children. James showed early promise of intelligence and choose not to follow the farming background of his family but to instead seek a career as a teacher. It was while teaching at Dromore in County Down that he met his wife to be, Anna Knox. The couple moved to Drogheda for a time, where James Porter taught and where the couple had two children.

Around the year 1784 he entered Glasgow College as a Divinity student, completing a theological course in 1786 or 1787. Licensed by the Presbytery of Bangor, he received a call to the congregation of Greyabbey in County Down and was ordained there on 31 July 1787, at the age of 34 years.

Supplementing his income through farming, Reverend Porter was also keenly interested in natural philosophy. His political leanings were reflected in his membership of the Irish Volunteers, a middle-class militia raised to protect against the threat of French invasion, which also espoused quite radical political views. In

1791 the radicalism of the Volunteers was superseded by the United Irishmen, who advocated constitutional reform but were forced underground in the mid-1790s and led a rebellion in 1798.

There is no evidence that Reverend James Porter was a member of the United Irish Society, but he was clearly sympathetic and delivered lectures ostensibly on natural philosophy which espoused United Irish principles. He anonymously wrote a biting satire entitled 'Billy Bluff and the Squire' in the United Irish newspaper, the *Northern Star*, and it was said that the seven letters in the series resulted in his death.

After the Rising had been quelled in Ulster, Reverend James Porter was arrested and charged with intercepting, opening and reading a military dispatch, a charge which he denied. He was tried by a court martial and found guilty on the evidence of a man who had been a United Irishman and was turned informer. In an address to the court, Porter professed his innocence, but it was to no avail and he was sentenced to death. His distraught wife took her seven children and sought to speak to Lord Londonderry, father of Lord Castlereagh, the Secretary of State for Ireland, at Mount Stewart and try and obtain clemency, but although his daughters were sympathetic, Londonderry – widely seen as being 'the Squire' in Porter's writings – would not assist her. Porter was duly executed on 2 July 1798, many of his congregation being forced to watch the proceedings. He was 45 years of age.

The eldest son of James and Anna, Alexander Porter, was 14 at the time of the Battle of Ballynahinch, and was said to have carried colours of the United Irishmen that day. He went to America after the Rising and became a judge in the American legal system and later Governor of Louisiana. Another son, James Porter, was to become the Attorney-General for Louisiana. Like many Presbyterian families connected with 1798, the family of James Porter rose to prominence in 'the land of the free'.[32]

James Orr, Bard of Ballycarry

James Orr was the son of a weaver and was born in 1770 in the County Antrim village of Ballycarry. He became the foremost of the Ulster Weaver Poets and was also a radical, contributing material and poems to the *Northern Star*, the newspaper of the United Irish Society.

In 1798 James Orr was among those who joined the '*Turn Oot*' as it was referred to in Antrim, marching with the local Broadisland Corps for Antrim town, where the Presbyterians would be defeated in battle. Orr was forced to flee from his native village, it is believed with a price on his head, and spent some time in the United States.

His poetry reflects this stirring period in Ulster Scots history, with a poem written on the eve of the Rising highlighting his views *(Prayer written on the eve of the unfortunate seventh of June)*, a second focusing on the events of the day

(*Donegore Hill*), a third highlighting the life of someone on the run (*The Wanderer*) and a fourth detailing the voyage of a political exile (*The Emigrant*).

After staying in the United States for a short time he returned to Ulster under amnesty and lived the remainder of his life in Ballycarry, where he died in 1816. His gravesite is now marked with a large sandstone memorial erected by the Masonic Order in 1831, of which he was a prominent member and a founder of the local Masonic Lodge.

James Orr was always regarded with suspicion by the local landlord, Richard Gervas Ker, who refused to allow him to join the local yeomanry on account of his involvement in the 1798 Rising.

Betsy Gray

Betsy Gray was one of those who lost their lives after the defeat of the Presbyterian United Irishmen at Ballynahinch in June 1798. History has added to her story, undoubtedly, and there is also some doubt as to her background, with at least two areas claiming to be her birthplace and childhood home.[33]

What is known is that Betsy was a teenager who probably got caught up in the excitement of the events of that June. Her brother and her sweetheart were involved in the United Irish Rising and all three accompanied the insurgent forces to Ballynahinch, very probably from the North Down area.

After the routing of the Presbyterian army in Ballynahinch, the three fled across fields but were unfortunate enough to come to the attention of the Hillsborough Yeomen, who, in pursuit of fleeing insurgents, murdered them in the townland of Ballycreen outside the town. A memorial was later erected at the spot by an American named James Gray, who claimed to be a descendant of Betsy Gray, although this may be open to some doubt. The memorial was unfortunately broken up in 1898, prior to a planned Home Rule demonstration at Ballycreen; highlighting that the memory of 1798 was no longer a shared one between Protestant, Catholic and Dissenter.

There is some doubt as to whether Betsy Gray and her two companions remained buried in the townland of Ballycreen, or whether she and her brother at least were interred in the Garvaghy parish churchyard at Dromara, burial place of a Gray family which was quite prominent and may also have been connected to those in North Down.

James Lowry of Greyabbey and Magheramorne

James Lowry, JP was a well-known Belfast businessman, and a member of a prominent Greyabbey family. He lived at Dalriada House, Magheramorne, County Antrim, and became a pivotal figure and benefactor to the local Independent Orange Lodge established in the area the following year. He was a Liberal in political persuasion and one of those behind the Magheramorne Manifesto in

1905, which appeared to support a measure of Home Rule for Ireland. It was through the influence of Lowry and Robert Lindsay Crawford, one-time Grand Master of the Independent Orange Order, that Twelfth demonstrations were held at Magheramorne. His residence was also used for early meetings of the Magheramorne Total Abstinence Association and Social Club, which was formed in the summer of 1904, and his wife was President of the body.

James Lowry was actively involved in Independent Orangeism and his portrait appeared on the banner of the local Independent Orange Lodge at Magheramorne. He died in 1909 and his remains were conveyed by train from Magheramorne to York Street, from thence it made its way to Greyabbey, the services being conducted by Reverend Thomas Bartley of Ballycarry and Reverend John Anderson of Greyabbey. Among the wreaths were those from the employees at Lowry, Lawson and McCormick in Belfast. An obituary which appeared at the time detailed how Lowry was a relative of David Baillie Warden, a student for the Presbyterian ministry, who was forced to leave Ulster after the 1798 Rising owing to his radicalism, and who later became US Government representative at the Congress of Vienna. Lowry was, it was said, "a man of broad and tolerant sympathies, and one of Nature's gentlemen". His background is interesting given the connections which the family had with 1798 and later radical politics in Ulster in the twentieth century.

The grave of United Irishman James Hope at Mallusk, County Antrim. Hope was a member of the Irish Volunteers before joining the even more radical United Irish Society.

James Hope

James Hope's family were of Scottish Covenanter stock and had settled in County Antrim, where Hope was born (at Templepatrick) in 1764, the son of John Hope and Sarah Speers.[34] Apprenticed as a linen weaver, he was fortunate in his early life to have employers who encouraged his wider education. Hope became greatly influenced by the American Revolution and the French Revolution. He enlisted in the Irish Volunteer movement, which was raised to protect against the threat of invasion by the French. Having served in the Roughfort company of Volunteers, after its demise he joined the Society of United Irishmen, being sworn in at Lowtown, Mallusk.

Hope wrote of this period, noting that many of those who were in the United Irishmen in his local area had formerly been Irish Volunteers (in June 1798 Volunteer standards were carried by some of those on their way to the Battle of Antrim).

Hope progressed in the movement, being elected to the central committee in Belfast and becoming close to leaders such as Samuel Neilson and Henry Joy McCracken. He was sent to Dublin in 1796 to assist the movement there and also mobilise the working classes in the city, establishing several branches of the United Irish Society.

When the 1798 Rebellion broke out, Hope was among a small group known as the Spartan Band who stood by Henry Joy McCracken following the Battle of Antrim, hiding out with him at Slemish for a time. He later described his life as "a scene of escapes."

Following the Rising, Hope refused to take up the terms of amnesty then offered to the United Irishmen, saying that to do so would be to renounce his principles and also accept that the punishment meted out on his associates was in some way just. He kept on the move, staying for some time in the counties of Meath and Westmeath and also Dublin, fleeing to England after the failed Emmet revolt of 1803.

James Hope is regarded as the most socialist of the United Irish leadership of the 1790s. His outlook is reflected in his targeting of manufacturers as well as landowners as enemies of radicalism. Such a stance must have sat uneasily with at least some of the middle class Presbyterian leadership in Ulster. Hope, who died in 1847, is buried at the Mallusk graveyard, his memorial stone stating:

> "One of nature's noblest works, an honest man. Steadfast in faith and always hopeful in the divine protection. In the best era of his country's history a soldier in her cause: and in the worst of times still faithful to it: ever true to himself, and to those who trusted in him he remained to the last unchanged and unchangeable in his fidelity …"

A measure of his loyalty to the cause of 1798 is evidenced in the fact that his two sons were named Robert Emmet Hope and Henry Joy McCracken Hope.

ENDNOTES

1 See Eliza O'Neill's letter in Crawford and Trainor, eds, *Aspects of Irish Social History*, Belfast: 1984, p44

2 McSkimin, Samuel; McCrum, ed, *History and Antiquities of the County of the Town of Carrickfergus*, Belfast: 1909

3 McSkimin; McCrum, ed, *op cit*, p90

4 See, for example, the toasts of the Belfast First Volunteer Company, in Hume, David, *'To Right some things that we thought wrong ...' The Spirit of 1798 and Presbyterian Radicalism in Ulster*, Lurgan: The Ulster Society, 1998, p50

5 Hume, *'To Right some things that we thought wrong ...' The Spirit of 1798 and Presbyterian Radicalism in Ulster*, *op cit*, p18

6 Smyth, PD, 'The Volunteers and Parliament, 1779-84' in Bartlett and Hayton, eds, *Penal Era and Golden Age, Essays in Irish History, 1690-1800*, Belfast: 1979

7 From Willie Wark's Song, by James Campbell, cited in John Hewitt, ed, *Rhyming Weavers and other country poets of Antrim and Down*, Belfast: 1974, p58–9

8 Stewart, ATQ, in his excellent history of the 1798 Rebellion in Ulster, *The Summer Soldiers: the 1798 Rebellion in Antrim and Down*, Belfast: Blackstaff Press, 1995, gives considerable attention to Hope.

9 'Declaration and resolutions of the Society of United Irishmen of Belfast', in Killen, John, ed, *The Decade of the United Irishmen, Contemporary Accounts 1791–1801*, Belfast: 1998, p20

10 There had, however, been less structured bodies after the Battle of the Boyne, the closest to the Orange Institution probably being Boyne Societies.

11 See McCoy, Jack, *Betsy Gray, Ulster's Joan of Arc*, Bangor: 1987

12 *Records of the General Synod of Ulster 1691–1820*, Volume III, Belfast: 1898, p208

13 Clifford, Brendan, ed, 'Henry Montgomery's Letter to Daniel O'Connell', *Belfast Magazine*, vol 4, no 1, undated

14 Walker, Brian, *Ulster Politics, The Formative Years 1868–86*, Belfast: 1989

15 See Hume, David, 'Events of 1869 help provide clues to a Bellahill mystery' in *Broadisland Journal*, 2002

16 Anecdote related to me by the late Hugh Reid of Magheramorne, who had been told of the incident by his father, David Reid, a member of the 'established' lodge in the area.

17 See, for example, Walker, *op cit*

18 The signatories and venue are listed on the Public Record Office Northern Ireland Covenant website. In Ballycarry one of the Presbyterian congregations was referred to as "Home Rulers", a sign that they were politically suspect to the local political establishment.

19 Locke argued that it was morally acceptable for James II to have been overthrown and as a consequence he was known as the 'Philosopher of the Glorious Revolution'.

20 See Barkley, John, 'Bottled in Ireland, uncorked in America', in *Free Thought in Ireland*, a supplement to *Fortnight* magazine, 1998

21 One of the examples of this, in 1913, was the formation of the Provisional Government of Ulster, which would undertake to control those areas which it could when Home Rule had been passed in parliament.

22 Quoted in Hume, David, *For Ulster and Her Freedom: the story of the April 1914 gunrunning*, Larne: 1989

23 Miller, David, *Queen's Rebels: Ulster Loyalism in Historical Perspective*, Dublin: 1978

24 MacDonald Fraser, George, *The Steel Bonnets: The Story of the Anglo-Scottish Border Reivers*, London: Harper Collins, 1989

25 David Noel Doyle in *Ireland, Irishmen and Revolutionary America*, Dublin: 1981, suggests 300,000 as a figure, based on factors including that because Ulster Scots settlers had Scottish surnames, many of them were classed as Scottish when they were not.

26 Stewart, ATQ, *The Summer Soldiers: the 1798 Rebellion in Antrim and Down*, Belfast: Blackstaff Press, 1995, p163

27 See Brims, John, 'Scottish Radicalism and the United Irishmen', in *The United Irishmen, Republicanism, Radicalism and Rebellion*, Dublin: 1993

28 Sibbett, RM, *Orangeism in Ireland and throughout the Empire*, vol 1, London: 1939, p266

29 Knox deliberately encouraged adherents to the recently established Orange Order to support his forces and many joined local yeomanry units as a result. This situation was not similar in areas around Belfast, the Sixmilewater Valley of Antrim and North Down and the Ards, where radical Presbyterians were not involved to any great number in the Orange Order but played a nurturing role in the United Irish Society and could certainly not be counted on by the authorities.

30 Gilmer Moss, Bobby, *Journal of Capt. Alexander Chesney, Adjutant to Maj. Patrick Ferguson*, South Carolina: 2002, provides a detailed account of the life and times in America of Alexander Chesney.

31 Webb, James, *Born Fighting: How the Scotch-Irish shaped America*, New York: 2004

32 Wharton, WJ, *The Reverend James Porter*, New Ulster, November 1994

33 See the excellent study on Betsy Gray by the late Jack McCoy, *Ulster's Joan of Arc, an examination of the Betsy Gray story*, Bangor: 1987

34 See *The Memoirs of Jemmy Hope: An Autobiography of a working class United Irishman*, Belfast: 1973

Chapter Eight

THE ULSTER-AMERICAN EXPERIENCE

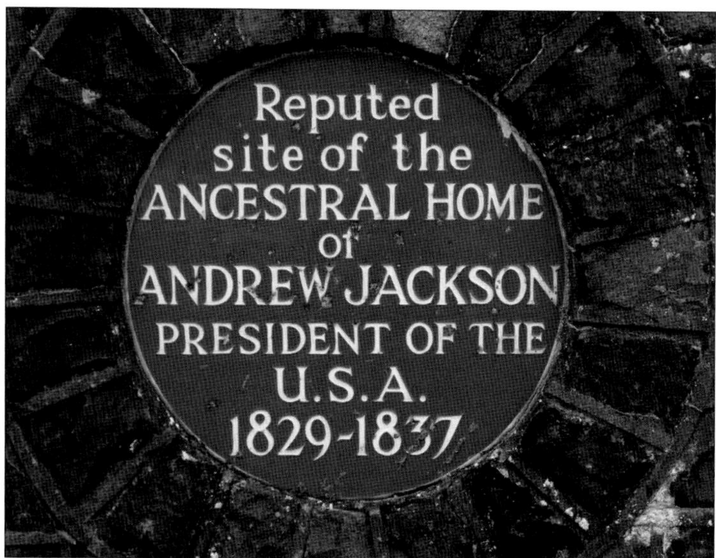

Commemorative plaque at Boneybefore, Carrickfergus, in honour of Andrew Jackson.

On a May day in 1717 a small ship named the *Friend's Goodwill* set sail from Larne on the coast of County Antrim, bound for Boston harbour. Unfortunately the passenger list has not survived, but what is known about the vessel is that she carried around 52 passengers and that she was certainly one of the earliest of the emigrant ships taking Ulster Scots to the New World in the eighteenth century. The voyage of the *Friend's Goodwill* would be eventful, and near the end it looked as if the supplies would run out. Two passengers died on the journey. In September 1717, the ship sailed into Boston Harbour, a welcome sight after the long months in the Atlantic. The *Friend's Goodwill* might have been the first, but she would certainly not be the last to make the voyage from Ulster ports to those on the other side of the Atlantic; Boston, Wilmington, Charles Town, Philadelphia, and Savannah among them.

The Ulster American Memorial in Larne, County Antrim.

It had been estimated that, prior to the American Revolution, a quarter of a million people had made their way from the north of Ireland to the colonies,[1]

but more up-to-date research has increased this figure to around 300,000 because many of those who arrived were described as Scottish, owing to a combination of surnames, accents and lack of knowledge of their origins. Ironically enough, many Americans still confuse those of an Ulster Scots background as being Irish; a confusion which led to the term Scotch-Irish being employed by them to describe themselves in the nineteenth century.

This drain of people concerned the authorities in Ireland at the time, and there were many areas which were left considerably deprived by the departure of families, friends and neighbours for a new life in America. For example, when Reverend James McGregor set sail for New Londonderry, New Hampshire, he took five ships and somewhere between 600 and 800 people. Similarly Reverend William Martin organised four or five ships and took several hundred Covenanters and their friends to the Carolinas.[2] Dotted across the United States were settlements founded by such emigrants, some of whose names remain, such as Belfast in Maine, New Londonderry in New Hampshire and Donegal in Pennsylvania. There were many other places, such as Russell Place (now Stoneboro[3]) in South Carolina, where the emigrants did not ultimately leave place names, but nevertheless left surnames, ethos and a strong clannishness to highlight their presence. "The importance of the Scotch-Irish pioneering tradition in Appalachia survives in some material culture. The ground plan of many Appalachian houses is identical to the traditional small Ulster farmhouse …" one author has noted.[4] It has also been suggested that the traditional log cabin, which was the first home built by most settlers, also has Ulster origins.[5] These factors are merely the 'material culture' and do not deal with the outlook and ethos which was passed on by the Ulster Scots settlers who were acknowledged as being tenacious and pioneering. Part of that ethos can today be traced across the region known as 'the Bible Belt'.

Faith clearly played an important part in the decision to leave their homes and embark on a journey across a wide ocean into unknown territory. William Moberg in his novel of Swedish emigrants in the nineteenth century, *The Emigrants*, notes the leap of faith for people used to solid earth under their feet taking ship across the ocean, where, for the duration of their voyage, nothing would be secure.[6] What probably sustained such emigrants, from wherever they came, was the faith that they would end up on the other side of the journey with solid earth and security once again. They also believed they would be better-off than they were at home, a major pull factor for all emigrants.

That is not to say that voyages were simply uneventful periods of transition. Robert Witherspoon, who was a young boy when his family took him from County Down to South Carolina in 1734, would recount events which would remain in his memory many years later when he compiled the so-called *Witherspoon Chronicle*:

> "We went on ship bord the 14th of September and lay wind bound in the Lough at Belfast 14 days. The second day of our sail my grandmother died and was interred

in the region Ocean which was an affective sight to her offspring ..." He continues his account, "We were sorely tossed at sea with storms which caused our ship to spring a leek. Our pumps were kept incessantly at work day and night. For many days our mariners seemed many a time at their wits end, but it pleased God to bring us all safe to land, which was about the 1st of December".[7]

A memorial plaque to Ulsterman John Witherspoon, founder of Williamsburg Presbyterian Church and pioneer of Kingstree, South Carolina.

John Blair, an emigrant from Larne in 1791, gave an equally interesting account of the journey to the United States, including the weather which he experienced:

"The horizon seemed all in a blaze with electric fire. About half an hour later it thundered in a most tremendous manner, accompanied with a very heavy squall which in an instant broke our foreyard, and split our main staysail; the sailors with great difficulty got the top sails handed which freed us from danger, at the hazard of their own lives, as some of the fire fell away convenient to the Quarter Deck ..."[8]

Not all would successfully reach the end of the voyage across the Atlantic; unfortunately, the *James and Mary*, which arrived in Charles Town, South Carolina, on 18 October 1772 had lost five children on the voyage from Larne.[9] This was not an uncommon situation, and often children born in America were named after those who had been left behind in time and memory.

Appalachian children from Tennessee at the Oconaluftee Pioneer Farmstead, Cherokee, North Carolina.

Those who did successfully reach the New World would find difficult and hard work awaiting them, and some would fare no better than they had at home. However, many did increase their ownership of land and their wealth. Although they may have left the Old World behind them, the Ulster Scots would never leave their identity and culture behind. They carried grievances against the authorities in Ulster, often assisted in memory by their clergy. The historian Francis Joseph Bigger said that lessons learned on many an Ulster hillside were not forgotten in America, referring particularly to the American Revolution.[10] The experience of Scots in Ulster had not always been a happy one, dating back to the 1630s, and in the aftermath of the Williamite campaigns, dissensions broke out between the Presbyterians and the Church of Ireland Establishment again. The feeling of grievance suffered by the Ulster Scots – combined with opportunity across the Atlantic – led to further attempts to emigrate, as had unsuccessfully occurred less than a century before with the *Eagle Wing* in 1636. The *Eagle Wing* had departed from Belfast Lough in September 1636 and returned in November. In the proceeding century, however, the ships kept sailing until they reached the American coast, and thousands disembarked there.

As at least one author has pointed out, the desire to emigrate is not fundamentally part of the human condition.[11] It is never produced, as an anonymous eighteenth century pamphleteer, wrote "without great pangs and struggles". The emigration from Ulster shores to America was, therefore, produced through individual and communal consideration, struggle, incentive and anxiety. Included among the factors which were relevant at the time was the fact that rents were increasing, and this was significant for two reasons: although rising rents are usually a sign of general economic prosperity, the rise was such as to make it untenable for many, with one commentator suggesting a fourfold increase in Ulster rents in the 50 years prior to the American Revolution. Secondly, as rents increased, the economic stakes were heightened for the tenant. But the price of wheat and oats – the main crop in the north of Ireland – did not increase correspondingly. The result was that tenants, already having difficulty paying the rent, were put on the margin of being sustainable if there was a bad year for crops.

What was taking place appeared to be the bursting of an economic bubble. Prosperity within the linen industry helped push up rents, but in a bad economic year it was difficult to meet the cost of rent, which resulted in the lure of a new life elsewhere becoming simply irresistible for many. Thus, profits in the industry provided the means to emigrate and economic downturn the motive. Even those who had not the means to pay their passage did not find a bar on their voyage, as they could become indentured servants for a period of years. They paid for their voyage by signing an indenture which allowed the ship's captain or another party to sell their service to the highest bidder on the other side of the Atlantic when they docked.

Linen, whatever the impact, was central in the lives of many emigrants. Decline of the linen industry, was rapid after 1770, while severe famines in 1727 and 1740 also prompted an influx to America: indeed periods of high emigration levels from Ulster coincide with periods of economic depression in the eighteenth century.[12]

Other economic factors were important in the decision to emigrate, such as legislation on exports and imports to Ireland, and wool being permitted to be exported only to England. However, more important to the mass of tenant farmers was the fact that they were being asked to pay higher rents for land they knew they, or their sons, would never own. A major pull factor for the rural community, which Ulster essentially was, was that cheap and available land awaited them in the New World. The American colonies were lands of promise, where hundreds of acres could be obtained by families emigrating, and where the potential for economic advancement, through hard work, was obvious. Thus in 1774, 298 of 518 passengers from Belfast for Nova Scotia in Canada, interviewed on reasons for emigration, outlined that they had done so because of the desire to seek a "better livelihood and employment".[13]

The positive accounts of emigrants who wrote to friends is also significant. James Murray, an emigrant to New York, writing home to Tyrone in 1737, stressed the cheapness and fertility of lands, as well as better opportunities and wages for labourers and tradesmen.[14] Such messages, while maybe not determining factors, would have certainly been among those weighed in the balance. A further and highly significant factor was the role of the Presbyterian communal bloc. One Ulster historian asserts:

> "The strength and compactness of the presbyterian bloc and the reality of the hold of the presbyterian church over the daily lives of its members had an important effect ... just as coals burn more brightly when in contact with one another, so did resentment rise among the closely-knit and numerically dominant presbyterian congregations in north-eastern Ireland. If that resentment did not of itself produce emigration, it helped the waverers to make their decision and lived in many minds long after temporal hardships were forgotten. Emigration in such a community was likely to be as contagious as a fever in an insanitary town: it was liable to become a local epidemic if the minister sponsored it."[15]

It was, therefore, a combination of economic, political, social and religious factors that pushed and pulled these people, known as the Scotch-Irish, into leaving their homes for a new land, where, asserts Rory Fitzpatrick, they became "God's Frontiersmen"[16] and pushed back the frontiers as the pioneers of their race.

The position which many in the Presbyterian community took in relation to the emigration can be gauged from the sermon of Reverend James McGregor, prior to the 1718 emigration from Coleraine and environs. He said that his group was leaving for a number of reasons, these being to avoid oppression, to shun persecution, and to be enabled to worship God according to their consciences. Although his reasons were religious, others undoubtedly had material or commercial reasons for going. However, when the revolutionary years came, the most radical of communities were often the Ulster settlements, such as Hanna's Town and Pine Creek in Pennsylvania, and Mecklenburg in North Carolina, from which early declarations of independence from King George were issued. At Mecklenburg, a resolution was signed by those with Ulster Scots surnames including Abraham Alexander, Adam Alexander, Charles Alexander, Ezra Alexander, Hezekiah Alexander, John McKnitt Alexander, Richard Barry, William Graham, James Harris, Zaccheus Wilson, Benjamin Patton, Matthew McClure, Robert Irwin, John Phifer, John Queary, and Colonel Thomas Polk. It declared:

> "... we, the citizens of Mecklenburg County, do hereby dissolve the political bonds that have connected us with the mother country and absolve ourselves from all allegiance to the British Crown, abjuring all political connections with a nation which has wantonly trampled on our rights and liberties, and inhumanely shed the innocent blood of Americans at Lexington ..."[17]

The Mecklenburg Declaration caused some historical controversy after it was published in 1819, since some phrases seemed similar to the later American Declaration, and some believed that Thomas Jefferson had used it as a basis for

Hezekiah Alexander House, Charlotte, North Carolina, built in 1774. The Alexanders of Mecklenburg County were strong supporters of the American revolutionary cause.

Alexander Chesney's grave in Kilkeel, County Down. An American Loyalist during the War of Independence, he lost his lands and came back to Ulster.

the latter, something he denied. In turn, others claimed that the Mecklenburg Declaration had been unheard of before 1819. Only the witness testimony of 88 year-old Captain John Jack that he had delivered a declaration of independent to the Continental Congress abated the argument. The Mecklenburg Declaration and its promoters had, perhaps, a greater part in the subsequent Revolution than has been realised.

In Pennsylvania, Ulstermen were mustering prior to the main declaration, and it was said that the first shots fired in anger during the Revolution were fired on the Alamance River in North Carolina from Ulster Scot muskets.[18]

Not all Ulstermen were American patriots during the Revolution, some such as Alexander Chesney of Ballymena remained loyal to the Crown and fought for the

King. Chesney and others who remained loyal found to their cost that they had backed the wrong side. Chesney lost his property and was forced to return to his native land, where the government found him a position as a customs official in Kilkeel in County Down.[19]

Chesney was at the Battle of Kings Mountain in South Carolina among other engagements, and he was one of the many that the government believed would flock to the colours as soon as King George's troops had gained control of areas of the Carolinas. However, the plan by Lord Cornwallis to defeat the rebels in significant numbers and impact and thus encourage the loyalists to come out from cover went awry at Kings Mountain and Cowpens, two battles of major importance. Following the British defeats in these battles, it was realised that the southern colonies of America could not be subjugated.

Prior to the Battle of Kings Mountain, rough mountain men from Virginia, Tennessee, and North and South Carolina gathered at Sycamore Shoals, Tennessee, to march on the Redcoats, then in the Carolinas. They were sent off by a fiery sermon from Reverend Samuel Doak, whose roots were in County Antrim. Doak epitomises the stance of many of his clerical brethren at the time. Reverend William Martin also encouraged members of his congregation to form patriot militia, while Presbyterian churches generally were known as 'sedition shops' by the authorities. The link between militiamen and churches was highlighted at Indiantown in South Carolina, where the rebels there formed the Swamp Fox unit under Francis Marion, attacking and then retreating into the virtually impenetrable swamps. The authorities linked the church and the Swamp Foxes to the extent that they burned the church.[20] It did not impact on the rebels other than to increase their resolve.

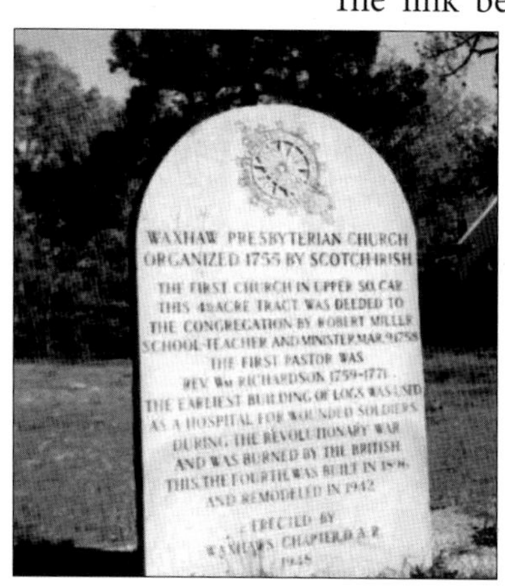

Waxhaw Presbyterian Church Marker highlights the events of the area during the Revolutionary War, when the church was burned down by King George's troops.

One element of the Ulster Scots character, the somewhat stubborn approach to life, was clearly visible in how the 'Upcountry' people were drawn into the war. There was a division between those on the coast in Charles Town, (now modern Charleston) who were predominantly Anglican, and the Upcountry settlers, Ulster Scots who were regarded by some as unruly and uncouth. Charles Woodmason, an Anglican cleric, had been sent as a 'missionary' into the so-called 'back country' of the Carolinas at one point, and returned with ringing condemnation of the people whom he had met:

> "[Their manners] are Vile and Corrupt – The whole country is in a stage of Debauchery Dissoluteness and Corruption – And how can it be otherwise? The people are compos'd of the Out Casts of all the other Colonies who take Refuge there".[21]

This antagonism was entirely mutual, not only in the personal but also the wider context. Thus, when those in Charles Town declared support for the American cause in the Revolution, the Upcountry people did not. This related much more to local prejudice than any political perspective. The Upcountry did not support the King either, but remained apart from it all, until one fateful day when American militiamen were ambushed by Tarleton's dragoons in the Waxhaws district. Banastre Tarleton's 'Green Dragoons' were notorious for giving no quarter and when the Virginians tried to surrender they were cut down without mercy. The wounded were nursed in the nearby Waxhaw Presbyterian Church by, among others, Elizabeth Jackson, mother of the future US president, and the response of the authorities was to burn the wooden church down. Afterwards, the Presbyterians in the area formed themselves into a militia and took up arms against the King. The support of the Scotch-Irish was crucial in areas such as the Upcountry, and they had soon mobilised in strength.

The legends surrounding some of those who took part in the Revolution remain strong in the United States. However, while the north may have had people like Paul Revere, the south's Ulster Scots community also had a few heroes. Andrew Jackson, who was a teenager at the time, was one of them. British troops were billeted on local families in the Waxhaws and at one point Jackson was ordered by an officer to polish his boots. The rebellious teenager refused and was struck in the face with a sword as a result, earning him the title of 'the Brave Boy of the Waxhaws'. Jackson's father died before he was born and he lost his mother and two brothers during the conflict. The Jackson family came to epitomise the sacrifice which was made during the American Revolution, although few would have to lose so much as the seventh president of the United States.

A historical marker highlighting Kate Barry near Walnut Grove, Spartanburg County, South Carolina.

One of the female heroes of the Revolution lived not a great distance from the Waxhaws. Catherine Moore Barry, known as Kate Barry, was married to a captain in the militia and lived at Walnut Grove, a beautiful plantation near the present city of Spartanburg. During the war Kate acted as a scout, keeping an eye to Redcoat movements and reporting back to her husband. She was active at the Battle of the Cowpens, at which the King's troops received their second major setback in the southern campaign. Walnut Grove also symbolises more than American opposition to the King; 'Bloody' Bill Cunningham, a well-known Tory, or sympathiser with the King, raided the Plantation, shooting one man dead inside the house, one of many acts across the area which earned him notoriety.[22]

There were many others who participated in the Revolution from the Ulster Scots community, and most of them were on the American side. The Wilsons, first generation Ulster settlers, provided seven sons for the American forces,[23] while at Mecklenburg in North Carolina, Ulster Scots as we have noted, particularly Alexanders, dominated those who were signers of the Declaration of Independence of May 1775, which predated the main American Declaration.[24] Andrew Porter, the son of General Andrew Porter of Londonderry, was born at Montgomery County in Pennsylvania and was one among the many of Ulster descent who played a prominent part in the Revolution. One observer from the nineteenth century, Judge Oliver Temple, could remark on the incident on the Alamance River in North Carolina in May 1771, when Scotch-Irish refused to comply with an order from the Governor to disperse:

> "The battle now became general, and lasted two hours, when the ammunition of the patriots failed, and they were driven from the field, stubbornly yielding to necessity. Of the royal troops, 9 were killed and 61 wounded; on the side of the patriots, 20 were killed, besides the wounded. This was four years before the battle of Lexington; and here was fired the first shot and fought the first battle by the Scotch-Irish in defense of popular rights on this continent."[25]

The same author could note that "These Scotch-Irish were everywhere tenacious and jealous of their rights."

It is a similar point which other authors have addressed in more recent times. The role of the Ulster Scots in the Revolution owed much to a view of history which placed a considerable emphasis on their dissent from the authorities but also saw them as a religiously faithful people. Thus it was that when a large force of rough mountain men set out from Tennessee to meet the forces of the Crown at Kings Mountain in South Carolina, they were sent off with that fiery prayer by Presbyterian minister Reverend Samuel Doak. A combination of strong faith, obstinacy and tenacity would lead them to achieve much during the revolution. They did not always win their battles, as some authors have pointed out, but they could be counted on to levy a heavy price on their opponents. They were, says one contemporary author, the people who, in the heat of battle, might bend but would never break.[26] Another author, US senator James Webb of Virginia, sees in the Ulster Scots, as alluded to in an earlier chapter, a historical characteristic of being 'born fighting' and never surrendering if the cause is right.[27]

An old postcard from Tyrone, Pennsylvania, one of the many locations in the United States to have an Ulster name.

The Town Hall in Antrim, New Hampshire, from an old postcard.

This situation goes some way to explaining the loss of identity of the Ulster Scots in America in the years after the Revolution. From time to time organisations have sprung up with the aim of highlighting their ethnicity, including the Scotch-

Irish Congress of America in the late nineteenth and early twentieth centuries. Largely, however, the crucial and formative role of the Ulster Scots in the American Revolution moulded them as Americans and their culture became the dominant culture of vast swathes of territory. The Bible Belt of the southern states today is probably the most prominent example.

Later Ulster and Irish Protestant emigrants into the USA, in the nineteenth and early twentieth centuries were small in overall numbers compared to the eighteenth century population, and in addition most of them appeared to settle in the north, which was dominated in terms of Ireland by Irish-American settlements of Roman Catholic emigrants, who did not always get on well with their Protestant counterparts. In the 1870s, for example, there were riots in New York when traditional Orange parades were held, and at one point the Governor of the State had to call out the National Guard to protect the Orangemen. The context in which this occurred was also related to the Draft Riots, during which Irish Americans had protested violently about plans to conscript them for service in the Civil War.[28] While the numbers of Irish-Americans might be strong in the cities of the north, the real bulk of the Irish emigration was largely a Presbyterian and certainly a Protestant one. The roll of Presidents with links to the British Isles generally shows clearly their domination, and they persistently interrelate to each other, although with few tangible signs that they saw themselves as ethnically linked. Andrew Jackson, seventh President, for example, had the Ulster Scot Carolinian John Caldwell Calhoun as his Vice President between 1829–32 (in true Ulster Scots style, they fell out …). Similarly, John Cabel Breckinridge, the descendant of a County Antrim emigrant family of Covenanter extraction, was Vice President under James Buchanan. Buchanan in turn had been US Secretary of State under President James Knox Polk and US Minister to Russia under President Andrew Jackson. Andrew Johnson, who entered the White House after the assassination of Abraham Lincoln, was in turn succeeded by Ulysses Simpson Grant, whose roots lay in County Tyrone. Such facts do not prove any conscious promotion of the ethnic community to which all belonged, but rather highlight the level of involvement of the Ulster Scots in political life in the United States.

A statue in Washington DC of President Ulysses Simpson Grant, whose ancestors were from County Tyrone.

Few would rise, of course, to high political office, as was obtained by Andrew Jackson, Andrew Johnston, Woodrow Wilson and others, although many would play prominent roles in local communities. Overall, they were well placed to do so because of the strength of numbers which they displayed. It has been estimated that the Scotch-Irish made up 14.3% of the total white population in 1790.[29] It is also suggested that settlement figures at this period equate to: New York 11%, Maryland 11%, North Carolina 13%, Virginia 14%, Pennsylvania 21%, South Carolina 24%, and Georgia 27% of the populations in those colonies.[30]

One historian, examining the history of part of Pennsylvania, notes:

> "The pioneer settlers in present Northampton County comprised a group of Scotch-Irish who, beginning in 1728, made a settlement at the forks of the Delaware in East Allen Township. Since William and Thomas Craig were prominent among these pioneers, the settlement was long known as the 'Craig settlement' or the 'Irish settlement', which by 1731 was sufficiently numerous to organise a Presbyterian church ... Somewhat later than the founding of the Craig settlement was the location of another group of Scotch-Irish in Lower and Upper Mount Bethel Townships in Northampton County, which was called 'Hunter's Settlement' after Alexander Hunter, a leader among them ... In 1738 it was large enough to organise Mount Bethel Presbyterian Church, and was developing rapidly. In 1752 there were six hundred Scotch-Irish in Northampton County".[31]

Robert W Ramsey in *Carolina Cradle: Settlement of the Northwest Carolina Frontier, 1747–1762* outlined the early Scotch-Irish settlements, including the earliest European speaking settlement so far from a navigable river. In 1749 there were at least 14 Scotch-Irish families there, and in the decade after March 1752 more than 100 families, most of them Ulster Scot, obtained lands there. They included Armstrongs, Strains, Douglas', Cowans, Locks, Galbraiths, Cunninghams, Dicksons and Stewarts. Many of these had come from Lancaster County, Pennsylvania, moving further south, often in search of better land. Among them were families from Coleraine, Derry and Donegal townships.[32] This movement of Ulster settlers from Pennsylvania resulted in the names of the counties they left being transported with them; in a great irony, Lancaster, York and Chester counties in South Carolina, known collectively as the Olde English District, were and are, heavily populated with Ulster Scots.[33]

Abbeville, South Carolina, was settled in particular by Ulster Scots from Monaghan and County Antrim.

South Carolina provides a good case study of the new life which awaited the Ulster dissenters when they crossed the Atlantic. The State of South Carolina today is quite small in US terms, comprising 31,113 square miles and being the smallest of the states in the Deep South and fortieth in size in the USA generally. However, in the seventeenth century the Province of Carolina comprised 850,000 square miles of territory, and most of the settled portions of what would become in the 1860s the Confederate States of America. The boundaries of 1665, established under Charles II, however, began to be whittled away as other settlements grew, among them North Carolina and Georgia. Landforms range from the coastal zone, on which Charles Town was situated to the Piedmont and the Blue Ridge mountains, the source of all three of the river systems which proved highly valuable to early settlers such as the Drumbo Witherspoons in allowing accessibility to areas further inland. In his chronicle Robert details the journey inland in an open boat, whose crew was an abomination to the pious County Down emigrants because of their "atheistical and blasphemous mouths". The boat journey along the Black River took the party to Potato Ferry, where they sheltered in a barn while the boat went further inland to Kings Tree with provisions and the men folk of the party set to the process of erecting basic houses, referred to by Robert Witherspoon as "dirt houses" or "potato houses".[34]

South Carolina was a rich province, dominated by Charles Town, but with other growing towns or settlements clustered around a country store. The road network, sometimes based on Indian trails, was also significant and important to early settlers and again the focus was on linking to Charles Town. The settlement was also the centre of culture in the colony, while pastimes in the Backcountry on Sundays included hunting and fishing, although it was said that South Carolina males did not need a special day for outdoor recreation. An occasional formal hunt would take place, but more often these were pastimes for individuals, family and friends. They could sometimes be dangerous pastimes, as was illustrated by the case of a sailor on the Stono River who decided to poke at an alligator for sport. He fell overboard and it was reported that the "Alligator made a good breakfast of him."[35]

Danger in South Carolina also lay in the climate and disease. Between 1670 and 1775 settlers faced some 59 major epidemics, including Yellow Fever, Smallpox, and Influenza. Malaria, while not necessarily a killer, could be fatal to young children and pregnant women and also weakened sufferers, making them more susceptible to a variety of other diseases and illnesses. In 1760 a smallpox epidemic affected 6,000 of Charles Town's 8,000 inhabitants, 730 of them dying as a result.

With a high infant mortality rate in the colony, the odds were against a woman seeing more than two of her children reach the age of 20. Perhaps because of such factors, families tended to be large. What was known as the Sickly Season (August to November, when temperatures were highest) was dreaded, adding as it did to the mortality rate. However, 'seasoning' was very important for settlers, and it was believed that if a person survived the first Sickly Season, he or she had a good chance of surviving thereafter.

Some relief was to be had living away from the coast and its mosquitoes, and in the Piedmont or Backcountry the temperatures were cooler, although still what Anglican preacher Charles Woodmason described as "excessive sultry" in September.

It was a climate with hot temperatures and humidity, and, in the winters, great cold. For those such as the Witherspoons it was a considerable change from the more moderate climate of County Down. Another change they would have found was the presence of slaves, which many families owned, and even churches used to hire out and thus obtain monetary return. Numbers of slaves varied, but in Charles Town the proportion to the white population was very high. In 1750 there were only 25,000 whites, around 10,000 of them adults, in South Carolina; by the end of the colonial period there were 75,000 black Carolinians, and their labours helped make the province the wealthiest colony in British North America.

Moore's Chapel Baptist Church, Spartanburg County, South Carolina, an area settled by County Antrim emigrants.

In terms of religious denomination a trend was already set by 1710 which would continue to develop. In that year Calvinists (Presbyterians, Huguenots and Congregationalists) comprised the largest religious grouping, with 45% of adherents, followed by Anglicans at 42.5% and Baptists at 10%, with 2.5% adhering to the Quaker religion. Scotch-Irish settlers founded 21 churches in the Backcountry in the early period, one of which, Long Canes Church, served 500 families and was probably the largest in the colony.

Although successful in establishing churches, Presbyterian insistence on university educated clergy made filling the pulpits difficult, and hence of the 21 only two had ministers. Baptists had no such criterion, however, leading to their predominance in many areas of the Upcountry, something which can still be traced in modern times.

Charles Woodmason, sent as a missionary to the Backcountry, was caustic about the behaviour of the Presbyterians there and set down to instruct the white "Savages" as he termed them, how to behave in church. His sermon "On Correct Behaviour in Church" had rules including: be on time, do not bring dogs to church, do not drink in church and when the Banns announcing a marriage were published not to make it a matter of sport.[36]

The colony, meanwhile, had other groups in addition to the White Savages of the Upcountry and the Black slaves. There were Native American tribes including the

Cherokee, who would fight the new settlers from time to time, often encouraged by others such as the French. Some tribes were happy to co-habit the territory, however, among them the Catawba tribes of York County in the Upstate.

The graves of the Ulster Scots McKeown family on their land near Blackstock, South Carolina.

Such was something of the kaleidoscope of South Carolina during the migratory period. Into this situation came many families from a very different landscape and background. Ulster settlers also made their way to many other parts of the American colonies, including New Hampshire, New York, Pennsylvania, Virginia, Tennessee, Georgia and elsewhere. Their assimilation into the American landscape is something which has often been viewed with bemusement by their modern cousins in Ulster, who feel that the identity of these settlers has somehow been lost. However to view matters in such a light is to miss the point somewhat: the early Ulster settlers became the first Americans and remained fervently loyal to the land they fought for. Francis Joseph Biggar may have been right in that they remembered lessons learned on Ulster hillsides when the Revolution came, but they also embraced a new identity which generally prevented them becoming hyphenated Americans. One contemporary Scottish author has provided the interesting assertion that one of the key elements in the success of Scots as empire builders across the world has been their ability to assimilate into the local culture.[37] Although there may be validity in this, the assimilation process is also something that many Ulster Scots in Northern Ireland lament upon when they feel the lack of support or indeed interest from their 'ethnic' community in the United States, compared to the strong sense of Irish-American identity, which comes across at an international level and has, unfortunately, in the past – from the nineteenth century onwards – in some cases reflected itself in support for violence on the *'aul sod'*.

One thing which remained a constant in both places, however, was the propensity to dissent from whatever the authorities said. In that propensity lay, if not the roots, then the nurturing, of the Ulster-American Revolution.

HISTORICAL QUOTES

The Witherspoon Chronicle

The account of Robert Witherspoon of the family emigration from Ulster in 1732, 1734, and 1736, reprinted by Williamsburg Presbyterian Church, 1981.

"May 8th, 1735 – My grandfather and grandmother was born in Scotland about 1670, they were cousins and both one sir name. His name was JOHN and hers was JANET. They lived in their younger years in or near Glascow and in 1695 they left Scotland and settled in Ireland in the County of Down and Parish of Drumbo, at a place called Knockbrackon, where he lived in good circumstances and in good credit until the year 1734 he moved with his family to South Carolina. We went on ship bord the 14th of September and lay wind bound in the Lough at Belfast 14 days. The second day of our sail my grandmother died and was interred in the region Ocean which was an affective sight to her offspring. We were sorely tossed at sea with storms which caused our ship to spring a leek. Our pumps were kept incessantly at work day and night. For many days our mariners seemed many a time at their wits end but it pleased God to bring us all safe to land, which was about the 1st of December.

But to return my grandfather and mother had 7 children, namely, JANET, DAVID, JAMES, ELIZABETH, ROBERT, MARY and GAVIN. Their daughter Janet was born in Scotland and was married to John Flemming in Ireland, they had a large family of children born in Ireland, they brought 7 with them to this place (viz Isabella, John, Elizabeth, James, Janet, Penelope and William). My uncle John died in the year 1750 in a good old age. My aunt Janet died 1761 in the 66th year of her age. My uncle David was married to Ann Pressley and brought to this place two children (viz Sarah and Janet). My uncle David died in the year 1759 in the 62nd year of his age. My aunt Anna died in the year 1772 in the 67th year of her age. My aunt Elizabeth was married to William James, they brought to this place four children (viz Mary, Janet, John and William). My uncle William died in the year 1750 in the 49th year of his age. My aunt Elizabeth died in the year 1750 in the 47th year of her age. My uncle Robert was married to Mary Stuart, and had two children (viz Mary and John). His first wife Mary died in Ireland. He married his second wife a short time before he left Ireland. Her name was Hester Jane Scot, and brought the aforesaid children to this place. My aunt Hester died in the year 1756 about the 40th year of her age. My uncle Robert died in the year 1758 in the 54th year of his age.

My aunt Mary was married to David Wilson and brought to this place two children (viz William and John). My uncle David died in 1750 in about the 50th year of his age. My aunt died in 1765 in the 58th year of her age. My uncle Gavin was married when he came over sea. It is to be remembered we did not all come in one ship, nor at one time. My uncle, my uncles William James and David Wilson and their families with Uncle Gavin left Belfast in the beginning of the year 1732 and Uncle Robert followed us in 1736.

As I said we landed in Charleston 3 weeks before Christmas. We found the inhabitants very kind. We staid in town till after Christmas and we put on board of an open boat, with tools and one years provisions, and one still mill. They allowed each hand upwards of 14 one axe, one Broad Hoe and one narrow Hoe. Our provisions was indian corn, rice, wheaten flours, beef, pork, rum and salt. We were much distressed in this part of our pasage, as it was the dead of winter we were exposed to the inclemency of the weather day and night and which added to the grief of all pious persons on board the atheistical and blasphimous mouths of our patrons and other hands.

They brought us up as far as potatou ferry. It turned us on shore, where we lay in Saml Commander barn for some time and the boat wrought her way up to the Kings Tree with the goods and provisions, which I believe was the first boat ever come up so high before. Whilst we lay at Mr Commanders, our men camp up in order to get dirt houses or rather like potatoe houses, to take their families to. They brought some few horses with them, what help they could get from the few inhabitants, in order to carry children, and other necessaries up, as the woods were full of water and most severe fronts, it was very severe of women and children. We set out in the morning, and got no farther that day than Mr McDonalds and some as far as Mr Plowdens, some to James Armstrongs and some to uncle William James. Their little cabins were as full that night as they could hold and the next day every one made the best they could to their own place, which was the 1st day of February. My uncle Gavin was married to Janet Wilson, sister to David and Robert Wilson (their fathers name was William, and their mothers name was Jane Witherspoon, sister to my grandmother) she died shortly after marriage and left no issue. He afterwards married Jane James, daughter of John James of Ox Swamp and brother to uncle William James, and had by her a large family of children. Uncle Gavin died in the year 1773 in the 61st year of his age. My aunt Jane died in 1774 in the 64th year of her age.

My fathers name was JAMES. He was my grandfathers third child and second son. He was born at the beginning of this present sentury and lived with his parents in Drumbow, until he was 25 years old, when he was married to my mother (in the 20th year of her age). Her name was Elizabeth McQuiod, daughter of Robert McQuoid. Her mothers name was Sarah Campbell. My grandfather, Robert McQuoid, died in Ireland in the year 1728 in the 86th year of his age. My grandmother died in Ireland also in the 80 year of her age. My father and mother settled in Grabo Parish near the Cunning Burn Mill, where they lived about nine years, when they sold their privileges there in order to embark for America. My father brought up his family to Grandfathers at Knockbracken about the 1st of May and left us there and went and wrought at the reed making trade until the 1st of September. They brought on ship bord four children (viz David, Robert, John and Sarah). Sarah died in Charleston and was the first buried at the Scotch meeting House Grave Yard. It was the 1st of February when we came to the Bluff. My mother and us children were still in expectation that we were comeing to an agreeable place, but when we arrived and saw nothing but a wilderness and instead of a fine timbered house, nothing but a very mean dirt house, our spirits quite sunk, and what added to our troubles, our pilot we had with us from uncle William James left us when he came in sight of the place. My father gave us all the comfort he could by telling us we would get all these trees cut down and in a short time they would be plenty of inhabitants, that we could see from house to house. Whilst we were at this, our fire we brought from Bog Swamp went out. Father had heard that up the river swamp was the Kings Tree, although there was no path, neither did he know the distance, yet he followed up the swamp until he came to the branch and by that found Roger Gordons. We watched him as far as trees would let us see and returned into our dollorus hut, expecting never to see him or any human person more, but after sometime he returned and brought fire. We were somewhat comforted but evening comeing on, the wolves began to howl on all sides, we then feared being devoured by wild beasts, having neither gun or dog, nor any door to our house. Howbeit, we set to and gathered fewel and made on a good fire and so passed the 1st night. The next day being a clear warm morning, we began to stir about but about mid day there rose a great cloud South west, attended with high wind, thunder and lightning. The rain quickly penetrated through between the powls and brought down the sand that covered over, which seemed to threaten to cover us alive. The lightning and claps of thunder were very awful and lasted a good space of time. I do not remember to have seen a much severer gust than that was. I believe we all sincerely wished ourselves again at Belfast but this fright was soon over and the evening cleared up comfortabel and warm."

Belfast News Letter account of the Revolutionary War in America, and particularly the Battle of Kings Mountain, December 19–22 1780.

"Several letters are received in town from South Carolina and Georgia, confirming the report of an action having happened with a large party of the rebels, at the extremity of that province, in which the Royalists gained a complete victory; a great number of prisoners were taken, and upon several of them were found to be similar pardons to those taken by Lord Cornwallis. The commanding officer in this engagement is reported not to have hesitated an instant upon the conduct he should pursue with those perjured traitors, and immediately ordered a certain number of them to be hanged.

The above party of rebels are the same which have been mentioned by Sir James Wright, the Governor of Georgia. In every one of his despatches sent to Government, he has constantly described them as keeping the whole province in continual alarm; as coming down in large bodies upon those estates situated at the extremities, driving off the cattle, plundering and burning the different planters habitations, and other like depredations. The defeat of this lawless banditti, it was hoped, would completely put an end to these depredations, and restore perfect tranquillity to the whole province of Georgia.

The dispatches from Quebec bring a confirmation of the success of Sir John Johnston, on the frontiers of New England and Albany, with the daily increase of his army.

Though no official accounts have been received from Lord Cornwallis of the disaster said to have happened to a body of Loyalists under Col. Ferguson in Carolina, yet we are sorry to hear, from particular private information, that there is too much reason to believe the fact; though the whole conduct of that business was totally against the opinion of the Commander in Chief."

Laurens, South Carolina

Petitions for Naturalization, Laurens County, South Carolina

Examples of citizens giving specific places of origin in Ulster. Recorded in Journals of the Court of Common Pleas and extracted by Mrs Bernice A George, Laurens (a copy of which can be viewed in the Public Record Office of Northern Ireland).

Samuel Austin, aged 60 years and a native of County Antrim (1821)
Alexander Austin Sr., arrived in Charleston from County Antrim in November 1804, along with James Austin Sr., James Austin Jr., and J. Alexander Austin Jr.

William Baxter, aged 26 in 1822, he was a native of County Antrim.

Robert Bell, from County Londonderry, aged 28 years in 1823, and had been a resident of South Carolina for around four years.

John Campbell, a native of County Antrim, who sailed from Portrush to America around 1820 and was 35 years old in 1825.

John Cannon, a native of County Donegal, aged 21, had been a resident of Laurens District about six months in November 1820.

David Graham, arrived in December 1788 from County Antrim.

Robertson Hamilton, who was born in County Tyrone at the end of the 18th century and filed for naturalization in November 1822.

Samuel Hamilton, who was a native of County Monaghan and who had arrived in Charleston in November 1816.

Andrew Kennedy and his family, natives of County Antrim, he was 40 years old in 1824, his wife Ann was 41. They had three children, Cunningham Moore Kennedy (17), born in Antrim, Isabella (14) born in Meath and John (13) born in Meath. They arrived in Charleston from Belfast in October 1823.

Rev. Alexander Kirkpatrick, arrived in Charleston from County Antrim in November 1816.

Thomas Kirkpatrick, a native of Londonderry, who sailed from Belfast to South Carolina in 1818 and was 28 years old in 1824.

Anthony McFaul (or McFall), native of County Antrim, aged about 26 years, had arrived in the US in November 1811.

Andrew Matthews, a native of the City of Londonderry, arrived in Baltimore in September 1818, moving to Columbia, South Carolina, in 1819, and taking the oath in Laurens in November 1823.

William Milligan, native of County Antrim, aged 60 years, resident of South Carolina for 20 years when he sought naturalization in 1823.

John Ranson, a native of County Monaghan, lived in South Carolina since 1818.

William Ranson, a native of County Monaghan, aged 36 in 1824, he had lived in South Carolina since 1812.

John Ross, a native of County Monaghan, lived in the USA since 1823.

Robert Sloan, County Antrim, arrived in Charleston January 7, 1800, and settled in Newberry for seven years, then moved to Laurens.

Alexander Stuart, petitioned April 16, 1806, stating that he was a native of County Antrim and had resided in the US for ten years and more, in South Carolina.

Samuel Thomb, a native of County Antrim, arrived in Charleston in June 1811 and settled in Laurens County.

Andrew Todd, a native of County Monaghan, who arrived at Charleston in 1816 and settled in Laurens County.

David Whiteford, from County Antrim, who filed naturalization papers in 1807 stating that he had been in South Carolina for around 17 years.

HISTORICAL FIGURES

Elizabeth Hutchinson Jackson

The wife of Andrew Jackson of Boneybefore, Carrickfergus, she had two sons in Ulster, Hugh and Robert, and her third son Andrew was born in the Carolinas, where the family made their home in the 1760s. When Hugh was four and Robert was two, and just before Andrew was born, their father, Andrew Senior died following an injury on their farm at the Waxhaws. Elizabeth Hutchinson, his wife, was left a widow, with two sons to raise and a third soon to be born.

Elizabeth's four sisters were also settled in the region, which was heavily populated with Ulster families: including the McKemey, Crawford and Lessley families. After Andrew's death, Elizabeth went to live with the Crawfords, her sister Jennet being married to James Crawford. Jennet suffered a disability and her sister looked after the eight Crawford children as well as her own three boys.[38]

Elizabeth Jackson statue, Waxhaws, South Carolina

During the American Revolution Elizabeth Jackson and other women in the Waxhaws became nurses, tending to wounded American soldiers. She would also be remembered, however, for an epic journey to a British prison in Camden, North Carolina, where she managed to have the freedom of her sons Andrew and Robert negotiated. Robert sadly died of smallpox not long after their arrival back in the Waxhaws. Hugh Jackson had already died of fatigue during the revolutionary campaign in South Carolina.

Elizabeth nursed her remaining son, but soon after left for Charles Town, where two of James Crawford's sons were sick on a prison ship. Elizabeth would never return, dying of a fever and being buried in an unmarked grave. When her son Andrew was President of the United States he made efforts to locate her remains, but unsuccessfully.

As a young boy, Andrew recalled sitting at his mother's knee and being told stories of his grandfather's participation in the siege of Carrickfergus and "the oppression by the nobility of Ireland over the labouring poor,"[39] but sadly little other references to what his mother imparted have been handed down through history. Her famous advice to her son to "Make friends by being honest, keep them by being steadfast" are a fitting testimony to an Ulster Scots mother. Elizabeth is commemorated by a statue at the Waxhaw cemetery in South Carolina, which notes her origins and her life in the region.

Charles Thomson

Charles Thomson was born of Ulster Scots parents in the townland of Gortrede in Maghera, County Londonderry, in November 1729. His mother died when he was ten years old and his father decided to emigrate to America with Charles and his brothers. Unfortunately tragedy would strike the family a second time when his father died during the sea voyage, leaving the boys – it is not quite clear whether there were three or four – as penniless orphans.

When they reached America the boys were to be separated, and Charles was taken charge of by a blacksmith in New Castle, Delaware, and educated in New London in Pennsylvania. An intelligent young man, in 1750 he became a tutor in Latin at the Philadelphia Academy and was also associated with Benjamin Franklin. When the American Revolution broke out, Charles Thomson was one of those actively involved in the Patriotic movement and he would become the secretary of the Continental Congress, serving for 15 years with unswerving dedication.

The first published version of the Declaration of Independence has Thomson's name as secretary and that of John Hancock, another Ulster Scot, as President of the Congress. Thomson was also active in foreign affairs and he and William Barton designed the Great Seal of the United States.

Thomson was not without critics, leading to one famous cane fight between himself and James Searle on the floor of the Congress, after the latter claimed he had been misquoted. It was said that the Maghera man had made enemies which prevented him winning a place in the new Government which was established after American Independence, and in July 1789 he resigned as secretary of the Congress and handed over the Great Seal. He spent the rest of his life working on a translation of the Bible and died in August 1824. The link with Ulster and the Declaration of Independence continues in that not only was it first written in the hand of the Maghera man, but it was also printed by John Dunlap, a native of Strabane in County Tyrone.

Alexander Chesney

The son of Robert Chesney or McChesney and Elizabeth Purdy, he was from Dunclug, Ballymena, and was born in September 1755. The family connection included Gillespie's, Fultons, Symontons and Pedens. Family members emigrated to Pennsylvania and South Carolina, and Chesney would follow this route, his parents and seven siblings setting sail on an emigrant ship from Larne in August 1772. One child, Peggy, who was eight months old, died of smallpox on the passage, but the remainder of the family arrived safely at Charles Town after a voyage of seven weeks and three days. They settled on lands at Grindal Shoals, on the north side of the Pacolet River in South Carolina.

When the Revolution broke out, Chesney showed sympathy to the Loyalists, and was captured by Patriots and forced to join them for a time, seeing some action at Charles Town, where he narrowly avoided injury. Returning home, he and around 200 others loyal to the Crown assembled when they heard that Charles Town had fallen to the British, and in June 1780 they reassembled at Bullocks Fork Creek, having heard that a force of American Patriots was intending to move against them. The company picked Chesney to be their commander and appear to have won some level of battle against their opponents. A few days later, Chesney and his men were put under the command of Major Patrick Ferguson, the British commander in the area, and continued to serve with him until the defeat of their forces at Kings Mountain on 7 October 1780, when he was Adjutant to Major Ferguson.

At one point Chesney was sent into an American camp on Cherokee Ford to obtain intelligence, and did so successfully, in an episode which would have cost him his life as a spy had he been detected. Following the American victory at Kings Mountain, Alexander Chesney was taken prisoner and treated badly. He was promised that he would not lose his property if he agreed to serve with the rebels for the period of one month and refused, being marched 150 miles almost naked as a result.

Chesney managed to escape and returned to Grindal Shoals, where he raised a company of militia which would take part in the second major battle of the region during the Revolution, Hanna's Cowpens in January 1781. Following the British defeat at Cowpens, Chesney is said to have returned home directly and took his wife and baby to the safety of the British lines at Charles Town. His wife would die, and his child was sent to Chesney's mother in the Piedmont region. He continued to serve the Crown, but his health declined and he returned to Ulster. Following the Revolution, Chesney lost his lands and property on account of his support for the King.

His loyalty was reflected in County Down, where he settled, and received a post as a customs officer. His house near Kilkeel was named Packolet (spelt differently than in South Carolina) in honour of his home across the Atlantic. He died there in January 1845 in the 88th year of his age.

He remains an interesting figure and a reminder of the divided loyalties which some of the Ulster Scots at least felt during the American Revolution.

Kate Barry

The daughter of Ulster emigrants to the Upcountry region of the Carolinas, Margaret Catherine Moore Barry was born in Ireland in 1752 and one of a family of ten children, two of them born in South Carolina. She was married as a teenager

The grave of Ulster Scot pioneer Kate Barry at Walnut Grove, Spartanburg County, South Carolina.

in 1767 to Captain Andrew Barry, whose family was also prominent in the region of Spartanburg County settled by County Antrim families. The couple would have 11 children.

During the Revolutionary War Kate Barry acted as a scout for her husband's militia, which was opposing the King's troops and those known as Tories – Americans who remained loyal to the Crown.

She would observe troop movements and then ride off to report to her husband, as well as conveying news to others. After the American victory at the Battle of the Cowpens, Kate rode from the nearby Tyger River shoals to a house 13 miles away where the anxious womenfolk of Nazareth Presbyterian Church were awaiting news of the outcome.

Kate often put herself in danger, as on one occasion when the Redcoats tied her up, lashing her because she would not tell them where her husband's militia was to be found.

On one occasion Bloody Bill Cunningham, one of the most notorious of the Tories in the area, attacked Walnut Grove and shot a wounded Patriot named Captain Steadman inside the Plantation house. He and two others shot near the Plantation House were the first people buried in the family cemetery at Walnut Grove.

Kate Barry's nephew was Senator William Taylor Barry, who served as Postmaster General under Ulster Scot President Andrew Jackson, and had served with Jackson in the war of 1812. He also became United States minister to Spain. The Walnut Grove plantation remained in the ownership of the family until 1961 when Thomas Moore Craig, the great great grandson of Charles and Mary Moore, gave it to the Spartanburg County Historical Association for restoration.

Today Kate Barry's grave is located in a quiet corner of the old Walnut Grove Plantation built by her Ulster ancestors.[40]

HISTORICAL TRAILS
SITES TO VISIT

Ulster American Folk Park, Omagh

The Pennsylvania farmhouse at the Ulster American folk park at Omagh, County Tyrone.

The Ulster American Folk Park at Omagh is an impressive facility, which tells the story of emigration from Ulster in the eighteenth and nineteenth centuries. An outdoor museum, it was established in 1976 to mark the bicentenary of the United States of America and includes many exceptional buildings recreating life in Ulster and on the American frontier. The park was built up around the original farmstead of Thomas Mellon, whose parents emigrated with him when he was five years old and made a new life in western Pennsylvania.

The Mellon family became extremely prominent in the business and commercial world and restoration of their Tyrone homestead was completed in 1968. Further work continued in the 1970s and since its opening in 1976 the park has grown rapidly, with original exhibit buildings dotted around the landscape near the visitor's centre.

Buildings include a Pennsylvania log barn, and an Ulster quayside, at which the visitor can step aboard an emigrant ship and experience the sights and sounds of life at sea. They step off in the New World and continue their journey through a very different architectural landscape. The park is also home to an emigration study centre, and an indoor exhibition on emigration.

One of the most impressive tourist attractions in Northern Ireland, the park is well worth a visit, but time should be allowed to fully appreciate everything on display, whether artifacts, exhibitions or living history.

American Memorial, Larne

The Memorial to the emigrants at Curran Park in Larne commemorates almost 300,000 Ulster Scots emigrants who set sail from 1717 onwards and found a new life and new fortunes in America. It was unveiled in 1993 by Professor Bobby Gilmer Moss of Blacksburg, South Carolina and is designed to show a family about to leave on an emigrant ship.

The first emigrant ship, the *Friends Goodwill*, set sail from Larne for Boston in May 1717, arriving in Boston harbour in September. The vessel carried 52 passengers, but unfortunately the passenger list has not survived.

The plaque on the memorial quotes Reverend WF Marshall, the Bard of Tyrone, who boasted that no other race in the United States could provide such a roll of honour as the Scotch-Irish.

The memorial is part of a heritage trail which highlights sites in the local area associated with prominent Americans including Presidents Theodore Roosevelt, Andrew Johnston, Vice President John Cabel Breckinridge, and General Sam Houston.

Jackson Cottage, Carrickfergus, the ancestral home of President Andrew Jackson.

Jackson Centre, Carrickfergus

The Jackson Centre commemorates the life and times of President Andrew Jackson, seventh President of the United States and the first President from Ulster stock. He was also the founder of the modern Democratic Party in the USA and is regarded as a hero of the common man. His father and mother emigrated from Boneybefore outside Carrickfergus in 1765, and settled in the Waxhaws region of the Carolinian Upcountry.

The Jackson centre is one of several small museums across Northern Ireland which commemorate Ulster-American Presidents. It consists of a fairly typical Ulster farmhouse of the period, with large open fireplace and small adjoining bedrooms. Although small, it gives something of a flavour of what life was like in rural Ulster in the eighteenth century, and includes displays on Jackson and his family. It is open by appointment and is operated by Carrickfergus Borough Council.

Adjacent to the Centre is the US Rangers Museum, which is an impressive centre of artifacts telling the story of the elite US Rangers unit, which was based in Carrickfergus during the Second World War.

The McConnell House at historic Brattonsville, South Carolina.

The school house at Brattonsville.

The plantation house at Brattonsville. The Bratton family were from Seskinore in County Tyrone.

Brattonsville kitchens.

Brattonsville, South Carolina

Located in the rural community of McConnells in South Carolina, Historic Brattonsville is a folk park based around the impressive plantation home of the Bratton family, who were originally from Seskinore in County Tyrone. There are many buildings in the park, including the McConnell farmhouse, a log cabin first built by the settlers, a schoolhouse, slave quarters and farm outbuildings.

Centre piece to the park, however, is the Plantation house of Colonel William Bratton, which provides an idea of what life was like for those at a higher level on the social scale than most.

The site was the scene for some of the filming of *The Patriot*, starring Mel Gibson, and gives an excellent idea of rural life in eighteenth and nineteenth century South Carolina.

The park includes a memorial to the Battle of Huck's Defeat, fought on 12 July 1780, during the American Revolution, and a re-enactment of the battle is held each year. Huck was a British officer whose unit was defeated by American patriots at the site, after they came in search of Colonel Bratton. There is also a stone in honour of Watt, the slave of Colonel William Bratton, placed there as a tribute by Bratton.

ENDNOTES

1 For example, Marshall, WF, in *Ulster Sails West* makes this assertion.

2 Jean Stephenson's *Scotch Irish Migration to South Carolina, 1772*, Washington: 1970, gives an excellent and detailed account of the migration and settlement patterns of those involved, including her own ancestors.

3 See, for example, Steen, Andee, *Stoneboro: An Historical Sketch of a South Carolina Community*, Spartanburg: 1993

4 Opie, John, in Williamson, JW, ed, *An Appalachian Symposium*, Boone, North Carolina: 1977, p115–116

5 Williamson, *op cit*, p116

6 William Moberg (1898–1973), wrote about Swedish rural society and its history, including Utvandrarna (*The Emigrants*) in 1949. Several of his novels have been turned into motion pictures.

7 'The Witherspoon Chronicle', as reprinted in Cooper, WJ, ed, *The History of Williamsburg Presbyterian Church*, Kingstree, South Carolina: 1981. The congregation was founded by the County Down emigrant group and remains an active church today.

8 Journal of John Blair, sailing on the *Sally of Savannah*, September 1791, held in the archives of the University of South Carolina.

9 Stephenson, *op cit*, p30

10 Bigger, Francis Joseph, *The Ulster Land War of 1770*, Dublin: 1910, p21

11 Dickson, RJ, *Ulster Emigration to Colonial America 1718–1775*, Belfast: 1988

12 See, for example, Leyburn, James, G, *The Scotch Irish, A Social History*, North Carolina: 1962, p159–160

13 Dickson, *op cit,* p16

14 Dickson, *op cit,* p17–18

15 Dickson, *op cit*, p5

16 Fitzpatrick, Rory, *God's Frontiersmen*, London: 1989

17 The Mecklenburg Declaration of May 1775 is the best known, being issued prior to the main Declaration of Independence. See Alexander, JB, *The History of Mecklenburg County from 1740 to 1900*, Charlotte, North Carolina: 1902

18 Fitzpatrick, *op cit*

19 Gilmer Moss, Bobby, *Journal of Capt. Alexander Chesney: Adjutant to Maj. Patrick Ferguson*, South Carolina: 2002

20 *Indiantown Presbyterian Church 1757–1957*, South Carolina: 1957

21 Woodmason, Charles; Hooker, Richard, J, ed, *The Carolina Backcountry on the eve of the Revolution*, North Carolina: 1953, p80

22 Today Walnut Grove is a historic monument in the care of the State of South Carolina. The Moores, who built it, were from County Antrim or County Down.

23 See, for example, Kennedy, Billy, *Women of the Frontier*, South Carolina: 2004

24 Mecklenburg Declaration signatories included James Harris, Richard Barry, Ezra Alexander, Zaccheus Wilson, Charles Alexander, Benjamin Patton, Matthew McClure, Robert Irwin, William Graham, Hezekiah Alexander, Adam Alexander, Thomas Polk, Abraham Alexander and John McKnitt Alexander.

25 Temple, Oliver, *The Scotch-Irish in East Tennessee*, Scotch-Irish Society of America third congress proceedings, Nashville: 1891, p167

26 Buchanan, John, *The Road to Guilford Courthouse*, New York: 1997

27 Webb, James, *Born Fighting: How the Scots-Irish shaped America*, New York: 2004

28 See, for example, Durney, James, *The Mob: The History of Irish Gangsters in America*, Naas: 1997, p44–51

29 See Wright, Louis, B, *The Cultural Life of the American Colonies*, New York: 1962

30 See, for example, Doyle, David, Noel, *Ireland, Irishmen and Revolutionary America*, Dublin: 1981

31 Dunaway, Wayland, *The Scotch-Irish of Colonial Pennsylvania*, originally published in 1944, Baltimore edition, 2002

32 Robert W Ramsey in *Carolina Cradle: Settlement of the Northwest Carolina Frontier, 1747–1762*

33 This area owes much to the settlement of five shiploads of Ulster emigrants led by the Covenanter cleric, Reverend William Martin, in 1772

34 Witherspoon, *op cit*

35 Edgar, Walter, *South Carolina, A History*, Columbia: 1998, p173

36 Woodmason, *op cit*

37 See Billy Kay, 'The Scots Ower the Sheuch', in Wood, ed, *Scotland and Ulster*, Edinburgh: 1994

38 James, Marquis, *The Life of Andrew Jackson*, New York: 1937

39 Rouse, Parke, Jr., *The Great Wagon Road*, Richmond, Virginia: 1995, p138–9

40 See Kennedy, Billy, *Women of the Frontier*, Belfast, 2004

Chapter Nine

STANDING TOGETHER: Ulster Scots and the Home Rule crisis

Ulster Volunteers on parade in Larne with some of the rifles landed on the Ulster coast in April 1914 during the Third Home Rule crisis.

On a September Saturday in 1912, tens of thousands of Ulster Protestants gathered in towns, villages, cities and hamlets, to express their opposition to governmental plans for a measure of devolution, or Home Rule, for Ireland. They signed a document which was a direct descendant of the Scottish Solemn League and Covenant of 1638. This opposition was largely based on fears and concerns as to their future as a cultural community under Home Rule, in an Ireland which they worried would be dominated by the Roman Catholic Church. The majority of those in the southern part of Ireland were Catholics, while the majority in Ulster were Protestants. For example, in modern terms, the Protestant population in Northern Ireland comprises 53% of the overall, while on an all-island basis the figure is reduced to 19%.[1] On 28 September 1912, unionists held church services and processions, and signed the Ulster Covenant, a clear return to the cultural and historical legacy from within the psyche of the Ulster Scots. It was also a significant underlining perhaps that the ethos of the Scottish Plantation settlement of the seventeenth century had permeated the overall Plantation population, the other major component of which was English.

Just as the original seventeenth century Solemn League and Covenant in Scotland was signed at a time when those concerned saw themselves as having to stand up for their faith and beliefs in a situation where they were beleaguered in the face of the authorities, a similar situation pertained in the Ulster of 1912. Unionists felt that their culture and faith systems were endangered, and they responded in historical fashion, thanks to the efforts of Thomas Sinclair, a liberal Ulster Scot

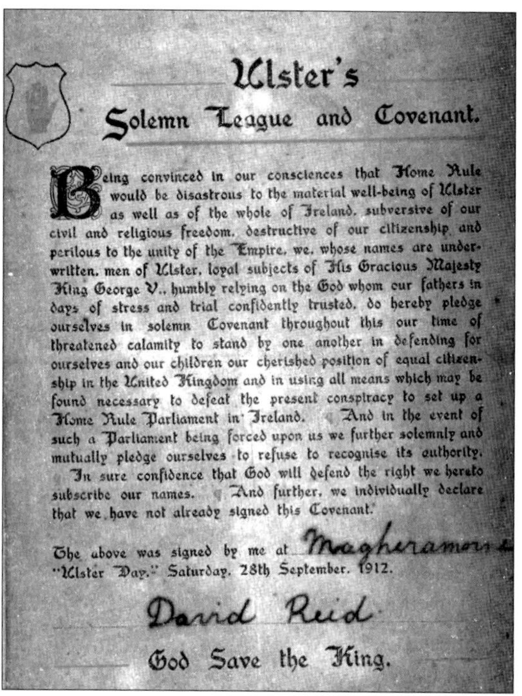

Ulster's

Solemn League and Covenant.

Being convinced in our consciences that Home Rule would be disastrous to the material well-being of Ulster as well as of the whole of Ireland, subversive of our civil and religious freedom, destructive of our citizenship and perilous to the unity of the Empire, we, whose names are underwritten, men of Ulster, loyal subjects of His Gracious Majesty King George V., humbly relying on the God whom our fathers in days of stress and trial confidently trusted, do hereby pledge ourselves in solemn Covenant throughout this our time of threatened calamity to stand by one another in defending for ourselves and our children our cherished position of equal citizenship in the United Kingdom and in using all means which may be found necessary to defeat the present conspiracy to set up a Home Rule Parliament in Ireland. And in the event of such a Parliament being forced upon us we further solemnly and mutually pledge ourselves to refuse to recognise its authority. In sure confidence that God will defend the right we hereto subscribe our names. And further, we individually declare that we have not already signed this Covenant.

The above was signed by me at Magheramorne "Ulster Day." Saturday. 28th September. 1912.

David Reid

God Save the King.

The Ulster Covenant, the document drawn up in opposition to Home Rule, drew heavily on the old Scottish Covenant of 1638. This one was signed at Magheramorne Presbyterian Church, County Antrim, by local man David Reid, who later took part in the 1914 gun-running.

whose roots went back to the original Covenants.[2] On Covenant Day a total of 471,414 signed the Covenants, women signing a separate declaration which contributed to that total. The Covenant was signed in Greyfriars Churchyard in Edinburgh, where the original Covenant had been signed in February 1638 and at many other locations including Dublin, where 2,000 men of Ulster extraction signed. It was even signed on a liner taking emigrants to Canada. The signing was backed up by support from others in England and Scotland, who amassed signatures on a British Covenant, supporters of which did not have to be born in Ulster.

The signatures on the men's Covenant were later to be used to recruit members of the Ulster Volunteer Force, which was under the control of the Ulster Provisional Government and was founded in 1913. Just over a year after its formation, the Ulster Volunteers were to show the Liberal Government in London that their opposition to Home Rule was neither bluff nor bluster. In his autobiography the author George Buchanan recalled his memories of life in the rectory at Kilwaughter outside Larne, where his father was incumbent in 1914.[3] His mother went into Larne on the evening of Friday 24 April that year to enjoy a theatrical performance. When she emerged from the building where the event took place, however, she found that she was witnessing another drama. The street was lined by members of the Ulster Volunteers, and among them she spotted a pedlar who, Buchanan informs us, had often called at the Rectory. Not surprisingly, the rector's wife asked him what was going on. "Heavy with pride in his duties," says Buchanan, "he says slowly: 'Go you home to bed and ask no questions'. She continues to ask him and he concedes: 'All you need to know is that the Ulster Volunteers are doing their duty. We're out all over the country tonight'..." On her way back to the rectory, Mrs Buchanan passed a stream of cars and lorries, heading with full headlights towards Larne Harbour.[4]

An old postcard showing an impression of the *Clyde Valley* arriving in Larne in April 1914.

In his autobiography, Buchanan recalls:

"And all through the night, on the road beside the rectory, we can hear the cars and we can see the trees constantly illuminated by their headlamps. In the morning it is understood that an extraordinary event has occurred. A ship from Germany landed a cargo of arms at Larne Harbour. The police barracks were surrounded and the telephone wires cut. Already the arms have been distributed to points throughout the province, some being concealed under chancel floors in Protestant churches. From this night the rebellion passes beyond the stage of play acting ..."

The landing of a cargo of thousands of rifles, bayonets and ammunition was part of the concluding chapter of a drama which had started much earlier and was written because of the perceived danger which Home Rule posed the unionists of Ireland, most particularly of Ulster. It was, perhaps, poetic justice that the ship which would be used to land the rifles in Ulster was named the *Clyde Valley* – even in this coincidental manner the links between Ulster and Scotland were being emphasised.

In their response to the perceived danger of Home Rule, Ulster unionists were every bit as radical in their outlook and actions as their ancestors had been in 1798. The common denominator in both events, which appear on the face of it to be diametrically opposed politically, is the sense of willingness to oppose the establishment. In 1798 the insurgents were prepared to take up arms against the government of the day. In 1914 the establishment was the Liberal Government and the Ulster unionists were signalling that they were a resilient and tough bunch to deal with. This time, however, the response to exterior political prospects was one of defence rather than attack.

The gravestone of Captain Andrew Agnew at Glynn cemetery in County Antrim. Captain Agnew played a key role in the 1914 gun-running.

The story begins in the nineteenth century, when the debate over Home Rule started almost as soon as the Act of Union united Ireland with the rest of Britain. By 1886, when a form of devolution was proposed by Gladstone, the arguments had already been well rehearsed. Although not all Protestants were unionists, the vast bulk were despite any misgivings they might have over the landed unionist elite which effectively governed them. At one point, in 1905, the Independent Orange Institution, representing an alliance of Protestant working class in Belfast and tenant farmers in North Antrim, appeared to be prepared to countenance Home Rule, a stance which owed much to resentments over land reform, and the position of conservative landlords within the official Orange Institution. However, by the time of the Third Home Rule crisis and certainly in 1912–14, any differences of opinion were, largely, although not entirely, subsumed in the sense that more was to be lost than gained by having a Dublin parliament govern Ulster.

In terms of reasons for opposition to Home Rule, James Loughlin, in his study *Gladstone: Home Rule and the Ulster Question 1882–93*,[5] provides a useful barometer of views from 1886. The main themes of opposition in speeches by Ulster Unionists have been analysed by the author and show that the main concerns were religious, economic and cultural. The issue of nationalists and the Roman Catholic priests, who were seen as largely controlling them at the time, persecuting the Protestant and loyal community was mentioned most of all, closely followed by Home Rule being inconsistent with imperial integrity, and relegating Ulster loyalists to representation by a subordinate parliament, thus depriving them of their imperial heritage and reducing their status in the world. Other issues which were prevalent included that Nationalists were perceived as having no respect for law and order, that their policies, such as protectionism, would mean social and economic ruin for Ireland, Home Rule would mean betrayal of Ulster loyalists, that an impoverished Irish assembly would not have the resources to finance the social and economic regeneration of Ireland, and that taxes in a Home Rule Ireland would concentrate on the area of greatest prosperity and industry – the north.

In 1893, when addressing a unionist meeting in the Orange Hall at Magheramorne, County Antrim, Reverend RC Oulton, of the Parish of Glynn, outlined his view that Home Rule would lead to higher taxation and was also to be given into the control of nationalist leaders such as Michael Davitt, who were in favour of land nationalisation by the state. "Suppose then, that a farmer with 20 acres were obliged to divide his land with every shoemaker, tinsmith, or labourer, how would he like it then?" he had asked somewhat rhetorically. Some years later, addressing a meeting at Chester Avenue Presbyterian Church in Whitehead, in January 1912, Reverend William Patterson, minister of May Street Presbyterian Church in Belfast, outlined his objections to Home Rule, which could be summarised as follows: the concern that all the prosperity which Ireland had obtained had been under the Union; worries that Home Rule meant Rome Rule, effective control of Ireland by the Roman Catholic Church of the time; the concern that Home Rule would bring financial ruin to Ireland, and that it would mean ultimate separation from the British Empire. Thus we can see that the arguments against Home Rule remained somewhat constant over the years from 1886 to 1914.[6]

Into this situation came the realisation by 1914 that the Liberal Government, including Winston Churchill who was lambasted by genteel elderly ladies at Larne Harbour a few years before chanting "Dun-dee traitor"[7] at him, appeared intent on confronting the Ulster unionists. This was on the basis of the mistaken belief that they were bluffing about fighting against Home Rule. Alongside, another battle was being waged, this one that of propaganda. Unionist associations formed twinning relationships with their counterparts in England and Scotland, sent speakers, canvassed at elections, and brought delegations to Belfast. One example comes from the Larne Unionist Club in 1911, which had linked up with the Newington Unionist Club in Edinburgh "for aggressive work in the campaign against Home

Rule."[8] Monaghan Unionist Club also had links with like-minded individuals in Scotland, being twinned with the constituency of Ross in the north of the country. At a meeting in the Hand and Pen Orange Hall in Monaghan in March 1912 one speaker, ME Knight of Clones, highlighted fears among the Protestant community in Monaghan that they would be swept aside politically, highlighting that there had not been a single Unionist on the County Council for years.[9] This sense of isolation is significant when we consider that the population of Northern Ireland in recent times is 53% Protestant and 44% Roman Catholic, that for the island overall being 19% and 75% respectively. The Ulster Scots in the Home Rule debate looked naturally to the east for support. The propaganda war they waged appears effective and impressive.

The old gunrunner *Clyde Valley* coming into Larne in 1968 (left) and in Nova Scotia just prior to the ship's voyage across the Atlantic to Northern Ireland (right).

At the root of it all was the fear that the question would not be settled on the doorsteps of Doncaster or Midlothian. In Ulster the Volunteers, numbering around 80,000, continued to drill in Orange Halls and private estates, supported by the knowledge that in England and Scotland support was being expressed through 'athletic clubs'. For example, in February 1914, it was reported that the Protestant Hall in Cowcaddens was not large enough to accommodate the Glasgow representatives of such clubs, while at Hamilton the local Volunteers were reviewed by Colonel Hickman, MP for East Wolverhampton and a prominent loyalist supporter.[10] That summer Hickman and General Sir Reginald Pole-Carew reviewed the Glasgow Volunteers, including cycling and signaling corps at Beechwood Park, the ground of Strathclyde Football Club. Pole-Carew told those present:

> "He knew there were many amongst them who were brothers in blood to those whom they were training themselves to help. He also knew that they being nearer to Ulster, were perhaps able to understand the question better than some of those in England."[11]

Undoubtedly the strong base which helped cement support in parts of Scotland for Ulster unionists included the Orange Order, which was very strong in Scotland, and the numbers of people in Scotland who were either first generation Ulstermen and women or their children. This aspect was brought home to me in 2008, while attending the Orange demonstration in the east of Scotland, at Grangemouth, when my host explained how he and his wife's antecedents had come across from County Antrim to find work, in that instance shale mines near Broxburn being what attracted many Ulster exiles. It would seem that the combination of Ulster blood connections and Orange Order membership were the key factors in the organised Scottish support for Ulster unionists. Efforts to appeal directly to Presbyterian links were not immediately successful, as one contemporary author has noted, "If Scottish support for Loyalist resistance to Home Rule was less than full-blooded in the years of the first two Home Rule Bills, the ambiguity remained during the period of the third".[12] There was clearly an attempt not only to focus on kinship but also on the value of the British Empire to Scots, as was the case when Captain Craig MP addressed a meeting at Hopetoun near Edinburgh in August 1912:

> "He said he had come there to appeal to his fellow-countrymen in that great Scottish constituency to have nothing to do with the great betrayal of their kith and kin across the Irish Sea … he felt confident that as the time drew nearer when the fatal step had to be taken, men of the North would stand by men of the North, and kinship would prove dearer than any political tie."[13]

Interestingly, in a contemporary community context, the author was among those involved in efforts to have a Church of Scotland clergyman become involved in commemorations for the first Presbyterian minister in Ireland (who was a previous incumbent in Drymen near the shores of Loch Lomond) in 1993. He found polite initial reticence in doing so, while efforts to enlist the support of the Church of Scotland in assisting development of cross-channel links proved fruitless; perhaps symbolic of the concerns which some Scots in the Kirk have about their co-denominationalists in Ulster in modern times.

In the context of the third Home Rule crisis, meanwhile, amid the drilling and organisation, one thing remained clear in Ulster. Dummy wooden rifles were being shouldered by most of the Ulster Volunteers and they would be of little consequence against the might of the army and navy.

Two factors developed to change this situation. Firstly, in 1914 the government did attempt to move troops into Ulster, it would appear with the aim of introducing martial law and confronting the unionists. However, what occurred instead was a major incident in modern Irish history, known as the Curragh Mutiny, when British army officers at a senior level made clear that they were unwilling to act against those seen by them as loyal subjects of the King and whose wish was to remain part of the United Kingdom.[14] The clear indication that some officers at least could not be depended on put the government in a quandary and may have effected future thinking: the issue of Home Rule for Ireland, it should be remembered, was one that divided the whole United Kingdom (when Lord Carson arrived in Liverpool in September 1912, after signing the Ulster Covenant, he was welcomed by an estimated crowd of 150,000 people).[15]

The second factor was the decision by the unionists to purchase a consignment of weaponry. This was planned by the shadowy Ulster Military Committee, which included figures such as Sir Samuel Kelly, the shipping magnate. In January 1914 the approach was made to Major Fred Crawford, already engaged in small-scale gun-running, and he was asked to undertake a much larger enterprise. The plans were duly set in motion. Weapons were purchased in Hamburg. A ship named the *Fanny* had been bought at Bergin in Norway. A seafarer named Captain Andrew Agnew from Magheramorne, County Antrim, was to be her captain on an epic voyage into the pages of history.

The ship was almost seized by the Danish customs, while in their territorial waters, which suspected that her cargo was weaponry. Officials took her papers as a precautionary measure, promising to return for a further inspection the next morning. The next day, with the benefit of a coastal mist, she set sail without her papers, was the object of search on the high seas, and was headline news on 1 April 1914 because it was believed, as the Reuters news agency put it, "the rifles are consigned to Ireland."[16] Since the ss *Fanny* was obviously a foreign vessel, a replacement was sought to bring her cargo into the Ulster coast. The *Clyde Valley*, a collier for sale in Glasgow and a familiar visitor to Belfast Lough, was purchased for £4,500 on the recommendation of Sir Samuel Kelly. She tied up alongside the Norwegian ship at the Tusker Rock in the Irish Sea and overnight the cargo was transferred while other vessels sailed past.

Donaghadee harbour in County Down, where guns were also landed.

There had been a number of plans for landing the guns. At a crucial point when, because of the publicity surrounding the event, Major Crawford was ordered to return with the ship to the Baltic, he threatened to ground the ship at Ballyholme and have the local Volunteers discharge her. This was judged too risky an operation and one likely to lead to failure. There was also a suggestion that the ship should sail to Belfast, where Volunteers would arrive by train, each leaving with a rifle apiece. Another option was to land most of the cargo at Larne, which would be sealed off, and to which the Motor Car Corps of the Volunteers would congregate. This was the plan which came to fruition, weapons also being distributed by the *Clyde Valley*, *Innismurray* and *Roma* to Bangor, Donaghadee and Belfast.

On 20 April an order went out to the Motor Car Corps from General Sir William Adair, County Antrim Divisional Commander of the Ulster Volunteers, detailing:

> "in accordance with your kind agreement to place a motor car at the disposal of the Provisional Government in a case of necessity it is absolutely necessary that your car should arrive at Larne on the night of Friday–Saturday 24th–25th instant at 1.00am punctually but not before that hour, for a very secret and important duty."[17]

The vehicles which would make the journey towards Larne that night would come from far across the province also.

When one major convoy of cars made its way through Ballyclare that night, it was recalled that locals ran to one another's houses, afraid that war had broken out.[18] The late Lily McKee, then a child at Larne Harbour, recalled how she stood and watched the long line of headlamps come down into the town from the hills that night, while the Harbour Volunteers, standing in the streets, had tea and sandwiches made by the womenfolk of the district.[19] It was an event unlike any other witnessed in Ulster, given the use of motorised transport.

The local newspaper correspondent of the time, TL Price, who witnessed the entire events of that night in the town, detailed:

> "... a vast transport of hundreds of motor cars, lorries and wagons drawn from their various centres came into the town ... It was an amazing sight to see this huge procession of cars nearly three miles in length descending upon the town with all their headlights ablaze. The people flocked to their doors as the seemingly endless procession filed past in the direction of the harbour."[20]

Price was, it was noted in an article in 1943, given a tip-off about events the day before (when, ironically, he was in Dublin) and saw everything that took place on the Larne seafront that night. The gun runners regarded the editor of the *Larne Times* as "a privileged spectator"[21].

The *Daily Express*, writing of the extraordinary events that night, likened the gun-runners to the participants in the Boston Tea Party:

> "On Saturday morning, in defiance of the Government, the Ulster Covenanters imported a vast quantity of arms and ammunition, deliberately hindering the police and the customs officers in the execution of their duty, in their turn deliberately defying the British ministry".[22]

The *London Times* could remark of the Volunteers that "Their orderly restraint compels the admiration of even their opponents ..."[23] while the *Larne Times* predicted that the event would find a permanent place in the history books and said it was "a deed of derring-do almost impossible of belief".[24]

On 30 May 1914, the *Weekly Telegraph* reported considerable activity in Fermanagh, where members of the Motor Car Corps of the Ulster Volunteers had been engaged in moving what was believed to be a large quantity of rifles and ammunition across the county. In one instance the police attempted to gain entry to private property but were told by a large body of men that they would not be permitted to do so, a sign that the Volunteers would not easily permit the seizure of their weapons. The legacy of the gun-running was clear; Carson and his Volunteers were not bluffing, and they had the vocal and often visible support of their cousins across the North Channel in Scotland, many if not most of them associated with the Orange Order there. For example, studies have found that throughout the nineteenth century and into the twentieth century, the membership of the Order in Scotland remained predominantly based on Irish Protestant immigrants. The course of events was changed by the arrival of the First World War. The Ulster Volunteers formed the 36th Ulster Division, and shed their blood like water, as John Buchan put it, for the freedom of the world.

A mural depicting the 36th Ulster Division at the Battle of the Somme in July 1916. The Division was created from the ranks of the members of the Ulster Volunteers founded by Carson and Craig in 1913.

In the late 1950s and 1960s obituaries started to appear of some of the gunrunners of 1914, among them David Bill of Templepatrick. Bill was 84 when he died in 1968. He had been a member of the Premier Unionist Club at Templepatrick, had carried the banner of the Club into the arena at Balmoral during the great Covenant Rally there in 1912, and later become a prominent figure in the Ulster Volunteer Force. Bill had taken a prominent part in the Larne gun-running, and was later involved after the War in the B Specials, serving as a District Commandant.

There was continuity in all of this. When David Bill died in 1968 the real legacy of his efforts was that Ulster remained part of the United Kingdom. David Bill, Orange and Presbyterian, had much in common with the fictitious Islandmagee farmer of 1914, Liberal and Presbyterian, who supposedly declared in his Ulster Scots tongue the night after the gun-running:

> "The mornin, when telt what happened, a felt it mair and mair
> That maybe – aye, just maybe – the buddies may be richt."[25]

HISTORICAL QUOTES

"Coming out from an amateur theatrical performance in Larne, my mother finds the main street lined with members of the volunteer force. She recognises and questions a pedlar who has often called at the rectory. Heavy with pride in his duties, he says slowly: 'Go you home to bed, and ask no questions.' She continues to ask him, and he concedes: 'All you need to know is that the Ulster Volunteers are doing their duty. We're out all over the country tonight.'

On her way home she passes a stream of cars and lorries, with full headlights, that are racing in the direction of the harbour.

And all through the night, on the road beside the rectory, we can hear the cars and we can see the trees constantly illuminated by their headlamps.

In the morning it is understood that an extraordinary event has occurred. A ship from Germany landed a cargo of arms at Larne Harbour. The police barracks were surrounded and the telephone wires cut. Already the arms have been distributed to points through the province, some being concealed under chancel floors in Protestant churches.

From this night the rebellion passes beyond the stage of play-acting …"

George Buchanan, *The Green Seacoast: An Autobiography*, London: 1959

Address on Ulster Day, 1912, by Reverend FJ MacNiece, St Nicholas Church, Carrickfergus, reflecting Protestant views on a Home Rule parliament.

"All sorts and conditions of men are united together; but the movement owes its strength largely to the fact that it is democratic. The working men who oppose Home Rule do not at all think alike on social and political questions. They know how to differ among themselves on questions affecting labour, wages and hours of labour. But they have a common conviction that Home Rule would be a death blow to the industrial life of Ireland. In this opposition they are joined by the farmers of Ulster, and may I add of Ireland …

There was a large emigration from Ulster to America. Many of those who went, carrying with them bitter recollections of the wrong done to them, were Ulster Presbyterians. In the American War of Independence many Ulster Presbyterians fought on the American side. Their brethren who remained in Ulster were then bitterly hostile to England – discontented and disloyal. The Ulster Presbyterians of our day are the descendants of men who suffered many a wrong, and who as a consequence were disaffected. But the Act of Union of 1800 had made a change. The Presbyterians of Ulster have experienced the benefits and blessings of the Union, and under it they have helped to build up great industries … when we think of the Presbyterians of a past time who were hostile and disloyal, and think of the Presbyterians of our own day, who under other circumstances are passionately loyal to the constitution of the United Kingdom, surely it is an argument for the belief that the policy that has affected such a change in them can effect a like change in others.

… has any Parliament predominantly Roman Catholic ever done justice to a Protestant minority? Is justice done today to the Protestant minority in Quebec? Was justice done to the Protestant minorities in Italy, France, Spain, so long as their governments were predominantly Roman Catholic? ..."

The Ulster Covenant, 1912 and the Women's Declaration

"BEING CONVINCED in our consciences that Home Rule would be disastrous to the material well-being of Ulster as well as of the whole of Ireland, subversive of our civil and religious freedom, destructive of our citizenship, and perilous to the unity of the Empire, we, whose names are underwritten, men of Ulster, loyal subjects of His Gracious Majesty King George V., humbly relying on the God whom our fathers in days of stress and trial confidently trusted, do hereby pledge ourselves in solemn Covenant, throughout this our time of threatened calamity, to stand by one another in defending, for ourselves and our children, our cherished position of equal citizenship in the United Kingdom, and in using all means which may be found necessary to defeat the present conspiracy to set up a Home Rule Parliament in Ireland. And in the event of such a Parliament being forced upon us, we further solemnly and mutually pledge ourselves to refuse to recognize its authority. In sure confidence that God will defend the right, we hereto subscribe our names.

And further, we individually declare that we have not already signed this Covenant.

We, whose names are underwritten, women of Ulster, and loyal subjects of our gracious King, being firmly persuaded that Home Rule would be disastrous to our Country, desire to associate ourselves with the men of Ulster in their uncompromising opposition to the Home Rule Bill now before Parliament, whereby it is proposed to drive Ulster out of her cherished place in the Constitution of the United Kingdom, and to place her under the domination and control of a Parliament in Ireland.

Praying that from this calamity God will save Ireland, we here to subscribe our names."

Account of Ulster Day in Ballynure, County Antrim, from the *Larne Times* and *Weekly Telegraph*, 5 October 1912

"Never in the history of Ballynure was there so much enthusiasm and determination shown as on Ulster Day, when the people of the village and surrounding district felt that they were assembling on no ordinary occasion. If their numbers were greater and their faces were sterner than usual it was because they felt that their civil and religious liberties, which had been purchased at such a price, were at stake, and their Protestantism was in danger of being handed over by unprincipled men to rebels and traitors. Hundreds in the district turned their footsteps towards the House of God, where they were to join together in a service of dedication … Divine service commenced at one o'clock in the Presbyterian Church by the singing of the hymn 'O God our help in ages past'. Rev. J. E. Mitchell took as his text Deuteronomy XXXII v.7 'Remember the Days of Old' and 1st Corinthians XVI, v. 13 'Watch ye, stand fast in the faith' …

Over 300 men signed the Covenant and almost 200 women signed the Declaration. When everyone had signed, a procession was formed for Ballyclare, where a splendid demonstration took place. In front of the Ballynure contingent was carried a large crimson banner bearing on one side the words 'Ballynure will not have Home Rule' and on the other side the motto 'Ulster will not our flag surrender' with a small Union Jack in the centre of the motto. The Ballygowan band led the procession and hundreds of men and women followed marching four deep. The Straid Flute Band, accompanied by the Straid Orangemen and members of the Straid Unionist Club, joined the Ballynure procession … In the village three cheers were given for Mr. Mitchell and the Loyalists of Ballynure and district and three cheers for the Ballygowan Band, after which all joined in singing the National Anthem. Thus ended a day memorable in the annals of Ulster and one not to be forgotten in Ballynure".

HISTORICAL FIGURES

The Crawford family grave in the city cemetery in Belfast, which has suffered vandalism.

Major Fred Crawford

Frederick Hugh Crawford was born in Belfast in 1861 and educated at Methodist College in the city and University College, London. After university he served as an apprentice at Harland and Wolff shipyard and spent some years at sea as an engineer.

In 1892 he became politically active during the Home Rule crisis, and formed a group called Young Ulster which imported small amounts of guns from England and was based on continental nationalist sporting clubs. By 1911 he was a member of the Ulster Unionist Council and involved himself in encouraging recruitment into the volunteers who were forming to resist Home Rule.

Crawford had served with the Artillery militia during the South African War, and his military and technical expertise was increased. During the Third Home Rule crisis, under the name of George Washington Graham, he undertook small-scale weapon smuggling into Ulster, but became convinced that the difficulties attendant on small-scale operations made it logical to plan a single major effort.

As it seemed apparent that the Liberal government of the day were intent on forcing their political plans for Home Rule through using force against Ulster Unionists, Crawford was asked to smuggle a large consignment of rifles and ammunition into Ulster. The story of the gun-running from Hamburg to Larne, Donaghadee, Bangor and Belfast is an epic, which could probably only have been carried out by someone of the calibre, tenacity and sheer stubbornness of Crawford. He died in 1952.

Andrew Agnew

A native of Magheramorne, County Antrim, Andrew Agnew was captain of the Clyde Valley, which landed a considerable consignment of weaponry and ammunition at Larne on behalf of the old Ulster Volunteer Force in April 1914. He had been skipper of the ss *Glendun* for many years, a ship of the Antrim Iron Ore Company fleet, and in 1885 was presented with a gold medal by the American government for saving the life of the crew of a US vessel. This award would be further added to when he was presented with the MBE by the King in 1920 for his services to the British Navy during the First World War. Despite the fact that his vessel had to continually pass through waters which were also home to roaming German submarines and hazardous also through the presence of mines, Agnew never missed a trip with his ship, regularly sailing between Belfast and the Tees, and visiting other ports including Stornoway, Dundee, Newcastle and West Hartlepool.

He would also be well-known for his part in the 1914 gun-running, during which he and Major Fred Crawford, brought the *Clyde Valley*, a former Kelly coal boat, up the Irish Sea and into the North Channel despite the watchful attention of the authorities, who were expecting an attempt to land guns for the Ulster Volunteers. Agnew steered the vessel safely, if slightly behind schedule, into Larne Harbour, where a vast motorcade of vehicles was waiting for her cargo to be offloaded.

In December 1928 he was presented with a salver and binoculars in appreciation of his services to the Ulster Volunteers as commander of the ss *Mountjoy II*, as the vessel was named prior to coming into Larne that night. Lord Craigavon, prime minister of Northern Ireland, handed over the gifts to Agnew saying:

> "Opportunity falls to the lot of few to exhibit such patriotism and courage as characterises Captain Agnew's action on behalf of the loyalists of Ulster, culminating on April 24 fourteen years ago ... When future biographers reveal the happenings of those stirring times his name will stand out in letters of gold ..."

Agnew died in Larne District Hospital in August 1932.

James Craig

James Craig, who was destined to be the first Prime Minister of Northern Ireland.

James Craig, 1st Viscount Craigavon, was the first prime minister of Northern Ireland and organised unionist opposition to the Third Home Rule Bill. He came from a wealthy family, his father having been a millionaire whiskey distiller, and alongside Sir Edward Carson he would become a leading figure in unionism.

In 1906 he was elected MP for East Down and after 1918 he represented Mid Down in parliament, stepping down in 1921. As a junior minister in the coalition government of Lloyd George between 1917 and 1921, he is credited with having had some influence and control over the government's Irish policy, and to have been one of those behind the Government of Ireland (1920) Act.[26]

Craig, who was a Boer War veteran, served as prime minister of Northern Ireland from 1921 until his death in 1940. His premiership has been criticised for not having done enough to encourage political pluralism (through abolition of proportional representation in local elections), but the early years of his term of office were dominated by attempts by militant republicans to destabilise his government, while nationalists refused to recognise Stormont.

In the early 1920s Craig met Michael Collins, a leading republican political and military figure, in an effort to reach agreement and reduce violence and tension. The Craig-Collins pacts of January and March 1922 achieved little, however, perhaps because the imperative behind them was pressure from the London government rather than any genuine spirit of compromise. Collins had secretly planned to have the anti-Treaty Irish Republican Army launch attacks on Northern Ireland while ostensibly recognising the northern state. He was shot dead in an ambush by anti-Treaty elements in County Cork on 22 August 1922, during the Irish Civil War.

Sir James Craig died in 1940 and is buried in the grounds of Stormont, along with Lady Craig.

Reverend James Brown Armour

Born at Lisboy, Ballymoney, in 1841, Reverend JB Armour was a Liberal Unionist who came to support Home Rule for Ireland. Some have suggested that his opposition to the unionism of the Third Home Rule crisis was more closely related to his views on the perceived domination by the Anglican establishment of politics and thus fits closely into the tradition of the Presbyterian radicals of 1798.[27]

Independent Orangeism and Liberal Unionism would generally fit this pattern of dissent in the early twentieth century.

Armour was originally opposed to Home Rule, taking a stance against William Ewart Gladstone's proposals for devolution in Ireland on the basis that he felt they would lead to separation and did not safeguard minority (ie Protestant) rights in Ireland sufficiently.

He also felt, however, that some changes were necessary in the government and came to view with disappointment the lack of Conservative support for land reform, which probably assisted in his view that nationalist co-operation would assist the Presbyterian tenant farmers – a viewpoint shared by many Presbyterians in North Antrim and elsewhere as well.

Something of a flavour of the period comes from a meeting which was addressed by Armour in Ballynure, County Antrim, in 1894. Armour told those present, said to number several hundreds, that he was sure "that a race of Presbyterians and Protestants worthy of the best traditions of our faith, will arise in the near future, with their minds cleared of Unionist cant, and blood purified from the rust of serfdom, and that they will claim to dwell in this land, not under the protection of the Saxon, nor by permission of the Celt, but in virtue of the services they will render to a country which we love and for whose welfare we pray."[28]

That not everyone in the strongly Protestant village agreed was evident by the fact that the local flute band paraded around the village while the tenant right meeting was taking place and stones were thrown at the Presbyterian Lecture Hall where Armour was speaking.

Armour supported Home Rule at the Presbyterian General Assembly in 1913 and helped organise a meeting of Protestant Home Rulers in Ballymoney town hall that same year. Ill health prevented deeper involvement in the politics of the period, and he last spoke at the General Assembly in 1924. He died in 1928.

Thomas Sinclair

The most prominent of the Ulster Liberal Unionists, Thomas Sinclair was a dominant figure in Ulster political and intellectual circles in the latter nineteenth and early twentieth centuries. He was born in September 1838 and educated at Royal Belfast Academical Institution and Queen's College, where he proved an exceptional student.

Despite his academic learning and ability, however, Sinclair entered the family business of J & T Sinclair, Provender Merchants, but would also play a major part in politics and in the Presbyterian Church, being the most prominent Presbyterian layman of his generation.[29]

Sinclair was deeply proud of his Ulster Scots ancestry, and saw Ulster Scots as heirs to the Glorious Revolution of 1688 and the American Revolution of 1776. He was the man who organised the 1912 Ulster Covenant, which provided a direct connection with the Scots Solemn League and Covenant of 1638. He was instrumental in the Ulster Convention of 1892 and was also active in canvassing Scottish Presbyterian opinion against Home Rule.

As a Liberal Unionist, Thomas Sinclair and his prominent ally Thomas Andrews supported land reform in Ireland and other measures intended to make society more equitable. He supported disestablishment of the Church of Ireland in 1869, and also non-denominational education in Ireland. He was an able representative of a radical, liberal tradition within Ulster Presbyterianism, which includes the 1798 tradition. By 1912, however, many of those within that constituency had come to view the Union as the best means of securing the future for all.

Thomas Sinclair, who devised the Ulster Covenant of 1912.

Thomas Sinclair ironically died in February 1914, while the Home Rule debate was still very much alive. Sinclair Seamen's Presbyterian Church in Belfast was built as a memorial to his uncle, John Sinclair, his father's business partner.

HISTORICAL TRAILS
SITES TO VISIT

The *Clyde Valley* Memorial at Larne Harbour, County Antrim was erected in 1964, the fiftieth anniversary of the gun-running.

Clyde Valley Memorial, Larne

The memorial to the Larne gun-running of 1914 is located at Chaine Memorial Road in the town, overlooking the mouth of Larne Harbour, into which the *Clyde Valley* sailed on two historic occasions. The first was in April 1914 on the night of the gun-running, and the second was when she was brought back from Canada in December 1968 and sailed again into the port.

The lamp on the memorial is one of those which originally lit the area in 1914. When the memorial was being erected to mark the fiftieth anniversary of the event, in 1964, one of the original rifles that were brought in the ship's cargo in 1914 was placed inside and sealed.

In 1989 a second plaque was attached to the memorial to commemorate the seventy-fifth anniversary of the Larne gun-running. The plaque was erected by the Ulster Society in conjunction with Larne Borough Council and was unveiled by David Trimble, chairman of the Society, who later became MP for Upper Bann and First Minister of Northern Ireland.

A recent mural depicting the *Clyde Valley*, at Bank Road, Tullygarley, in Larne.

Parliament buildings at Stormont.

Parliament Buildings, Stormont

The Northern Ireland parliament buildings at Stormont in East Belfast have a number of prominent reminders of the Home Rule period and its outcome as far as Northern Ireland is concerned.

In the front of the building is an impressive statue of Sir Edward Carson, the unionist leader whose campaign won six counties of Northern Ireland the right to be separate from what would become the Republic of Ireland. Standing in a striking pose, the statue has Sir Edward overlooking the city whose unionist population took the Dublin barrister to its heart.

Inside the parliament building, at the top of the central stairway is a magnificent bronze statue of Sir James Craig, who would become the first prime minister of Northern Ireland in 1921 and served until his death in 1940.

In the grounds to the east of the building is a small enclosed garden which contains the tomb of Sir James Craig and Lady Craig, the only grave in the grounds of the parliament buildings.

Somme Heritage Centre

The Somme Heritage Centre outside Newtownards in County Down is an excellent facility at which to learn more about the Battle of the Somme and the soldiers who fought there.

There are fascinating displays of artifacts relating to the First and Second World Wars, and the culmination of any visit to the Centre is a walk through the front-line trenches, where the visitor is surrounded by the noise of a tremendous artillery barrage as well as seeing an audio visual presentation on the Battle of the Somme.

Located near to Helen's Tower at Clandeboye, where the Ulster Division trained, the centre tells the story of the 10th (Irish), 16th (Irish) and 36th (Ulster) Divisions. It is also expanding into Second World War coverage. The Centre is operated by the Somme Association, which is also responsible for the management and care of the Ulster Memorial Tower at Thiepval on the Somme battlefield in France.

Ulster Tower at Thiepval, France

Located close to the site of the old German front line in July 1916, this First World War memorial and its grounds are a small part of Ulster in a foreign field. The Tower is based on Helen's Tower at Clandeboye, where many of the soldiers of the 36th Ulster Division trained in 1914–1915, prior to their participation in the Great War. Many did not return. The Tower was dedicated on 19 November 1921, and remains a focus for many Ulster visitors to the region.

The 36th Ulster Division attacked from Thiepval Wood on the morning of 1 July 1916, entering the Schwaben Redoubt and securing the lines of trenches which had been their objectives that day. Unfortunately, however, other units failed to push sufficiently forward and the Ulstermen were left isolated. Although they held stubbornly to their positions, causalities mounted and ammunition ran low, resulting in them being pushed back in a German counter-attack. The causalities for the Division that day alone were in the region of 5,500 killed, wounded and missing.

In the grounds of the Ulster Tower is a plaque commemorating the nine members of the 36th Division who were awarded the Victoria Cross for their valour during the Battle of the Somme. The first of them was William McFadzean, a bombardier, who threw himself on two unexploded grenades which had accidentally fallen out of their box on the morning of the Battle of the Somme. He was mortally wounded, but saved the lives of those around him by his action. Willie McFadzean's family lived on Belfast's Cregagh Road and he had been a member of the Young Citizen Volunteers, formed to oppose Home Rule for Ireland before the War.

There is also a memorial at Thiepval commemorating the members of the Orange Order from across the British Empire who were killed in the Battle of the Somme and in the overall conflict. This included members from Ireland, England, Scotland, Canada, and Australia.

At the nearby Connaught Cemetery and Mill Road cemetery are the graves of Ulster Division soldiers who fell on 1 July 1916.

ENDNOTES

1 See article by Jean Agnew in Institute of Ulster Scots Studies, Working Papers, vol 1, p60

2 Lucy, Gordon, 'Thomas Sinclair', in Great Ulster Scots leaflet series, published by the Ulster-Scots Agency, undated

3 Buchanan, George, *The Green Seacoast, an Autobiography*, London: 1959

4 Buchanan, *op cit*, p45

5 Loughlin, James, *Gladstone: Home Rule and the Ulster Question 1882–93*, New Jersey: 1987

6 *Larne Times* and *Weekly Telegraph*, 20 January 1912

7 This was related to me by an informant whose elderly aunts were apparently responsible for the uncharacteristic outburst.

8 *Larne Times* and *Weekly Telegraph*, 9 December 1911

9 *Weekly Telegraph*, 23 March 1912

10 'The Home Rule Crisis. What Scotch Orangemen are doing', *Larne Times* and *Weekly Telegraph*, 21 February 1914

11 *Larne Times* and *Weekly Telegraph*, 18 July 1914

12 See Walker, Graham, *Intimate Strangers, Political and cultural interaction between Scotland and Ulster in modern times*, Edinburgh: 1995, p35

13 *Weekly Telegraph*, 17 August 1912

14 'House of Commons Hansard, Government of Ireland Bill', 27 and 28 April 1914, give an informative flavour of the debate surrounding the Curragh events.

15 Stewart, ATQ, *The Ulster Crisis*, London: 1967, p66

16 'Strange Story from Denmark', *Belfast News Letter*, 1 April 1914, p7

17 Buckland, Patrick, *Irish Unionism 1885–1923: A documentary history*, Belfast: 1973, p249

18 Stewart, *op cit*, p205

19 Related in Hume, David, *'For Ulster and Her Freedom' The Story of the 1914 Gun-running*, Larne: The Ulster Society, 1989

20 Hume, *op cit*, p28

21 *Larne Times*, 21 January 1943

22 Hume, *op cit*, p32

23 Hume, *op cit*, p32

24 *Larne Times* and *Weekly Telegraph*, 2 May 1914

25 Killen, John, *John Bull's Famous Circus: Ulster History through the postcard 1905–1985*, Dublin: 1985, p69

26 Connolly, SJ, *The Oxford Companion to Irish History*, Oxford: 1998, p124

27 Connolly, *op cit*, p25

28 Armour, WS, *Armour of Ballymoney*, London: 1934, p134–135

29 See the leaflet on Thomas Sinclair in the Ulster-Scots Agency 'Great Ulster Scots' series.

Chapter Ten

CONSERVING AND PRESERVING THE ULSTER SCOTS IDENTITY

There are differing aspects to the heritage of the Ulster Scots community, something which, in itself, is a healthy indication of a culture that is alive and well, adapting to survive in changing circumstances throughout history. There were different strands to that community through its history, of course. This is probably highlighted by the fact that, in 1798, while Presbyterian Ulster Scots in Antrim and Down were in rebellion against the Crown, those in the west took a very different stance. Indeed, even in the eastern part of Ulster, where the influence of the Presbyterian radicals was strongest, there were also many who shied away from the event. The weaver poet James Orr, in his poem *Donegore Hill*, talks of how while some prepared to go to war, others "hade like hens in byre nuiks" and were reluctant to be involved. The Orange Order, founded in 1795, formed yeomanry to defend against the United Irish rebellion and among the early leaders there were Presbyterians (although the leadership soon passed to Anglican gentry, where it would rest for a considerable time). During the American Revolution, when Ulster Scots played such a prominent part, there were members of their community who remained loyal to the Crown; indeed, in one predominantly Scotch-Irish settlement, at Queensborough in Georgia, it has been estimated that one quarter of the population was loyalist.[1] The lesson of Queensborough was not a positive one for such loyalists, since many lost their lands and eventually the name was seen as being too royalist and was changed to Louisville.[2] Collectively, however, there is an overall heritage which ostensibly starts in Scotland with the identity of the Scots (although the original Scots were from Ulster anyway) and which reflects the majority and overwhelming bulk of the community.

The Alphabet Angel, Dundarave, Bushmills, County Antrim.

It is useful to note, as one recent writer on heritage generally has explained, that the French definition of the word heritage relates to legacy and that one dictionary definition is "That which has been, or may be, inherited".[3] Another historian writes, "Our times and our thoughts are largely shaped by the past. That shaping is the reason we study history … To study the past may help us to understand better how we came to be who we are."[4] In the context of the Ulster Scots there have been many aspects which have formed part of their cultural heritage and identity over the generations. Some of that heritage is highly visual, not least the existence of Presbyterian churches on the landscape,[5] place names, and surnames which can, of course, be reflected in the world of business very visibly through shop signs, advertisements and even on vehicles.[6] In the rural community outside the small city of Clover in South Carolina, you can drive up to a crossroads and see McGill's Stores along the road, a reminder that, although the spelling may be different (Magill in Northern Ireland), the roots are the same, wherever Ulster families have ventured. Pipe Bands are another clear indication of a Scots linkage, and there are probably more pipe bands in Northern Ireland than in Scotland in proportion to the population. In modern times, Ulster pipers and drum majors have proven themselves to be world champions, highlighting the strength of and continued interest in the pipe band tradition in Northern Ireland.

Raphoe Pipe Band on parade.

Not all contacts with Scotland were always appreciated in the past. One small reminder of this from local history, for example, is how, in 1848, the arrival of a Scottish plough manufactured at Addington near Glasgow caused some debate in the rural community around Ballycarry in County Antrim. James Davison, whose father had bought the plough to work on his lands at Bellahill near the village, was challenged by a local blacksmith named John Ewans, that he could make a more effective plough than any made by Mr Gray. On 21 January 1848 a ploughing contest was arranged, the prize being the one pound waged by the blacksmith, at Kilroot near Carrickfergus. A large gathering of people assembled for the occasion, including members of the local farming societies. Three judges adjudicated on the outcome of the event, and determined that the Scottish plough of the Davison's was superior.[7] It was not a good result for the local blacksmith and possibly one with long-term implications. The episode certainly highlighted the influence of Scotland among farmers in the east, an area which also witnessed regular rural migration to assist with the Scottish harvests and supplement incomes on the western side of the channel. For example, the 1840 Ordnance Survey Memoir for the parish of Templecorran, in which Bellahill is sited, noted that there were six individuals in 1839 who migrated annually, all of them to Glasgow.[8] In the nearby parish of Raloo, there were five individuals who migrated annually to labour, three women and two men, and all of them also went to Glasgow.[9]

The Scottish coast is within sight of the highest points in Bellahill, where the unique ploughing match originated in 1848, and geography has undoubtedly played an important part in the linkage with Scotland and the development of Ulster Scots. At its most basic, this spurred the development of cross-channel sea links in the nineteenth century, when the Belfast and Northern Counties Railway Company saw the potential to create a sea link which could be utilised on the other side of the North Channel. Directors of the company, along with a representative of the London and North Western Railway Company arrived in Larne by special train to discuss the capabilities of the harbour in 1869, and in future weeks Stranraer Council would also become involved in the lobby to develop such links.[10] The links had, of course, already been operating through small boats on the Scottish and eastern coast of Ulster for centuries, but development of modern ferry links increased the potential for trade, travel and for tourism on a much larger scale. Towards the end of the nineteenth century and for some years in the early twentieth, there were even proposals to develop a tunnel linking Scotland and the east coast of Ulster. In 1913 an American engineer, HG Tyrrell, from Chicago, assessed four possible ways of constructing a tunnel across the North Channel, settling on the prospect of a 'floating tube' tunnel, which would lie in quiet water about 60 feet below the surface. The cost of the proposal at the time would have been between £5 million and £6 million, but one problem which was identified was that the tubes would eventually have to be replaced, as they would rust.

The idea of a tunnel to link the two parts of the kingdom had in fact gone back to the 1880s, when there was a suggestion for a tunnel between Portpatrick and Donaghadee. By 1913 it was anticipated that the terminus on the Ulster side would have been at Islandmagee in County Antrim. In proposing the tunnel, the promoters did not see it in isolation, highlighting that it would integrate the prospect of cross-Atlantic travel by linking to the west coast of Ireland by rail. One suggestion was to develop Portush in County Antrim as a major transatlantic embarkation port, which would further allow the railway system from Belfast – via the cross-channel tunnel – to be more fully utilised. Harbour improvements at Portrush could have converted the Antrim port "into an excellent shipping port for American steamers" according to the *Belfast News Letter*.[11] Among those arguing for such a project was a distinguished London engineer named Harrison Hayter, whose firm had constructed the Severn Tunnel in England, representatives of the Belfast Chamber of Commerce and others including Arnold Foster MP, who said that "Engineering science had brought such a scheme [as a tunnel] within reasonable bounds of probability at comparatively moderate cost." By February 1915, although the suggestion was not completely lost, Prime Minister Herbert Asquith informed Gershom Stewart, who was Unionist MP for Wirral in Liverpool that it was "hardly practicable" in the "present circumstances to draw up estimates of the cost of a tunnel between Ireland and Great Britain so as to ensure constant means of communication between the interior of Ireland and the Atlantic ports of the west coast."

The proximity of east Ulster to Scotland which spurred the unrealised thoughts of a tunnel, undoubtedly assisted in the large proportion of Scots settlers there in the years prior to and including the period of the Plantation of Ulster. In the Cairncastle and Killyglen areas north of Larne, for example, it was estimated that the proportion of Roman Catholics to Protestants in 1840 was one to 16, and that of Episcopalians to Presbyterians was one to 37, highlighting the extent of the Scottish influx into the area. "From about the year 1573 to the year 1610, the Scots continued to arrive and settle themselves in this parish, and in a very few years became the sole possessors of it," the Ordnance Survey Memoir for the parish noted. This settlement pattern, which was outwith the official Plantation of Ulster, was to see a major population of Scots settle in North Down and the Ards and the east Antrim areas in particular. Although not part of the official Plantation in name, they were to all intents and purposes an integral part of it – indeed, perhaps, the integral part of it, given the numbers involved and the long-term impact which they ultimately had.

While there seems little controversy over the issues of place names, population settlement and other geographical manifestations of the Ulster Scots identity, one element which has led to considerable debate has been the Ulster Scots language. There are some who remain clearly unconvinced that the language is any more than a dialect of sorts, even though it is recognised by as a European Minor language. The source of the dispute probably owes something to the fact that language, notably the Irish language, has been used by some (but not a majority of language enthusiasts) as a political weapon, expressed through street signs, wall slogans and murals, and so on. There are some who have seen the resurgence of Ulster Scots language as having had similar political motivation behind it. It may be true that, at a time when the unionist community felt politically isolated and threatened, this revival had some grounding in the overall situation. This would hardly be surprising in itself, since it is not uncommon for people to seek to defend something which they see as being threatened or about to be lost. It is probable that the politics of the situation from the mid 1980s were catalystic in encouraging unionists to look again at their culture and heritage and who they were. This did perhaps assist the revival of Ulster Scots but it may not have been the only factor. Equally, it would be more realistic to see the overall revival in Ulster Scots as being about a desire to highlight community culture and in such a circumstance the language issue naturally fell into that cultural kaleidoscope. Those who are not overly enthusiastic supporters of the language may, moreover, view it as important to preserve what is left, but not to expect Ulster Scots to end up as a spoken language across nine counties.

The language has often been a source for ridicule from the nationalist community, and in 1996, for example, a report in the nationalist daily newspaper, the *Irish News*, focused on how a study from the European Office of Lesser Used Languages had found few native speakers. While the findings of the study would clearly be debated by Ulster Scots language enthusiasts, the newspaper was entitled to report on the issue. Sometimes it seems that the lines become a little blurred between journalistic coverage and partisan comment, however, and in the case of this report this is highlighted by the fact that the report referred to Ulster Scots by saying that "European funding of the obscure Ulster Scots 'language' will only continue because of its political links with the unionist community, a leaked European report claims". In a journalistic sense, the language was designated as "obscure" in the report by the newspaper, something which the report itself did not appear to attribute to the leaked document.[12] The European document was, however, quoted as saying that the world was not made aware of Ulster Scots language until formation of the Ulster-Scots Society[13] in 1994. This was clearly ill-informed.

Ulster Scots can be traced back to a common linguistic root – Anglo Saxon and Germanic – as can English, but it was clearly different until the point in the seventeenth century when English became the language of officialdom. The presence of the Weaver poets and other literary efforts also show that Ulster Scots was not merely invented in 1994. However, equally there is a story from within the Ulster Scots community of how one of its number was asked at one point what the Ulster Scots term for telephone was and responded that it was a *"lang blether"*.[14] The truth is, as is the case with the Irish language, that some words in the modern world do not have an equivalent in the language, which is no big deal. Unfortunately the criticism of the language has probably resulted in some feeling under pressure to try to defend it in ways which are less than appropriate, as outlined above. We should not be about the business of invention. Equally, there must be some greater degree of understanding in the wider community about Ulster Scots. However, given that the wider public is informed by the media, there is a level of responsibility which can be expected and is not always met.

In October 2003, the BBC, whose output, perhaps ironically, includes Ulster Scots programmes, carried an article on its *Talkback* programme claiming that an inappropriate Ulster Scots translation had been given in a newspaper article for a teacher for children with special needs. The article claimed that the wording in Ulster Scots described children with special needs as "wee daftie weans". Following challenge from MLA Nelson McCausland, the BBC broadcast a retraction and subsequently the BBC Northern Ireland Controller wrote to the MLA accepting that "no such advertisement existed, or that any translation appeared in the form suggested by our programme … we regret that the programme broadcast this item."[15]

To denigrate a language which existed very strongly in the seventeenth century and eighteenth centuries, and then gradually declined at the hands of educationalists and polite society, is to be, at best, rather chauvinistic. To suggest it did not exist is plainly foolish. On occasions I have been asked, when participating in media programmes, to speak in Ulster Scots. I am never incredibly comfortable doing so, as in my generation the language had declined to such an extent that it was not common currency other than in words and phrases. For the perimeters of expression on Ulster Scots generally to be set so specifically is not really appropriate, especially since the language has suffered so much and lost so much. I have my own proud example of a survival in terms of language:

When I was a young boy the main attraction of the lint dams on our farm was the search for tadpoles. My father, who was born in 1911, used to refer to the area of the lint dams as, and here it is written as he pronounced it, *"the squaws"*. Although this conjured up thoughts of a western prairie, in later life I began to wonder about that unusual name. I knew that it could have nothing to do with Native Americans. I had never heard it used locally for any other location, adding to the sense of mystery. I never got to explore with my father why he called that piece of our farm such a strange name. When I eventually started to enquire, it was to no avail. I asked folklore experts, local historians, Irish speakers, and others, all in an effort to find what the strange name on our farm meant. Most fields were named, as was common practice in bygone generations with cattle as well as property. But the names were functional; the dam field, where a small dam was located, the low fields, which lay on an incline to the east, the quarry field, where stone and earth had been extracted in bygone years.

And it was the functional side of farming language which was the clue. I had consulted grammars and dictionaries,[16] again to no avail. There was no mention of the word *squaw*. I decided a different approach. I stopped looking for *'squaw'* being spelt in that way. It had always been a dubious proposition in any case. And there was the answer. In the County Antrim Ulster Scots dictionary,[17] flicking through the Q section, I found the solution to the whole mystery. The word *qua* was a good old County Antrim Ulster Scots term. And it referred to wet places. The lint dams were, of course, clearly a wet place, but the topography of the area suggested that there had previously been a marshy area, which had been deemed appropriate to create lint dams and feed the water into. That this area pre-dated the lint dams suggested that the turn of phrase in referring to it went back further too. So when my father, and probably his father, had referred to the *(s)qua's*, they were using Ulster Scots to describe an important part of the landscape of their farm. This basic example ties in with others of unexpected appearances for letters in Ulster Scots. Hugh can, for example, be delivered as *'shooey'* in Ulster Scots[18]. James Fenton, in another example, informs us that the word *quuster* (based on twist/quust) was used for a straw-rope twister.[19] And in Aldfreck townland of Ballycarry, they used *squa's* instead of *qua*, making, it would appear, a subtle change to standard County Antrim Ulster Scots. They were custodians of not only land their forefathers had ploughed, but also of a language dating back to centuries long gone. I remain extremely grateful to them for bringing what could have been a long-forgotten word down safely to my generation.

At a language course which I conducted in Ballycarry, County Antrim, in 2007, several words emerged which were all but lost in the local area. These included *shirroy*, which referred in the local case to an indefinable number of people, although it could also mean a batch, a commotion, or a noisy gathering in County Antrim.[20] One of the class members, Roy Marsden, recalled it having been used with him many years before by one of the blacksmiths in the location:

A had tae help tha blacksmith, but a got there kinna late.
A said "Sorry am late".
He said "Hmmm, tha wa tae hell is paved wi guid intentions".
A axed "Wur ye busy this morning?"
"Hmmm, a hale shirroy o folk here, an you worney."[21]

Interestingly, Ballycarry, which is a settlement dating back to seventeenth century Scots, has few of its townlands highlighting this connection in terms of Ulster Scots terminology. Only one townland had an overtly Ulster Scots connection, this being Cairnbrock, a *brock* being an Ulster Scots word for badger. However, there were other placenames in the locality which were more localised and did highlight Scottish origins, including *brae* and *burn*. A study in Greyabbey, County Down, in the 1990s[22] highlighted that the rural landscape was dotted with Ulster Scots names, including those which used the name *fiel* or *fiels* as part of their title. These were cited as Blair's Fiel, Well Fiel, Lint Hole Fiels, Plantin' Fiel, Fitba Fiel and Stack Garden Fiel. Another local name was *Mairs* (pronounced 'mares'), a Scottish word for uncultivated land and rough ground, while *Knowes* (pronounced 'nows') is a Scottish word referring to a knoll and usually used in the plural to signify a rough field. *Knowe* is a familiar term for laneways or roads.

Ulster Scots was (and, it would seem, still is) essentially a rural language and one that survived by word of mouth from one generation to another. It was not generally a written language in bygone generations, apart from a few periods, and it was often a language looked down upon by those with a better education. Because it was not written, it had the ability to change from one area to another, much in the same way as spelling of surnames changed from location to location depending on how people thought the names were or should be spelled. Thus appears another of the apparent contradictions of Ulster Scots; that the language changes within short geographical areas and is therefore seen as being merely pigeon English, poorly spelled. The real story is somewhat more complex.

James Orr, Bard of Ballycarry, gives a fine example of the disparaging outlook on Ulster Scots in his day, and how this outlook impacted on the ordinary people of his locality. In his exceptional poem *The Irish Cottier's Death and Burial* he talks of how the clergyman came to visit the house of the deceased. The minister would, along with the schoolteacher, have been among the most educated and influential of figures in any Ulster Scots community. When the minister came to call, the country folk tried to impress him with their knowledge. Orr tells us that they:

"try to quat braid Scotch, a task that foils their art;

For while they join his converse, vain though shy
They monie a lang learn'd word misca' an' misapply"[23]

The country folk could not escape their heritage. Nor did they avoid their destiny to pass down something of an ancient language to new generations. Of course, they would not have known that the language they were speaking was believed to be west Germanic in origin and possibly related not only to Scots emigrants but also Old Norse settlement and trade. Such information was for the scholarly and those who had got to college. Simple folk had no need to think on such matters. Their task was a basic and practical one; they passed on the language to another generation.

In a world which is often geared up to academic achievement and obtaining grades and qualifications, there is a distinct and overwhelming irony in that the precious heritage of language was almost destroyed through better education, while the less well educated clasped and held it for the future, then passed it on to a younger generation.

Some years ago, I was engaged by a local council to undertake some historical work with a youth group. In doing so I provided a standard list of Ulster Scots names for parts of the body (*fizog, e'en, neb, fit, hunkers, shanks*, etc) to see how much the young folk recognised. This was in a working-class Protestant estate in East Antrim and I did not expect great things from teenagers who knew little, as it had transpired, about their history generally. It was, therefore, somewhat of a surprise when, working together in groups, they came back quickly with all 12 of my Ulster Scots words correctly identified. These were words they had heard in their homes and among their peers in ordinary conversation. All of this gives hope for the continued revival of Ulster Scots language. It has been severely damaged over the generations and the decades. Sentence structures have been lost to the point where often only words or phrases remain. But each word and phrase that has survived can and no doubt will be used to build again the foundations of the language and its future. It has been encouraging to see some areas highlight the language in recent years.

North Street, Greyabbey.

In 1996 the Greyabbey and District Historical Society successfully lobbied Ards Borough Council to have street names in Ulster Scots in the village, which became the first in Northern Ireland to have official street name plates promoting the Ulster Scots language. The names included *Schuil Loanen* (School Lane), *The Big Raa* (Main Street) and *Meetin House Brae*, while the village Ulster Scots name of *Greba*, as many locals refer to it, also featured.[24] Among those backing the move was local councillor Jim Shannon, who would later become MP for Strangford and deliver his Maiden Speech in the House of Commons in Ulster Scots.

The School of Ulster Weaver Poets to which James Orr belonged provided a major strand of Ulster Scots writing. Orr was the foremost of the Weaver Poets, and the language which he used was clearly that which was understood and spoken by the average person in his community. Orr, who was writing in the latter eighteenth and early nineteenth century, reflected the linguistic situation in that his poems are both in standard English and also Ulster Scots. In the same context, the twentieth century Ballycarry poet and songwriter William James Hume (my grandfather) was also reflecting language usage in the 1930s and 1940s when he wrote poems such as *The Aul Wa's*, about an ancient landmark in the locality:

In the evening when my work is done
at Aldfreck's towering brae
I take a trip by the aul Burnside
and land at the Aul Wa's
To hear the news and have a laugh
for the folks could not be beat
I tell you their names a' in a train
of those merry boys I meet.

chorus
Archibald Burns and Henry Burns
and Nelson from Loughanlay
and James McCausland from the moss,
David Craig from the Lady Brae
William John Craig and John Gardiner
an odd straggler an that's a'
and a' that happens in the worl
is tak'd at the aul wa's

Hume's verse shows overwhelming use of English, but also incorporation of Ulster Scots such as *aul wa's*, *brae* and *tak'd*. It is a useful indication of the state of the spoken and written language in the 1930s and 1940s in a segment of County Antrim. In some ways the use of English and Ulster Scots together is not so different from the work of James Orr, who was writing well over a century before. It could be argued that Ulster Scots had found an accommodation whereby some elements of the language could survive alongside standard English. Again, this is the sign of a living culture, which adapts to changing circumstance in order to ensure its preservation.

The Ulster Scots community has produced many poets, their work in most cases generally more relevant in their own localities than on a wider basis. Often communities had their own designated bards – for example, Orr was the Bard of Ballycarry and Samuel Thomson was the Bard of Carngranny. James Campbell, who was born in Cairncastle in the latter 1750s and died in Ballynure in 1818, was referred to as a familiar entertainer in the East Antrim area. "He was to the poor on this side of the Moyle's deep waters what the immortal Burns was to his from the Tweed to John o' Groats", it was prosaically remarked.[25] James Loughridge, a formidable representative of literary output in Cullybackey, County Antrim, was described as one of a steady stream of writers in the area from the mid nineteenth century until well into the twentieth.[26] These men are only examples among many. In their generation poetry and writing was entertainment and those who excelled were undoubtedly not only those able to write, but also able to perform. As the century developed and television and radio moved into a centre stage for entertainment, a number of things happened: firstly, the traditions of storytelling and 'yarns', of soirees in neighbours houses, were largely overtaken by the new exciting medium. And secondly, the new exciting medium was generally about 'proper English' and did little to promote local linguistic traditions. Thus the process of modernity resulted in the isolation of Ulster Scots speech. It was the equivalent of the Pictish language being sidelined by the Scots in ancient times, only for the fact that Ulster Scots was not completely wiped out.

Language is, of course, only one aspect of the legacy and heritage of Ulster Scots, and unfortunately a definition of Ulster Scots would appear to have evolved which expects language to be at the crux of the whole culture. This is perhaps a deliberate ploy by some, for there have been those who have been caustic about Ulster Scots to the point of denying there ever was a language. Others have been content to refer to Ulster Scots as 'nothing but Scotch mist'.[27] However, all of this somewhat misses the point. The Ulster Scots language was spoken by the early Scots settlers in Ulster and has been diluted and threatened virtually ever since. From about 1650 onwards, Ulster Scots written forms were generally discarded in favour of English. The language, as a consequence, largely survived until the latter eighteenth and early nineteenth century in oral form only. But there were revivals, when the language was written, as during the period of the Ulster Weaver poets such as Orr, Campbell, Beggs, Thomson and others. The language was rural and belonged to the lower classes, which resulted in it being viewed by officialdom as a rude and unlearned dialect, something which played no small part in encouraging people to abandon it. It is disingenuous to suggest, having subtly almost extinguished the language in the classroom, workplace and social setting, that because of that process it never really existed in the first place.

As mentioned previously, language is only one aspect of the legacy and heritage of Ulster Scots, and the loss of many elements of the Ulster Scots language through the process of modernisation in society does not undermine the essential cultural elements which the Ulster Scots community possesses. These include faith, outlook, music, literature and other aspects. Revivals have been occurring in many of the cultural fields of the Ulster Scots community, including Scottish dancing, particularly in this case among communities which would not have previously probably been involved. The Royal Scottish County Dance Society, which marked its sixtieth anniversary in Northern Ireland in 2006, has several hundred members, but probably the greatest sense of new engagement with Scottish dancing has come through groups in areas such as, prominently, the Strabane area, and in East and South Belfast. Young dancers there learning Highland dance have excelled themselves in the space of a few years, and in the case of the Sollus Highland Dancers from Bready in County Tyrone, girls have even performed at the Edinburgh Tattoo.[28]

Left: Scottish Dancing has won more adherents over the past number of years as an Ulster Scots cultural revival continues.

Courtesy of Peter Rippon.

Right: The bass drummer of Moyne Pipe Band, County Donegal.

In terms of desire for knowledge on Ulster Scots identity, and assistance in its promotion, many groups have been founded from the 1980s across Northern Ireland. These engage in various activities, including lectures and talks as well as dance classes and other aspects of Ulster Scots heritage. While some criticism has been leveled that groups have emerged solely to try and claim grants, this is rather unfair, not least since the availability of grants is what has made it at least possible for groups to stage events. The fact that they may have organised in response to the realisation that grants were attainable does not negate the fact that Ulster Scots identity was there in the first place. However, there is also undoubtedly a question in relation to some groups as to the actual depth of the understanding of Ulster Scots and desire to strategically promote it.

For several years there has been a rumbling dissent in some quarters of officialdom that Ulster Scots is simply a cover for Orange groups seeking funding;

the development of many groups in Orange Halls has assisted this perception, which has to be tempered by the fact that a majority of members of the Orange Order in Ulster are probably from the Presbyterian and Ulster Scots tradition.[29] Thus there is indeed a legitimacy in these groups staging and promoting Ulster Scots events. It is clear that in the past Orange groups which sought funding from government departments were, either unthinkingly or otherwise, referred to the Ulster Scots Agency. This action by senior civil servants begs the question why other civil servants would then seek to say that Ulster Scots is merely a cloak for Orange events, given that encouragement was given to such a process in the first place.

Where a real problem may exist, however, is that these groups may have their main focus on the Orange tradition as opposed to any long-term consideration of the Ulster Scots side of their tradition. It is of some interest that while one Ulster Scots community group at Ballycarry has consistently raised the issue of east-west funding and development of strategic links with Scotland – including with three successive DCAL government ministers – little of such a lobby appears to have come from the other groups who would be considered to belong to the same cultural genre. In fact, it would appear that progress on east-west links has been lamentably slow and remain, at officially supported level, almost if not completely non-existent. This is a curious lapse on the part of those who would see themselves as genuine Ulster Scots groups. Ultimately if they are to have any relevance, it must surely be through their ability to highlight their identity through once again connecting with the *'Mither land'*.

Mid Argyll Pipe Band on parade at the Broadisland Gathering in Ballycarry.

The case of the Broadisland Gathering in Ballycarry, County Antrim, is a good example of community-driven Ulster Scots activity. I was one of the founders of the Gathering,[30] which was first staged in 1993, having been promoted by the local community group, which was not singularly Ulster Scots, although based in an overwhelmingly Ulster Scots community. With the support of the local council, the Gathering was intended to reflect the strong Scots history of the area, which had the first Presbyterian minister and congregation in Ireland, as well as being the birthplace of James Orr, the foremost of the Ulster Scots weaver poets. The first Gathering included pageantry which reflected the arrival of the first Scots in the area in 1609, the event being officially opened by a re-enactor depicting William Edmonstone, founder of the community, and elements which were developed over the years including a Common Riding of the Marches around the village,[31] re-enactors in period dress, pipe bands in concert and on parade,

Ballycarry townland banners on parade, a new tradition in County Antrim.

and the area's unique townland banners, which highlight the heritage of the local community. The townland banner parade at the Broadisland Gathering is proud to boast that it is the only townland banner parade in the world, the unique banners reflecting the history and landscape of each townland (rural area) in the community.[32]

The Gathering has been a focal point for Ulster Scots from near and far, and has welcomed international visitors from Commonwealth countries as well as the United States, one of its key selling points being the family atmosphere which prevails. The Gathering has transformed the village over the years, and on occasion police estimates have suggested that the visitors on the day (5,000) outnumbered the local population by at least four to one.

The Broadisland Gathering was ahead of its time, taking place even before the establishment of the Ulster Scots Heritage Council, an umbrella body which aims to develop Ulster Scots culture and language, and which, in 2008, became the Ulster Scots Community Network. There are many other areas which are now staging similar festival days, and in 2006 the 400th anniversary of the Hamilton and Montgomery settlement provided a major injection for pageantry and re-enactment in North Down and the Ards. Such events, although some may remain highly localised, all have in common that they serve to highlight the Ulster Scots identity of their own areas. Inevitably, in a small community, they also draw on others from the wider Ulster Scots community, through the fields of music, dance, literature and culture, and therefore help to emphasise and cement the sense of commonality which is highly pertinent in the modern age. The potential for continued development of the Ulster Scots culture and heritage is a strong one. The possibility of a heritage trail which would not only highlight areas in Ulster, but also extend east to Scotland and west to the United States and Canada, with a few other locations elsewhere, is something which could be innovative in a global and international sense. The tourist, educational and cultural possibility of such a trail would be enormous, but would require international contacts, goodwill and co-operation, something which may be difficult to co-ordinate. I recall using the occasion of a speech in East Kilbride in 1993 to call for such a trail,[33] but level of

Fiddlers with the Ulster Scots Folk Orchestra. The revival of interest in Ulster Scots culture has assisted in the flowering of arts and music within the Ulster Scots community.

co-ordination is a daunting prospect and would require commitment at governmental levels.

There are, nevertheless, strong possibilities for benefit through the forging of links with areas which are Ulster Scots in ethos and history. This should be something which develops between Ulster and Scotland, with linkage for communities and groups on either side of the channel. But it could also be extended to areas of high Ulster Scots concentration in countries such as Canada and the United States. In the 1990s I was involved in assisting the twinning process of Larne in County Antrim with an area of strong Ulster Scots concentration in the Carolinas, a small town named Clover and adjoining York County. This was an area which had clear connection with Ulster through history, surnames and churches, and the twinning, signed up to by both areas in 1997, was progressed with moderate success, with limited exchanges between the two areas, and some tourist efforts on both sides. Subsequently, further developments took place through an international twinning agency, the Sister Cities programme. The most impressive element of the twinning on the American side was undoubtedly development of the annual Clover festival known as *Feis Clobhair*: A Clover Kinntra Gatherin, which attracts several thousand visitors each year in June for a day of pipe bands, games and entertainments, the naming of a civic building in Clover after its Ulster twin, and the similar naming of a school in the US city (Larne Elementary School[34]).

Above: The Piedmont Highlanders at the Clover festival, South Carolina.

In June 2000 the name of County Antrim was brought to wider attention in South Carolina by the naming of the Antrim Business Park off Lyle Boulevard on Interstate 77 at Rockhill, South Carolina. Eddie Williams, President of Williams Engineering Inc, who owned the land on which the park – representing a $220 million investment – was to be sited, told *The Herald* newspaper, that he was aware of the history of the area. The paper reflected:

> "Plenty of York residents can trace their roots back to the people who fled County Antrim in Northern Ireland more than two centuries ago to settle in upstate South Carolina" Historian Sam Thomas was quoted as saying "We call them patriots. They formed the backbone of the whole rebellion against the British crown."[35]

On the Ulster side the erection of a permanent bronze memorial in Larne's Curran Park to emigrants from Ulster has become a fixture on the tourist trail for many Americans visiting Northern Ireland.

Below: The unveiling of the Ulster-American Memorial, Larne, County Antrim, in 1992. Those included in the official party are Cllr David Fleck, Cllr. Roy Beggs, Cllr Amelia Kelly, Mr John Hunter, Dr David Hume, Prof Bobby Moss, Alderman Rosaline Armstrong, Mr Gordon Lucy, Mr Liam Kelly, DL, JP, Mrs Vera Love, Mr Ronnie Hanna and Mrs Jenny Brennan.

Courtesy of the *Larne Times*.

The twinning has not been without difficulties, however, and these have included the distance factor and different cultural approaches to various matters. One of the aspects which did not successfully develop as it was envisaged, for example, was a youth exchange, which had the aim of allowing young people from both areas to learn from each other. This sense of twinning between communities, as opposed to merely 'structural twinning' between the respective local authorities (involving, for example, delegations of officials from one area to another) has, whatever the reasons, probably including distance and cost factors, unfortunately not been realised to any great degree among the wider populace. Hopes of increased cross-Atlantic tourism and investment have not largely been realised either, although this is something largely outwith the capacity of authorities in both areas to regulate. Based on the strong Ulster Scots connection, the twinning aimed to provide all the people from the area with potential to interchange and visit, irrespective of their background, and was, however, an honest attempt to have the Ulster Scots community open beneficial doors for others. It perhaps raises questions as to how effective such links can be, given the distance factors and the economic factors involved, but that does not negate the potential they can have to bring major benefits.

American visitors Vance Stine, then Mayor of Clover in South Carolina, and Sam Thomas of York County Historical Commission explain to schoolchildren in Larne the distance between the two areas during a visit to Northern Ireland.

The opposite impact of internationalism is, of course, that in an age which has seen the threat of globalisation, all cultural communities have been adversely affected, and Ulster Scots has been no different. The concerns over the impact of mass communication have been felt in areas which are also cultural homelands of the Ulster Scots, such as the Appalachians, but it is equally true that often cycles occur in human history. Just as creeping globalisation has threatened indigenous cultures, particularly through the pervasive impact of American television, food chains and brands, so too there has begun to be a response which some heritage analysts are referring to as 'glocalisation', which is a desire to return to more localised roots.[36] It is to be hoped that this will indeed be more and more the case for cultural communities who have suffered through the global aspect of communications, culture and the media. One common aspect in all of this, however, is that if the young people and children of any community do not learn their culture then it will be forgotten.[37] In this sense, the *wains* of Ulster hold the future of their cultural community in their hands.

Historian Robert Bewley says, "... it is interesting to contemplate why as a species homo sapiens, we are so interested in our past; we seem to have an innate desire, even a need, to know from whence we came."[38] Ulster Scot folksinger Robbie Gilbert, from the town of Edneyville, North Carolina, put it in layman's terms when he told me during discussions at a re-enactment at the Elijah Clark

Clover, South Carolina, which is twinned with Larne in County Antrim.

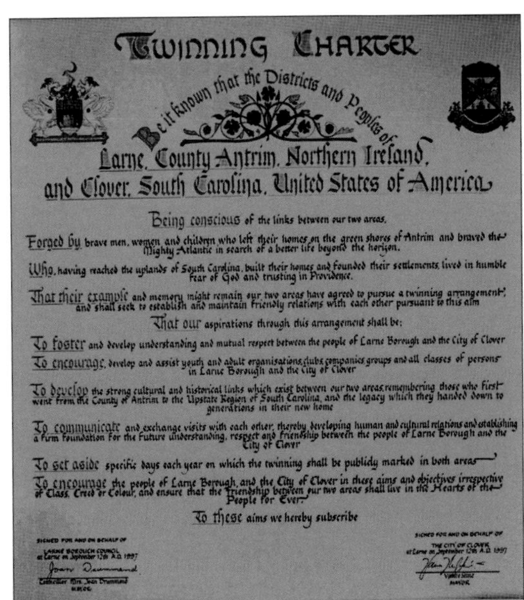

TWINNING CHARTER

Be it known that the Districts and Peoples of
Larne, County Antrim, Northern Ireland,
and Clover, South Carolina, United States of America

Being conscious of the links between our two areas,

Forged by brave men, women and children who left their homes on the green shores of Antrim and braved the Mighty Atlantic in search of a better life beyond the horizon.

Who, having reached the uplands of South Carolina, built their homes and founded their settlements, lived in humble fear of God and trusting in Providence.

That their example and memory might remain our two areas have agreed to pursue a twinning arrangement, and shall seek to establish and maintain friendly relations with each other pursuant to this aim

That our aspirations through this arrangement shall be:

To foster and develop understanding and mutual respect between the people of Larne Borough and the City of Clover

To encourage, develop and assist youth and adult organisations, clubs, companies, groups and all classes of persons in Larne Borough and the City of Clover

To develop the strong cultural and historical links which exist between our two areas, remembering those who first went from the County of Antrim to the Upstate Region of South Carolina, and the legacy which they handed down to generations in their new home

To communicate and exchange visits with each other, thereby developing human and cultural relations and establishing a firm foundation for the future understanding, respect and friendship between the people of Larne Borough and the City of Clover

To set aside specific days each year on which the twinning shall be publicly marked in both areas

To encourage the people of Larne Borough, and the City of Clover in these aims and objectives irrespective of Class, Creed or Colour, and ensure that the Friendship between our two areas shall live in the Hearts of the People for Ever.

To these aims we hereby subscribe

SIGNED FOR AND ON BEHALF OF LARNE BOROUGH COUNCIL at Larne on September 12th A.D. 1997

SIGNED FOR AND ON BEHALF OF THE CITY OF CLOVER at Larne on September 12th A.D. 1997

MAYOR

Larne and Clover Twinning Charter.

State Park in Georgia, USA, "I kind of look at it like, if you don't know where you've been, you can't know where you're going to …" As an Ulster Scots community and as individuals, we need to be assessing where we are and where we are going. We simply cannot do so if we do not know where we have come from.

One thing which is important for us to address as a community is what appears to be our short-termism compared to, say the nationalist community in Ireland. Sometimes criticised for being able to look back through 800 years of perceived injustice, nationalists have more than a march on the Ulster Scots community, which is unionist. It is often difficult to identify that the latter has a sense of more than the most immediate past, apart from a passing knowledge of the Battle of the Boyne in 1690, at which the Protestant William of Orange was victor, establishing constitutional rights which remain in the United Kingdom, and also impacted on the United States of America, as US author Michael Barone has pointed out.[39] Similarly, perhaps this inability of many to have a historical knowledge is also matched by inability to address any long-term strategic thought for the future.

Political observers in Northern Ireland have remarked in the past that nationalism, which wants to see the goal of a united Ireland realised, appears to have a more coherent political strategy than unionists, whose wish to remain part of the United Kingdom is not as demonstrably apparent in terms of political developments. It is easier, perhaps, for an opposing team to progress towards a goal than the home team to always defend the goalmouth, for example. This sense of strategy is clearly illustrated by the republican leadership in Ireland's adoption of the theme of 'a long war', one which would last for decades before their goal had been realised. The unionist psyche may be reflected in the Ulster Scot approach in the American colonies, as recent authors have pointed out.[40] Because the Ulster settlers were essentially squatting on land, they did not expect to be in any particular place for a considerable time, and were more likely to be moving on (or be moved on) in a relatively few years. This led to a psyche which was more concerned with the short-term than anything else. But the more important aspect of outlook may be the Calvinist one, which expounds the idea that as individuals we are only temporarily in this world. Given such a viewpoint, which is central to the Protestant outlook, long-term plans for community could seem superfluous. Individualism, which some Ulster Scots take to the far extreme, does not assist in any long-term strategic thought of a communal nature. Thus, it may be engrained into the psyche of the Ulster Scots not to consider long-term strategies for community education and health as relevant. This viewpoint is not helpful. Indeed, it may be causing irreparable harm and terminal damage. We need as an Ulster Scots and Scots Irish community to get beyond it, to work together as the first pioneer communities of our people worked for the betterment and the future of all.

The Belfast Agreement of 1998 promised the unionist community that east-west links would be developed in tandem with cross-border links with our neighbours in the Republic of Ireland. However, in all the years since, the development of those east-west links is yet to take place. Despite many attempts to highlight this, community groups and unionist politicians seem unable to effect any change, even at ministerial level when there have been promises to review the matter at the North South Ministerial Council.[41] The Minister with responsibility for Ulster Scots in 2010, Nelson McCausland MLA, himself a long-term enthusiast of the Ulster Scot culture, stressed the potential for links to be developed "to the mutual benefit of both communities", that is to say communities in both Scotland and Ulster.[42]

Ulster Scots has a considerable potential in terms of cultural development, geographical links and tourism. In 2010 the Broadisland Gathering in Ballycarry showed that it was not a stereotypical Ulster Scots event by inviting Coisir Og Dhail Riata, a Scots Gaelic youth choir from mid Argyll, to be guests at the longest-established Ulster Scots event in Northern Ireland. The Scots Gaelic community highlights the ancient connections with the Kingdom of Dalriada and not the Plantation of Ulster to which so many Ulster Scots would look in terms of cultural heritage. The Argyll connection, however, is an important and wider aspect of cultural heritage, for it relates to what was a much earlier Plantation, in the fifth and sixth centuries. The settlers from Dalraida – the original Scots – took with them a language now alien to most Ulster Scots, only one aspect of the difference which time has created. The presence of the youth choir, however, helped underline that language should not be seen as the preserve of one community or the other, something which has unfortunately in the context of Northern Ireland, all too often been the case. Interestingly, the Gaelic language found no opposition at the event, in a 92% Protestant community heavily influenced by Ulster Scots, perhaps a sign that, as General Sir James Steele, one of the village's famous native sons, said, there was nothing small about a Ballycarry man or woman and they were able to look beyond their own boundaries.

There is perhaps a message here for the Ulster Scots community generally, which has been portrayed by some as being highly political, single dimensional and inert. The Ulster Scots community must not allow itself to be placed in such cultural boxes, whether by the critiques of others or by the actions of its own. Cultures are always changing and they should be always challenging. It is clear in the context of Northern Ireland that various cultures borrow from each other and have done so historically. In Ulster the term 'kirk' is usually seen as referring to a church in Scots, however there is evidence of use by earlier Anglo-Norman settlers also, showing the cross currents between historical and cultural communities.[43] A major part of the Ulster Scots identity is its Calvinism, its Ullans language and its strong sense of Britishness, but it must also be strong enough and confident enough not only to explain its identity to others but also to explore those aspects of its identity which differ from the norm. In the period between 1905 and 1912, for example, there were Ulster Scots who were prepared to support Home Rule for Ireland. In 1798 they were even more prepared to oppose the King during the United Irish Rebellion as their cousins had opposed the King during the American Revolution. That these things are so should not be ignored for they are at the crux of our identity as a community of dissenters.

This identity of dissent is matched by the tenacity to carry through on whatever path is taken. I am always struck by the story of the Witherspoons of Drumbo, who emigrated to South Carolina in the 1730s. At one point as the pioneer family of Robert Witherspoon, who was just eight years old at the time, made their way to a rudimentary cabin, the fire which they had carried in a small container into the wilderness went out. Without this fire they would not only have no heat for the night ahead, but would also have no protection against wolves and other nocturnal animals. Robert recalls how his father James set out on his own to find another farmstead. He had no idea how far through the swamp it was, but somehow managed to safely locate the cabin of Roger Gordon, and return with fire. His wife and children had given up hope of seeing him again, but James probably saved his family that night – for as they sat in their dirt hut without a door, the large fire they burned outside kept wolves and wild beasts at bay.

James Witherspoon found himself in a new circumstance, but with at least one certainty. Preserving his family required urgent action. The cultural welfare of the Ulster-Scots community family requires no less a response. The flame which has been passed down now needs to be preserved. The legacy of modern Ulster Scots is a rich one, the heritage they bequeath to those following them must be equally so. The ancestors and the children of the Ulster Scots of today are dependent on them to keep the fire burning brightly for the future. The matter rests.

HISTORICAL QUOTES

The Scottish element in North East Ulster
Quote from the *Larne Reporter*, 19 April 1890

"Ulster has much to be proud of as well in relation to days far in the distance as those of the present, and not the least interesting chapters of its history may be found in the kindly spirit of hospitality that ever marked the genial relations which the natives displayed towards the fugitives that fled from persecutions in other lands. The province was very thinly populated in the first part of the seventeenth century when a considerable number of immigrants from the Northern side of the Tweed had settled in the lower districts of the country. It was not, however, until after 1641 that the full tide of immigration set in, and that the port of Carrickfergus became thronged as the landing place of men, women and wains from Ayr, Lanark, Argyle and Aberdeen … These sturdy people sought new homes for themselves in different countries, but especially in Down and Antrim … The Scotch farmers were all members of the Presbyterian Church, and as they did not look over the landmark that divided their creed from that of their neighbours, and pursued with energy the course of agricultural industry, they became the best friends of all around them. As farmers, they were very much ahead of the natives both in skill and perseverance, and the example they set was very generally followed. A wide gulf had existed between many of the people of opposite sects, the Protestants felt bitterly the devastations committed on them by the Roman Catholics during the rebellion of the Celtic chiefs and their armed followers, but gradually the unobtrusive powers of conciliation which the Scotch farmers gently exercised brought about a better state of feeling, and toleration on both sides did its missionary work …

Pipe Majors on parade at Rossnowlagh, County Donegal, Republic of Ireland.

The people of Holywood, Bangor, Newtownards and Donaghadee in their colloquial intercourse did not differ in the slightest degree from the usual phraseology current with the denizens of the towns of Ayr, Kilmarnock, or Irvine, and although of late days the patois has considerably changed and become more Saxonised there may yet be found a fair proportion of the original style of language in those sections of Down."

HISTORICAL FIGURES

WF Marshall

Reverend William Forbes Marshall is known as the Bard of Tyrone and did much to highlight the heritage of the Ulster Scots people and the general British population of Ulster. His poem *Me an' me Da* provided an excellent introduction to Ulster Scots language through humorous verse:

> (The deil the man in this townlan'
> wos claner raired than me
> but I'm livin' in Drumlister
> in clabber to the knee).

He also wrote *Ulster Sails West*, which told the story of the Ulster Presbyterian emigration to America in the eighteenth century and often brought the subject of the United Irishmen into sermons to fellow members of the Orange Order. He in many ways epitomises the transition of the Ulster Scots community, looking back with pride on the men of 1798, but also being strongly in support of the Union with the rest of the United Kingdom, being a member of the old Ulster Volunteer Force and later the Ulster Special Constabulary.

Marshall was born in 1888 near Omagh in County Tyrone and was educated at Sixmilecross, where his father was teacher, the Royal School in Dungannon and Queen's College in Galway. In 1912 he was licensed by the Presbytery of Omagh and he ministered at Aughnacloy and First Ballymacarrett Presbyterian Church in Belfast before being installed in 1928 at Castlerock in County Londonderry. He died in 1959.

There is a WF Marshall Centre at Sixmilecross in County Tyrone, which aims to highlight the life and legacy of this outstanding preacher and poet.

Professor RJ Gregg

A native of Larne, County Antrim, Professor Robert J Gregg (1912–1988) can justly be regarded as the man who laid the firm foundations of study and acceptance of the Ulster Scots linguistic and cultural heritage.

The research and surveys which he conducted on the Ulster Scots language from the 1950s through the 1980s were seminal. They began at an important stage in the history of the language, when many rural dwellers continued to speak Ulster Scots. Gregg used a 600 point questionnaire to develop his research and underscore his findings.

In so doing he essentially charted how the Plantation of Ulster and arrival of Scots settlers had effectively mapped out for future generations the basis of geography and cultural heritage in Ulster.

Gregg's work in Counties Antrim, Down, Donegal and Londonderry, helped to highlight the strongholds of the Ulster Scots language in the twentieth century, and did much to ensure that the culture of his people was placed on an academic footing. The research which he carried out highlighted the strong geographical placement of Ulster Scots, and also the fact that the language was cross-community in its reach and usage.

Robert Gregg taught languages in Belfast and Newtownards grammar schools before he emigrated to Vancouver in British Columbia, Canada, in 1954. He founded the Department of Linguistics at the University of British Columbia, but always retained a strong interest in his homeland, returning to visit family and friends and maintaining a high level of academic study which will be long-lasting in the context of Ulster Scots.

HISTORICAL TRAILS
SITES TO VISIT

Broadisland Gathering, Ballycarry

The Broadisland Gathering was established in 1993 as the first Ulster Scots Gathering in Northern Ireland and regularly attracts Ulster Scots and international visitors as well as focusing on many varied aspects of Ulster Scots identity and culture.

The Broadisland Gathering was established in 1993 and is the longest-established Ulster Scots festival in Northern Ireland. Organised by the Ballycarry Community Association, it also includes several evening events in the run up to the first Saturday in September.

On the Gathering day itself, there is, typically, a country fair, piping, drum major displays, dancing displays, exhibitions, talks, band concerts and musical groups, vintage military and other vehicles, re-enactors, children's events, and pageant parades.

The townland banner parade which takes place at the Gathering is unique. The banners portraying the history and geography of the local townlands converge from several areas to a central point to form the main pageant parade. The first townland banner was created in 1996 and one was unveiled each successive year. There is also a banner commemorating two townlands – Holmanstown and Spierspointstown – whose names have disappeared from the area (they were possibly Norman in origin).

Ballycarry is bedecked in Scottish flags for the event as well as flags from across the British Commonwealth. Visitors from across Northern Ireland as well as further afield including, in the past, the United States, Canada, Australia, Hong Kong, mainland Europe and elsewhere have boosted numbers present, which in 2007 were estimated at 5,500.

In 2010 the Culture Minister, Nelson McCausland, said of the Gathering, "It is a great credit to the folk in Ballycarry. To know that it has been going for 18 years in the way that it has is a great credit to them." The DCAL Minister has been one of several senior figures to have visited the Gathering, others have included former Ministers Edwin Poots and Gregory Campbell MP, and John Reid MP when he was Secretary of State for Northern Ireland. Bands which have performed at the event in the past include the regimental band of the Black Watch, Raphoe Pipe Band (Donegal), Clontibrit (Monaghan), Uphall Station (East Lothian) and Mid Argyll Pipe Band.

Alphabet Angel, Dundarave.

Bushmills Sculpture

The Alphabet Angel in the Dundarave estate in Bushmills, County Antrim, became the first ever Ulster-Scots community sculpture when it was unveiled in 2004. Artist Ross Wilson created the impressive sculpture based on the wishes of local people and schoolchildren in the area, and was inspired by his own Ulster Scots connections. The project took two years to complete and was funded by European Peace Funding, Big Lottery and the Ulster-Scots Agency. The Angel represents a messenger, a traveller and a guardian and the pathway which leads to the sculpture has the words of a poem by Ulster Scots poet James Fenton.[44]

The sculptured figure holds in its left hand the letter A, representing Alpha, the beginning of communication and the origins of word making and language, and in his left a trumpet, calling for recognition and awareness of the unique sound and rhythm of the Ulster Scots tongue.[45] The Alphabet Angel is believed to be the first cultural sculpture based on the Ulster Scots dialect in Europe.

Historic Athenree Homestead at Katikati, New Zealand, was built in c.1878 by Ulster settlers Captain Hugh and Mrs Adela Stewart. It is open to the public every Sunday during January and February and the first Sunday of each other month.

Courtesy of Barbara McKernon.

For more information visit: www.athenreehomestead.org.nz

Katikati, New Zealand

Located around 20 miles from the town of Tauranga, at the Bay of Plenty in New Zealand, Katikati was settled by an emigrant group from County Tyrone in 1875. The promoter of the emigration was George Vesey Stewart, from Ballygawley.[46] He is believed to have encouraged several hundred people to settle in New Zealand, and he received early support for the venture from the Grand Orange Lodge of Ireland and also from the Orange establishment in Auckland at the time. Stewart made plain that he welcomed everyone to participate in the emigration, so long as they harboured no feelings of bigotry or religious discord. It is highly likely that the economic potential of the settlement encouraged Stewart to persist in progressing it, as one New Zealand historian of the settlement has pointed out.[47]

The plan was well thought out, encouraging landed gentlemen who would provide capital to sustain the settlement, and tenant farmers who would work the new lands. The settlement was successful and today there are many families in the Katikati area who have their roots in County Tyrone.

Today Katikati is a very vibrant community and there are a number of homesteads which serve as folk museum buildings. In July 2007, the museum celebrated July twelfth with an Orangeman's Day event, at which flags sent from the Grand Orange Lodge of Ireland to commemorate the link with New Zealand were prominently on display.

ENDNOTES

1 This was one reason why British strategy during the war was to control the southern states, on the expectation loyalists would readily flock to the colours. This was, perhaps, an over optimistic expectation.

2 For a good study of this settlement see McReynolds, Alister, *Challenging the stereotype and defying hagiography – the Rea Brothers and George Galphin in colonial George*, Institute of Ulster Scots Studies, Working Papers 1, p42

3 Howard, Peter, *Heritage: Management, Interpretation, Identity, Continuum*, London: 2003

4 Morris, Richard, *A Short Guide to writing about history*, Harper Collins: 1995, p7

5 Although in many of the southern states of the United States, Baptist churches are the more prevalent indicator of the presence of the Ulster Scots, who found it difficult to maintain themselves as Presbyterians when their church insisted on university educated ministers on the frontiers.

6 Hume International Transport from Randalstown (unconnected with the author) is a visible reflection on the roads of Scottish ancestry, as is Montgomery Transport, for example.

7 *Belfast News Letter*, 8 February 1848

8 OS Memoir, Parish of Templecorran, p132, Institute of Irish Studies, 1994. Their names were given as William Armstrong (23), James McMurthry (26), James Greer (23), Samuel Morrison (25), Samuel McKinstry (40), and Frank McCue (35).

9 OS Memoir, Parish of Raloo, Institute of Irish Studies, 1995, p129. Their names were given as John Gault (35), Alexander McFall (24), Sally McFall (35), Eliza Tippin (20), and Henry Gallagher (25); all but Gallagher, who was Roman Catholic, were Presbyterians

10 *Larne Weekly Reporter*, July 10, 1869

11 *Belfast News Letter*, August 1886; Hume, David, 'Plans for tunnel to Scotland were floated but sunk without trace', in *The Ulster-Scot*, April 2007

12 O'Toole, Michael, 'Ulster Scots "language" rubbished', *Irish News*, 11 September 1996

13 This presumably is a reference to the Ulster Scots Language Society.

14 Communicated to the author by an informant within the language community.

15 'BBC apologies – Ulster-Scots ad was a myth!' in *The Ulster-Scot*, April 2004

16 Dr Philip Robinson's *Ulster Scots Grammar* is the definitive book on the subject, while James Fenton's *The Hamely Tongue* is an excellent dictionary for County Antrim.

17 Fenton, James, *The Hamely Tongue*, Newtownards: 1995

18 This example is from Hume, ed, *The Aul Leid*, Ballycarry: 2008, p5

19 Fenton, *op cit*

20 Fenton, *op cit*, p139

21 Hume, ed, *The Aul Leid*, *op cit*

22 *Ullans 1*, Ulster Scots Language Society: Spring 1993

23 Orr, James, 'The Irish Cottier's Death and Burial', in *Collected Poems*, Ballycarry: 1935

24 *Belfast Telegraph*, 29 June 1996

25 'A County Antrim poet', in *Larne Times* and *Weekly Telegraph*, October 30, 1909

26 A collection of Loughridge's poems, *The Inconstant Nymph*, was published in Belfast in the 1950s.

27 Opinion piece by Dennis Kennedy in the *Belfast Telegraph*, 6 December 2002

28 Bready, County Tyrone and Bright Lights and Southcity dancers from Belfast are excellent examples of the dancing revival among children and young people.

29 University of Huddersfield survey on the Orange Order.

30 Co-founder of the event was Mrs Valerie Beattie, whose grandmother Elizabeth Briton was Scottish.

31 This was later to fall foul of insurance issues, which also prevented a tug o' war taking place, a sign of the modern claim culture in which we live.

32 'Ulster Scots provide a new innovation for a shared heritage', *The Ulster Scot*, November 2004, p15

33 Reported in the *News Letter*, 16 June 1993

34 An article in the *Larne Times*, 27 May 2010, highlighted hopes of linking two local primary schools with the new elementary school, which opened in 2009.

35 'Land owner celebrates Irish ancestry by naming business park after county', *The Herald*, Rock Hill, South Carolina, 8 June 2000

36 Howard, *op cit*

37 Williamson, J, ed. *An Appalachian Symposium*, Boone, North Carolina: 1977

38 Bewley, Robert, *Prehistoric Settlements*, London: 1994

39 Baronne, Michael, *Our First Revolution*, New York: 2007

40 Brown, Stephen, *et al*, *Two Continents, One Culture, The Scotch-Irish in Southern Appalachia*, Tennessee: 2006

41 In a letter to the Broadisland Gathering committee in July 2010, for example, Minister Nelson McCausland MLA, outlined that a major review of the issue was underway and that the legislative remit of the Ulster Scots Agency, the government body charged with development of Ulster Scots, was part of the review.

42 *Ibid*

43 Hughes, AJ, and Hanna, RJ, *Place Names of Northern Ireland*, vol 2, The Ards, Northern Ireland Place Names Project: p73

44 See, for example, Glynn, Elinor, 'Standing tribute to Ulster-Scots', *News Letter*, 19 November 2004

45 See, for example, *The Ulster Scot*, November 2004, p5

46 A detailed account of the Katikati settlement is given by NC Mitchell in 'Katikati: an Ulster settlement in New Zealand', *Ulster Folklife*, vol 15/16, 1970

47 See Jasmine Rogers' dissertation 'A Little corner of Ulster in New Zealand'. This can be accessed on the Internet at http:/jasmine.co.nz/katikati. See also Gray, Arthur, *An Ulster Plantation*, Wellington, New Zealand: 1938, and subsequent reprints.

Memorial at Ballyboley to General Sam Houston, whose ancestors farmed there in the eighteenth century.

EAGLE'S WINGS INDEX